BISMARCK
and His Times

G E O R G E O. K E N T

Southern Illinois University Press: Carbondale and Edwardsville

Feffer & Simons, Inc.: London and Amsterdam

Library of Congress Cataloging in Publication Data

Kent, George O. 1919–
    Bismarck and his times.

    Bibliography: p.
    Includes index.
    1. Bismarck, Otto, Fürst von, 1815–1898. 2. Statesmen—Germany—Biography.
3. Germany—Politics and government—19th century. I. Title.
DD218.K36   943.08′092′4 [B]   78-2547
ISBN 0-8093-0858-4
ISBN 0-8093-0859-2 pbk.

Contents

Preface

This book presents a short account of Otto von Bismarck's life and policies against the background of nineteenth-century Germany and is based on the literature that has appeared since the Second World War. The aim of this study is to acquaint undergraduate and graduate students and the general reader with a summary of that literature.[1]

A generation ago a similar task would have been relatively easy. Then, historians were preoccupied with political history, particularly German nationalism, and with few exceptions, they considered Bismarck one of the greatest statesmen of all time. World War II changed their outlook and their emphasis. Today, though political history still provides the basis and general framework for any Bismarck biography, it is being complemented by economic, social, constitutional, and most recently, psychological history.[2]

As Lincoln and the Civil War dominated United States history in the late nineteenth and early twentieth centuries, Bismarck dominated German political thinking and historical writing from his death in 1898 to the outbreak of the Second World War. As another historian has noted, the changes in the historical interpretations of Bismarck reflect the heights and depths of German historical scholarship in this period.[3] It was only after Germany's defeat in the Second World War that the personality and policies of Bismarck and the events leading toward German unification ceased to be a political issue for German historians. This change in emphasis led to the post–World War II reappraisal and rewriting of modern German history.[4]

The historiographical Notes and Bibliographical Essay in this volume will provide the serious student of history with a guide to the intricacies of historical scholarship pertaining to Bismarck and his

PREFACE

times. For the general reader, the main text presents a picture of the man, the issues, and the age in the light of modern research.

GRATEFUL ACKNOWLEDGMENT IS EXTENDED TO the publishers for permission to quote from the following: Koppel S. Pinson, *Modern Germany: Its History and Civilization* (New York: The Macmillan Company, 1954), Copyright, 1954, by The Macmillan Company; Fritz Stern, *The Failure of Illiberalism: Essays on the Political Culture of Modern Germany* (New York: Alfred A. Knopf, Inc., 1972), Copyright © 1955, 1960, 1967, 1969, 1970, 1971 by Fritz Stern; Fritz Stern, *Gold and Iron: Bismarck, Bleichröder, and the Building of the German Empire* (New York: Alfred A. Knopf, Inc., 1977), Copyright © 1977 by Fritz Stern.

I am grateful to a great number of people who helped me in the preparation of this study, among them some anonymous readers whose comments and criticisms improved earlier drafts and the staff of the McKeldin Library of the University of Maryland, which provided valuable assistance. My greatest indebtedness, however, is to Marthe— *sine ea nihil*.

George O. Kent

Washington, D.C.
June 1977

Bismarck's Youth

Otto von Bismarck was born at Schoenhausen in Brandenburg-Prussia on April 1, 1815, during the Hundred Days, and he died at Friedrichsruh near Hamburg, on July 30, 1898, while the European powers were partitioning Africa and extending their dominion over large parts of Asia. His life spanned almost a century, an important period in the development of modern Europe and a crucial one for Germany. To understand the changes which occurred during Bismarck's lifetime, it is necessary to consider the European situation at the time Napoleon was sent to his first exile.

The Congress of Vienna (September 1814–June 1815) settled the political upheavals which followed the revolutionary and Napoleonic wars; in the process, the Congress created a new order in central Europe which survived for almost half a century. This order was based primarily on a new political and territorial arrangement in which the Austrian Empire predominated, and the Kingdom of Prussia (enlarged in the west to form a barrier against France) became the second largest power. Austria, Prussia, thirty-three other principalities, and four free cities formed the German Confederation. Of these thirty-three states, Bavaria, Wuerttemberg, Baden, Hanover, and Saxony were the most important, and these states were usually called the "lesser German states" or the "Third Germany."[1] The confederation was a loose grouping of sovereign states which had its permanent meeting place in the Federal Diet at Frankfurt. The architect and leader of the confederation was the Austrian chancellor, Prince Clemens von Metternich, who lent his name to this system and the period during which it operated.

Napoleon's defeat brought little change in the economic and social conditions in central Europe, though the revolution in France, the French occupation of large parts of Germany,[2] and the wars of liberation had left their marks. What changes occurred were uneven, and they were generally more extensive in the west than in the east. The gradual spread of the industrial and agricultural revolutions was accompanied by an equally gradual abandonment of the vestiges of the feudal system, a decline which benefited the landowners and the bourgeoisie more than the peasants.[3]

The peasants, who were usually unable to support themselves on the land left to them,[4] turned to home industries—primarily weaving and spinning—and when these were taken over by machines in the 1830s and 1840s, these peasants joined the ranks of the discontented landless and urban masses who played such an important role in the initial stages of the mid-century revolutions.

The gains of the bourgeoisie were primarily economic, occasionally social, and rarely political. That the bourgeoisie in central Europe did not gain political power despite their economic achievements (in contrast to the English pattern) led subsequently to the major constitutional and political conflicts in Germany in the second half of the nineteenth century.

The privileges and powers of the nobility remained intact. Land, especially in the east, was still the major source of wealth, and although the influence of the French Revolution had curtailed some noble privileges, the nobility retained its social position. The Stein-Hardenberg reforms of 1807–8 had only been an abortive beginning toward a more equitable social order.[5]

In the *Altmark*, home of the Bismarcks for over five centuries, conditions were no different from those in the north and east of Prussia. At the beginning of the eighteenth century, the Bismarcks acquired Schoenhausen, an estate surrounded by sand and pine forests on the floodplain of the Elbe near Tangermuende and Stendal. It was here that Otto von Bismarck was born. His ancestors came from the nobility and the upper bourgeoisie. On his father's side, the family could be traced back to the thirteenth century, a part of the Brandenburg nobility whose members fought in the Thirty Years War, in French and Swedish armies, all over Europe. They stayed close to the land, served as sheriffs and judges, led frugal and sober lives, and seldom had higher aims. Though loyal to their sovereign, they were an independent lot. Frederick Wilhelm I once noted that the Bismarcks, the Schulenburgs, the Knesebecks, and the Alvenslebens were particularly disobedient toward their sovereign, and advised his successor to keep a sharp eye on them. August Friedrich, Otto's grandfather, was known for his roughness and his drinking capacity, and also for his prowess as a hunter, horseman, and soldier. Otto's father, Ferdinand, of milder disposition, was more interested in improving his estates. When he was thirty-five, he married the seventeen-year-old Wilhelmine Mencken at Potsdam (July 6, 1806).[6]

The Menckens (of whom H. L. Mencken, the American literary critic, was a descendant) came from an Oldenburg merchant family, some of whom became prominent in literary and academic fields during the eighteenth century. The family's most illustrious member, Anastasius Ludwig (born 1752), became a diplomat and secretary of cabinet to Frederick the Great. As a high state official, he proposed some of the administrative changes which provided the basis for the reforms of Baron vom Stein. His daughter Wilhelmine, Otto von Bismarck's mother, shared her father's humane outlook and keen intelligence.[7]

Thus, the nobility, army, and civil service, the classes which dominated Prussia, were prominent among Otto von Bismarck's ancestors; this legacy was to play a considerable role in his own life.[8] His childhood, while not unhappy, held few fond memories for the man. At seven he was sent off to a Berlin boarding school which was considered very progressive. There he stayed until the fall of 1827, when he entered the *Gymnasium* (roughly the equivalent of a preparatory school) and lived in the family's Berlin flat, supervised by a housekeeper and a tutor. In the spring of 1832 he passed his examinations. He was a slightly better than average student and did well in German, Latin, and history; he was average in mathematics, physics, English, and French. He showed no special interests that hinted at his later career, and when his mother suggested that he prepare for the diplomatic service, he did not object. He apparently never considered a military career.[9] In the summer of 1832 he went to the University of Goettingen to study law but left in the fall of the following year. While he does not seem to have accomplished a great deal scholastically, he did apparently have a good time joining the Hanovera fraternity, fighting many duels, and making friends with some foreign students, among them John L. Motley, the American writer and historian.[10]

In October 1834 he registered at the University of Berlin and studied French literature, philosophy, and political science during the fall semester and law during the summer. The following fall he registered for some economic courses but apparently attended only a few lectures. He probably studied with a tutor, for he passed his final examination in Roman and canon law on May 22, 1835. While in Berlin he attended many social functions and was often invited to Court. His mother, an ambitious and strong-minded woman, realized that he lacked the makings of a scholar and wanted him to choose a military career, but Bismarck declined. Though dreaming of the life of a country squire, he entered the Prussian civil service and in June 1835 became a junior official at the Berlin City Court. He was none too happy interviewing witnesses and keeping records and intended to stay only a few years before entering the diplomatic service. A year later, in the summer of 1836, he was assigned to the Aachen district administration. Bismarck himself had chosen Aachen because the district governor, Count Arnim-Boitzenburg, a well-known and highly respected official, was a friend of the family. At Aachen, Bismarck worked in the estate and foresty departments and the military and communal sections. His inquiries about entering the diplomatic service were not well received in Berlin. The Prussian foreign minister, Ancillon, suggested that Bismarck complete his civil service assignments and then enter the foreign ministry laterally, through the German Customs Union section. The implication was unmistakably clear: there was no place in the ministry's European section for a backcountry squire from Pomerania.[11] Though disappointed, Bismarck accepted Ancillon's suggestion, and with the help of Arnim, prepared himself for still another examination.

His social life during this period was noteworthy for two love affairs, both involving English girls, and one of which seriously interfered with his official duties. He took several months' leave without permission from his superiors and followed his ladylove all over Europe, only to lose her, in the end, to an English major. When his request for additional leave (presumably to recover from this affair) was denied, he asked and was given permission to transfer to Potsdam. He arrived there in December 1837.

Bismarck's assignments in Potsdam were no more exciting than those in Aachen, except that he was closer to home and to Berlin. His father urged him to fulfill his military service and though Bismarck dreaded the drill and loss of freedom it entailed, he joined the guard battalion at the end of March 1838. He was becoming increasingly disillusioned with his prospects in the civil service and longed for country life. Thus, when his mother became ill and his father offered to give part of his estate[12] to his two sons, Otto jumped at the chance, obtained leave from the army (September 1838) and resigned from the civil service a year later.

Bismarck's career had so far been a disappointment. Lack of private funds, slow advancement, and most of all, his desire for independence and self-fulfillment had made government service quite unattractive to him. As he wrote to his cousin, "I should like to make music as I want to, or I shall make none at all."[13] He had also incurred many debts, more than he could afford, and another reason to leave the service was to find an independent income to be able to pay his debtors back.[14]

Bismarck's mother died in January 1838, and two years later his father divided the estate between Otto and his brother. Otto now had Kniephof to himself, and he slowly managed to improve the estate's finances.[15] It was during this period that he became known as the "mad Junker." His wild parties, many duels, heavy drinking, and especially his practical jokes provided endless gossip for the Pomeranian squirearchy. This was also his romantic period of "storm and stress." He admired Lord Byron and loved the "revolutionary" music of Beethoven; he developed a deep feeling for Shakespeare's works and was interested in republican ideals and ideas.

At the same time, he was appalled by the mobs at the Hambach Festival (a patriotic meeting on May 27, 1832, which demanded German freedom and unity and advocated revolutionary action if peaceful measures failed) and by the Frankfurt riots.[16] During this time he also had an unhappy affair with Ottilie von Puttkamer (no close relation to Johanna von Puttkamer, Bismarck's future bride), and to get over it, he traveled abroad, visiting England, Scotland, France, and Switzerland from July to October, 1842. He even thought of going to Egypt and India, but this plan was abandoned when his travel companion, Oscar von Arnim, met and decided to marry Bismarck's sister Malvine.[17] Bismarck was restless, bored, and dissatisfied with country life, and possibly as a diversion, he became an official of his district, acting in this capacity as one of the two representatives of the local district chief (*Landrat*).

Bismarck's political views were no different at this time from those of his conservative neighbors. He believed in the moral precepts and Christian ideals of his class and the traditional prerogatives which made him free and independent on his estates and assigned him God-given authority in matters of law, police powers, and economic affairs. He believed that only the nobility had the right and the competence to govern in a German and Christian state, and that these rights had to be defended against outsiders, such as Jews.[18]

In November 1845 Bismarck's father died and Otto moved to Schoenhausen. There he became involved in numerous local matters; as dike reeve (*Deichhauptmann*) on the Elbe, he engaged in an extensive correspondence with local authorities on the proper conditions of the Elbe dikes, suggesting methods to improve them.[19] More significant for his later career, however, was his involvement in a fight for the preservation and reorganization of patrimonial jurisdiction in his district. This and another legal remnant of feudalism, patrimonial police power, were still widely used on the landed estates of Prussia, Silesia, Brandenburg, Saxony, and Pomerania in the first half of the nineteenth century. Police powers were exercised directly by the nobility, while juridical powers were delegated to trained lawyers and jurists who were appointed by, and responsible to, the lord of the manor. The higher state courts supervised the system, which by the late 1830s and early 1840s had generated considerable dissatisfaction all around. Peasants and tenants became increasingly unhappy with the judgments rendered, the nobility was irritated over the time and expense connected with these duties, and the state courts, jealous of their prerogatives, wanted to take over the entire system. Some noblemen, such as the Buelows and the Thaddens, Bismarck's neighbors, defended these rights as part of their manorial duties toward their dependents. Bismarck favored patrimonial jurisdiction in the interest of maintaining manorial privileges and independence and suggested a clear delineation of the powers involved, rather than a doctrinaire defense of the issues. In a circular of January 8, 1847, to the nobility of his home district, Bismarck explained his position in great detail and argued that the loss of manorial jurisdiction would also involve a loss of noble influence and prestige. At the same time he suggested that the nobility should be given an extension of their powers as well as some financial relief. His views became widely known and, when it appeared that manorial police powers might also be abolished, he was asked to lead the opposition in a regional fight against such reforms. Thus Bismarck acquired a reputation as a strong conservative in his district and beyond, and when his name was suggested as the district representative to the United Prussian Diet in 1847, it was not unknown.[20]

During this same period, two incidents occurred that were of considerable importance in Bismarck's life. Through the friendship and influence of Maria von Thadden and Moritz von Blanckenburg, his religious outlook changed, and he became a devout Christian (he had earlier professed atheism, announcing at age sixteen that he had stopped saying his prayers), and through them, too, he met Johanna von Puttkamer, whom he later married (July 28, 1847).

Bismarck's religious conversion and his numerous subsequent expressions of piety are in sharp contrast with his later pronouncements as statesman and politician. This discrepancy might be explained by his often expressed belief that service to king and country was, in the Lutheran tradition, also service to God. Moreover, he believed that the state and the existing order were divinely ordained, and that governments were instituted to defend Christians from non-Christians as well as from evil, a theory that led logically to his conviction that those with responsibility had been charged by God to defend their subjects with the sword against their enemies. He was also aware that there were times when, as a statesman, he had no choice but to sin; he was always confident, however, that whenever he made such a choice—invariably in pursuit of honorable causes—God would forgive him.[21] He often said, and there was no reason to doubt his sincerity, that his only responsibility was to king and God. This was really an ideal solution; it made Bismarck's egoism and quest for power appear to be God's will, and at the same time, spared him pangs of conscience. "I am God's soldier," he wrote to his wife in 1851, "and must go wither He sends me, and I believe that He sends me and shapes my life as He requires."[22]

Bismarck's religious conversion is also of interest in connection with his betrothal. Both occurred at about the same time, in the summer of 1846, and as was the custom, he wrote a formal letter to Heinrich von Puttkamer, Johanna's father, asking permission to marry her. This letter has become famous. Its style and content foreshadow the statesman; its arguments, the diplomat. Bismarck's life and reputation until then had not been such as to inspire confidence even in a sympathetic and unprejudiced person; Johanna's father, a bigoted, narrow-minded conservative, was aghast at the thought of his daughter even considering marriage to this "mad Junker." Bismarck was, of course, aware of old Puttkamer's attitude, and he set out to overcome this formidable obstacle. Using a tactic that he was to employ regularly in the future, he confounded the unsuspecting gentleman with unexpected and complete frankness; rather than asking "for Johanna's hand because he was worthy of God—this would have seemed presumptuous to a Pietist [such as Puttkamer] in someone far more religious"—Bismarck asked for Johanna's hand "because only God could make him worthy." He went on to describe his youthful religious indifference and his recent struggle to find faith in God. What was the father to do? "To reject him would have indicated not lack of faith in the suitor, but an absence of trust in God." In reply, Heinrich von Puttkamer quoted several passages from the Bible which had consoled him in his sorrow and extended Bismarck a lukewarm invitation to visit. When Bismarck arrived at Reinfeld, the Puttkamer estate, he found Johanna's parents ready for further negotiations. In no mood to accommodate them, Bismarck not only embraced Johanna when they met, to the astonishment of all concerned, but later at an informal dinner brazenly announced his intention of marrying her.[23]

Bismarck was, without a doubt, pleased with his conquest and wrote his brother that "speaking frankly [I am] marrying a woman of rare spirit and nobility, charming and easy to live with as I have never known another woman to be. In matters of faith we differ, somewhat more to her sorrow than to mine, though not as much as you may think . . . certain internal and external events have brought about changes in my outlook . . . so that I consider myself now a Christian . . . furthermore, I love Pietism in women."[24] These remarks seem to cast doubt on the sincerity of Bismarck's religious conversion but only if one applies generally accepted standards of ethics. This would be unfair, because Bismarck himself recognized no standards except those that he applied himself; for example, he never accepted the good faith of an opponent, or the validity of any argument not his own. "It was not that Bismarck lied . . . but that he was finely attuned to the subtlest currents of any environment and produced measures precisely adjusted to the need to prevail. The key to Bismarck's success was that he was always sincere."[25]

In May 1847, between his betrothal and marriage, Bismarck was sent as the first alternate delegate to the United Prussian Diet, when v. Brauchitsch, the original delegate, became ill. This was the real beginning of Bismarck's career, and it became obvious that the political arena was his chosen field. He had found himself at last. At the Diet, Bismarck was moderately conservative. He defended the government against the opposition and the nobility against the liberals. His first speech, on May 17, 1847, caused a minor sensation. It was directed against the liberals, whose demand for a constitution was based on the premise that the wars of liberation against Napoleon had been inspired by liberty and patriotism, and that the popular uprising had freed the fatherland from foreign occupation. Bismarck almost contemptuously asserted that one could not demand rewards for having resisted after a prolonged beating. The liberation movement had been a patriotic one, he said, but it had nothing in common with liberty and constitutionalism. During the uproar that followed his speech, he turned his back to the Diet and read a newspaper until the noise subsided. This incident brought him some prominence, and he became a favorite at the royal court and with the ultra-conservatives.

Always defending the government, he soon became an outspoken opponent of Vincke, the liberal leader. Only on the question of emancipation of Jews, an issue which found some favor with the government, did Bismarck disagree with the government's position. He took his stand on medieval Christian principles and against what he called humanitarian and sentimental trash. All European states, he declared, were religious Christian states, and without religious principles they would disintegrate. His views were not based on racial grounds but rather on rural Junker prejudices and on personal experience with

Jewish moneylenders.[26] The Diet recessed on June 26, 1847, and Bismarck, instead of rushing to Reinfeld to see his fiancée, tended to political affairs while visiting friends and colleagues.

In this, Bismarck's initial experience in politics, certain aspects of the attitudes and style that became characteristic of the future chancellor could already be seen: his eagerness to participate in political debates, his love of a good fight, his desire to influence people, his confidence in his own judgment, and his disdain of majority opinions. His political and social views were those of the Prussian conservative nobility of his region, passionately defensive of the status and privileges of the landed aristocracy and the monarchy. At the same time he was keenly aware of the realities of power and was determined to uphold the power of the Prussian state against what he considered to be the narrow interests of political—and especially liberal—parties. The style of his speeches and writings also emerged. It was expressive and to the point, original in concept and economical in language. It was most effective because he unerringly used those arguments which appealed to his listeners without being too obvious. At Court he became the favorite of the royal princes, especially the prince of Prussia, later Wilhelm I, though King Friedrich Wilhelm IV was less impressed with this young and radical deputy. Yet when they met during Bismarck's honeymoon in Venice (the wedding had been on July 28, 1847), the king let Bismarck know that he approved of his activities in the Diet. To the liberals, however, Bismarck was the personification of the conservative, reactionary Junker.

Bismarck
and the
Revolution
of 1848

The central European uprisings of 1848 began when news of the successful revolution in France reached Berlin and Vienna. In contrast to France, the course of the revolution in central Europe was complicated by nationalism, a force which simultaneously threatened to dissolve the Austrian Empire and unify the German states. The revolution's resulting crosscurrents of nationalism, liberalism, and particularism defy simple explanation and obscure a common pattern. The initial successes of the revolutionaries can be attributed to the ineptitude of the local authorities rather than the strength of the revolutionary movement. This was not recognized at the time, and the misjudgment of the relative power of the revolutionaries and their foes contributed to the revolution's ultimate failure.

Liberalism, the most influential creed of the revolutionary and unification movement in the Germanies, was supported by the professional and business classes. Its roots lay in the early phases of the French Revolution of 1789, and its ideals were those of English parliamentarianism. The number and wealth of German businessmen had increased considerably in the decades of the early nineteenth century; conscious of their rising economic strength and importance, they demanded an appropriate share of political representation. They opposed the arbitrary powers and privileges and the corrupt and inefficient methods of aristocratic government; they advocated constitutional, representative, and limited monarchy, abolition of the remnants of the feudal system, equality before the law, extension of the franchise to the propertied classes, and freedom of thought, speech, and association. They did not advocate violence and revolution but aspired to equality with the nobility; like the nobility, they were apprehensive over the growing number of illiterates and workers, who might threaten life and property if not restrained.

The economic demands of the bourgeoisie paralleled their political demands. They advocated abolition of the restrictions and regulations of the mercantilist system (especially those affecting labor and production), freedom of movement for men and goods, repeal of internal road and river tolls (toward which the Prussian Customs Union of 1834 was a promising beginning), uniformity of currency, weights, and measures, and a common law of commerce. These last provisions linked economic reforms to political issues because every businessman realized that national unification would provide a powerful stimulus to business and industrial expansion and lead to abolition of countless local customs and usages left over from the Middle Ages. The liberal merchants and businessmen also demanded noninterference by the government in matters of business and trade, which became known as the laissez faire doctrine.[1] A similar attitude toward government interference was also noticeable in the field of social welfare. The liberals were opposed to any type of welfare legislation, such as child labor laws or the shortening of the working day, and favored instead freedom of contracts and the abolition of usury laws, which set low rates of interest. This attitude of unrestrained individualism, in the face of the increasingly inhuman working conditions in factories and mines, aroused the hostility of the workers against the middle classes and inspired socialist writers to attack liberalism from the very beginning.[2]

The intellectuals, whose freedom of expression had been suppressed after 1812, reemerged after the 1830 revolution in Paris, and at the Hambach Festival in May 1832, they staged the first mass demonstration in the Germanies; they denounced the repressive measures of the Metternich system, such as censorship of press and publication and restriction of the right of association, and demanded a reunited, republican Germany and the liberation of Poland, Hungary, and Italy. The German governments, prodded by Metternich, responded to these demands with more repressive measures which, in turn, popularized the Young German movement. This movement, one of many similar European-wide movements (Young Italy, Young Ireland, and Young Poland) was inspired by French revolutionary ideals and dissatisfaction with the repressive and reactionary measures of the Metternich regime.

A new generation of writers began to use criticism and satire as political weapons and they attacked conditions in Germany in essays, letters, and travel accounts. In doing so they spared neither Goethe, who had died in 1832, nor the romantic movement. They favored the present over the past and had no use for Romanticism's glorification of the Middle Ages, Catholic piety, or the ancient Germanic tribes. Instead they admired Luther, the Reformation and the Enlightenment, Kant, Voltaire, and Schiller and considered liberty the most priceless possession.

Contrary to the movements in Poland, Hungary, Italy, and Ireland, which were primarily nationalistic and directed against foreign occupation, the Young Germans were not, as a whole, in favor of German unification. They were cosmopolitan ("I hate any society which is smaller than the human society," Boerne wrote) but could not agree on what form the ideal state should take. Some preferred a constitutional monarchy, others a republic.

Led by Gutzkow, Buechner, Herwegh, Freiligrath, Boerne, and Heine, the Young Germans laid the foundations of political journalism.[3] But their political influence on events in the Germanies was limited because two of their best known advocates, Heine and Boerne, were exiles in France. Their praise of French culture and criticism of some of the more exaggerated romantic notions of their compatriots were unpopular in this period of rising nationalism. That they and a number of their followers were Jewish did not help the Young German movement.

Another protest movement, smaller in size but more influential, was the group known as the Young Hegelians. Even more radical and critical than Hegel himself, the Young Hegelians considered themselves guardians of rationalism and champions of humanity. They objected to the religious revival, opposed ultramontane Catholicism, the Pietism of the Protestant churches, and the alliance between throne and altar. Initially they considered Prussia the best and most promising state in Germany but were appalled by the Prussian government's handling of the Cologne disturbances in 1837 and by Friedrich Wilhelm IV's concessions to the Catholic church after 1840.[4]

Most intellectuals, like the bourgeoisie, were not true revolutionaries but advocates of peaceful reforms whose native liberal roots
could be found in the writings of Kant and Wilhelm von Humboldt.
Their beliefs were reinforced in the Rhineland and in southern Germany by French ideas, and in northern Germany by English liberalism. Hanover was tied by personal union to the English crown from
1714 to 1837, and the University of Goettingen, in southern Hanover,
became a center of English constitutional studies and a link between
German and English Protestantism. The case of the "Goettingen Sev-
en" became famous throughout Germany: seven professors from the
university were dismissed in 1837 because they refused to take an oath
to the new Hanoverian constitution which omitted the liberal provisions of the old one.

At about the same time, the reading habits of the romantically inclined public turned from the medieval castles of Sir Walter Scott to
the slums of Charles Dickens and Victor Hugo, who glorified the workers and derided the philistine bourgeoisie.[5]

Throughout the late 1830s and early 1840s, many Germans were
aware that the number of poor had increased, that class conflict was
spreading, and that many people sympathized with the ideas of socialism. It was also widely believed that the proletariat, product of
the new industrial age, was incapable of improving its economic and
social position and would, therefore, resort to revolution to overthrow
the existing order.

Economically, the 1840s were particularly bad; poor wheat and rye
crops and a potato blight had disastrous effects throughout western
Europe. Rising food prices, increasing unemployment, and lower
wages combined with widespread business failures to bring about a
severe depression in 1846–47. Popular unrest led to food riots, and
demonstrations and revolts were expected everywhere. Thus, the
specter of socialism became a real one and most governments expected
a revolution to break out at any moment. When the revolution finally
did come to central Europe, the governments bowed before the inevitable.

Following the initial success of the Revolution of 1848 in Austria,
Prussia, and central and southern Germany, an assembly of representatives from all parts of the country was called to Frankfurt on the

Main to prepare for elections to a national parliament, which would, in turn, draft a constitution and organize a government for a united Germany. This preliminary parliament (*Vorparlament*) met in St. Paul's Church on March 31, 1848. Its delegates were asked to choose between a moderate program—a federal union under a liberal monarch with a constitution drafted by a national assembly—and a radical program— a republic, which called for universal manhood suffrage and the abolition of aristocratic privilege. This latter program was decisively defeated. The preliminary parliament recommended, instead, that the delegates to the national parliament be elected by direct, universal suffrage; this provision was largely ignored by the various states, with the result that most delegates were chosen by electors and came from the propertied classes. The great majority of the delegates were political and economic liberals, without any revolutionary fervor, but anxious to achieve national unification. They met on May 18, 1848, under the presidency of Heinrich von Gagern for the opening session of the Frankfurt Assembly.

The Frankfurt Assembly has for a long time (and especially in Germany history textbooks) been derisively labeled the "professors' parliament," mocked for its long, useless speeches, pointless debates, and lack of practical achievement. This characterization, used primarily by conservatives to discredit liberalism and democracy in Germany, has only recently been corrected. It is now fairly well established that there were more lawyers and judges than university professors among the delegates who, on the whole, did not differ in their professional and occupational background from any similar European legislative body of the period. (There were 49 university professors, 40 school principals and teachers, 200 jurists, 35 writers and journalists, 30 merchants and industrialists, 26 clergymen, and 12 physicians.)[6] There were certainly long, learned debates and numerous committee meetings, but the establishment of parliamentary procedures, the drafting of a federal constitution, the discussion of fundamental rights, and the organization of a provisional federal executive had never been discussed in Germany on a national level before, and these were topics and measures that could not be hurried along.

In the end, the Frankfurt Assembly failed not because it discussed useless theoretical concepts, but because the two major powers in

Germany, Austria and Prussia, had recovered their military strength and refused to put their armies under the leadership of Archduke John, the Assembly's elected executive officer (*Reichsverweser*). Without an army, the Frankfurt Assembly lacked the power to enforce its laws and decrees. Parliamentary impotence became especially apparent in the Schleswig-Holstein question.

In the late spring and summer of 1848, German public opinion was aroused over the plight of the German minorities in Schleswig and Holstein and demanded that German troops defend the minorities against an invading Danish army. In accordance with a resolution by the Frankfurt Assembly, Prussia, Hanover, and Brunswick sent troops into the duchies and expelled the Danes. When the defeat of the Danish army seemed imminent, Russia and Britain, alarmed at German expansionist designs, threatened to intervene. Confronted with this threat, Prussia and her allies withdrew and signed an armistice at Malmoe on August 26, 1848. Members of the Frankfurt Assembly and German liberals everywhere considered the armistice a major national defeat and urged the Prussian government to continue the war, but to no avail. The powerlessness of the Frankfurt Assembly became painfully obvious to liberals and conservatives alike, and the Assembly never recovered from the loss of prestige occasioned by the Schleswig-Holstein affair.

There were other issues as well. The question of Austria's exclusion from, or inclusion in, the new Reich—and whether Austria or Prussia should assume the leadership—had agitated German nationalists for a long time. In general, the Protestant population of North Germany was pro-Prussian, while the Catholics south of the Main River were pro-Austrian. At Frankfurt the problem was solved temporarily when the Czech delegates from the Austrian provinces of Bohemia and Moravia refused to join the Assembly, which reduced Austria's delegation to 120, while that of Prussia remained at 198.[7]

The old Grand Duchy of Poznan, divided since 1815 between the Prussian provinces of West Prussia and Posen, which contained about 800,000 Poles, 400,000 Germans and 76,000 (mostly Germanized) Jews, presented another problem. Before the revolution, German liberals strongly supported Polish claims for independence and the Prussian government was ready to grant concessions to the Polish population in the two provinces. When, however, the Poles took control of the local administration in March–April 1848, the German population resisted and, with the help of Prussian military detachments, suppressed the Polish insurrection.

The debates on the Polish question in the Frankfurt Assembly (July 24–27, 1848) centered on the degree of autonomy the Prussian Polish provinces should be granted in the future, and specifically, on whether and how many Germans should come under the jurisdiction of local Polish officials. Only two delegates, Arnold Ruge, a leader of the extreme left, and Janiszewski, the only Polish delegate, pleaded the Polish cause. Wilhelm Jordan, a Berlin Democrat, spoke for the German minority in Posen. His strongly nationalistic speech can be considered "an early example of that fusion of liberal nationalism and Prussian power politics which was completed between 1866 and 1871."[8] An overwhelming majority, 342 to 31, voted to uphold the rights of the German minority, and those areas with a large German population, such as East and West Prussia, the Neisse district, the city of Posen, and the surrounding area to the west of the city, were incorporated into Germany. The area east of Posen, which had an almost exclusively Polish population, was left out of the newly constituted German state though it was still part of Prussia and would be able to adopt whatever degree of autonomy the Prussian government was ready to grant. The predominant attitude in evidence at the Frankfurt Assembly in the Schleswig-Holstein and Polish questions, the ascendancy of nationalism over liberalism, foreshadowed the widespread popular support for Bismarck's foreign policy.

By the end of March 1849, the Frankfurt Assembly had completed its work. It advocated a federal state with a constitutional monarchy, a bicameral parliament (members of the lower house to be elected by universal, direct, and secret ballot; half of those of the upper house to be chosen by the state governments and half by the lower houses of the state legislatures), and a federal supreme court. On March 28, the Assembly offered the crown of the prospective German state to King Friedrich Wilhelm IV of Prussia, who refused it saying that no king by divine right would stoop to the gutter for an imperial crown. In any event, this was an empty gesture because the revolutionaries had been defeated everywhere, and in Bohemia, Hungary, and Austria the old order was once again in command.

For Bismarck the revolutionary events in Prussia were of particular significance. When news of the successful uprising in Berlin reached Schoenhausen on March 19, 1848, Bismarck was incensed. He became even more distressed when he learned that the troops, undefeated and loyal to the king, had been ordered by Friedrich Wilhelm IV to leave the city and retreat to Potsdam, and that the king himself was a prisoner of the revolutionaries in Berlin. Bismarck's deep-seated Prussian royalism was outraged; he felt compelled to do something. After surveying his estates and the neighboring countryside and assuring himself of the loyalty of the peasants, he decided to mobilize the country against the revolutionary towns, march on Berlin, free the king, and crush the revolution. Before carrying out his plans he went to Potsdam, which had not been occupied by the revolutionaries, to learn at firsthand what had actually occurred. There he stayed with his friend Albrecht von Roon, who shared Bismarck's feelings and believed that the revolution could be defeated if only a man could be found to lead the loyal troops. (It never occurred to Roon that Bismarck, then barely thirty-three, could be that man.) Having agreed on a solution, the two friends set out to find Prince Wilhelm, a strong conservative and next in line to the throne, whom they thought would be the man to rescue king and country. But the prince could not be found; there were rumors that he had left the country because of his unpopularity with the people of Berlin.

When Bismarck called on Princess Augusta, Wilhelm's wife, to inquire of the prince's whereabouts and to tell her of their plans, he met with a cold reception. Augusta insisted that her husband was loyal to the king and would not act against the king's orders; she made Bismarck promise that he would use neither her husband's nor her son's name in any disloyal undertaking. It seemed that Augusta had plans of her own. An admirer of Louis Philippe and the July Monarchy in France, she was said to have established contacts with the liberal party in the Prussian National Assembly. Friedrich Wilhelm IV, according to these plans, would abdicate while her husband, Prince Wilhelm, would renounce his rights to the throne, and she herself would be installed as regent for her son. It seems likely that Bismarck learned of Augusta's plans and considered them nothing short of treason, a perversion of the Prussian monarchy, and an opening toward constitutionalism. Bismarck's enmity toward Augusta and her intense dislike of Bismarck took root at this time.[9]

But the king was still a prisoner and the revolutionaries remained in control in Berlin. In the opinion of the army and its officers, the king was not free to act in the best interests of his country, but without royal orders they could not move. Was it possible to save the royal house in spite of itself by acting without, or even against, the king's orders? Could General Yorck's decision at Tauroggen in 1812, when he concluded an agreement with the Russians without the permission of the Prussian government, be repeated? The only man willing to make such a decision was Bismarck. It was inconceivable to Bismarck that a Prussian king would order the army to refrain from firing on a revolutionary mob of his own free will; therefore, the king was being held a prisoner by the mob. Therefore others who could act for the good of Prussia and the royal house must do so for king and country. Bismarck apparently questioned various army commanders in the provinces about their attitude, and though a few seemed ready to go along with his plans, others opposed them. The whole scheme collapsed when Friedrich Wilhelm IV appeared at Potsdam on March 25, 1848, demonstrating that he was not a prisoner, and exhorted his troops once again to abide by his orders and not to fight the revolutionaries in Berlin.

Bismarck returned to Schoenhausen in despair. "The peasants here," he wrote in his diary, "were enraged over the Berliners, but who can support a building whose main support is rotten?"[10] How much the failure of his plan influenced Bismarck's view of subsequent events is difficult to say. In his opinion, the initial success of the revolution was caused by the cowardice of the civil service, the indecision of the crown, and the timidity of the majority of the population which, though loyal, was frightened by barricades and popular assemblies. The roots of revolution, according to Bismarck, were to be found in the new industrial system and the spirit of the times, which was antireligious and questioned authority. It was this spirit that had infected the intellectuals and the bureaucrats. The people, Bismarck believed, were not inclined toward revolution, and the "enemy" was the bourgeoisie. He apparently perceived, early on, the possibilities of an alliance between workers, peasants, and aristocracy against the middle class. For these reasons he believed that the revolutionaries should have been confronted immediately with force of arms and not with negotiations.[11]

For the time being Bismarck was out of favor with his own conservative colleagues, for he was not asked to participate in the organization of the Prussian Conservative party or in founding the conservative newspaper, the *Kreuzzeitung*. His only support came from the prince of Prussia; the king, though recognizing Bismarck's loyalty, considered him too wild and too reactionary and refused to appoint him to a responsible position. There is a trace of ruthlessness in Bismarck's letter to his mother-in-law in November of 1849, in which he dismisses her sympathy for the Hungarian revolutionaries and defends the mass executions of revolutionaries in Austria. She was, he wrote, only following the principles of Rousseau which had guided Louis XVI when, by his reluctance to execute one man, he assumed the guilt for destroying millions.

The years immediately after the revolution were, for Bismarck, contemplative ones. His views and attitudes matured, and he turned from a narrow defense of his own interests, and those of his class, toward a more general conservative outlook, against bourgeois capitalism and intellectual liberalism. His Prussian particularism, however, remained unchanged, and he refused to recognize German nationalism.

In the February 1849 election, Bismarck won a seat in the lower Prussian chamber and on April 3, 1849, when King Friedrich Wilhelm IV refused to accept the imperial crown offered to him by the Frankfurt Assembly, Bismarck defended the king's action. To accept the crown, Bismarck declared, would be to subordinate the monarchy to popular sovereignty and drive Prussia into a war with Austria at a time when the revolution was meeting defeat everywhere in central Europe. Bismarck preferred an independent Prussia to a Germany united under the Frankfurt constitution.

Only a strong and independent Prussia would be able to play her part in Germany and in Europe. This meant a continuous expansion of Prussia's military and economic power north of the Main achieved through military conventions with the lesser states and an extension of the Customs Union. Independence would be achieved with or without Austria.[12] The implications were clear: "with" Austria meant that Prussia would be equal and not subordinate to Austria, and "without" Austria really meant against her. Thus Bismarck's future policies toward Austria, first as Prussian delegate at the Frankfurt Diet and later as Prussian prime minister, began to take shape. For the time being, however, he opposed the king's plan for a German Union, conceived by Radowitz, as much as he had opposed the plan of the Frankfurt Assembly of which the Radowitz plan was but a variant. This plan envisaged a union of north and central German States under Prussian leadership in a wider German federation under Austria. Prussia would have had to submit to a federal executive, and to this Bismarck objected. The Prussian Union project foundered on Austria's objections, for Austria saw in it an attempt to challenge her claim for supremacy in Germany. This situation, combined with the Schleswig-Holstein and the Hessian problems,[13] almost led to a war between Austria and Prussia in the fall of 1850. Only Friedrich Wilhelm IV's submission to combined Russian and Austrian pressure prevented war. With the agreement of Olmuetz, November 29, 1850, Prussia officially abandoned her Union project and recognized the reestablishment of the German Confederation and the Diet at Frankfurt.

Bismarck first attacked the government for giving in to Austria. Following the example of his hero, Frederick the Great, he would rather have gone to war. "In foreign policy," he told his friend Ludwig von Gerlach, "he [Bismarck], like Frederick the Great in 1740, recognized no rights, only conveniences."[14] But Bismarck soon changed his mind. Whether he recognized that Prussia's army was inferior to Austria's or that Friedrich Wilhelm IV was not a Frederick the Great is difficult to determine. In any case, in a speech to the Prussian Parliament he defended the government's policy forcefully on the ground that Prussia could not go to war against two major conservative powers, Austria and Russia, in defense of an unworkable constitution and the principles of the 1848 Revolution.[15] "According to my [Bismarck's] conviction, Prussian honor does not consist in Prussia's playing the Don Quixote all over Germany for the benefit of mortified celebrities from parliament. . . . I look for Prussian honor in Prussia's abstinence before all things from every shameful union with democracy."[16] Bismarck's speech had important consequences.

Unable to agree on a reorganization of the Confederation, the German states decided to return to the prerevolutionary system, and the problem of whom to send as Prussian representative to the Diet at Frankfurt arose. In the aftermath of Olmuetz, this job would have been a thankless task for any man, and many candidates declined. At this point, Ludwig von Gerlach, Bismarck's friend and mentor and the king's chief adjutant, remembered Bismarck's spirited speech in the Assembly and suggested his appointment to the king. Friedrich Wilhelm, mindful of Bismarck's lack of experience in diplomatic matters, was initially reluctant but later agreed, with the proviso that the Prussian minister at St. Petersburg, von Rochow, be transferred temporarily to Frankfurt to familiarize Bismarck with the intricacies of protocol and negotiations with the Austrians. When Bismarck readily agreed to accept the position, the king complimented him on his courage in assuming this difficult assignment. "It is the courage of Your Majesty," Bismarck replied, "to trust me with such a position. I have the courage to obey, if Your Majesty has the courage to give the orders."[17]

Frankfurt
St. Petersburg
Paris
1851–1862

The relationship between Austria and Prussia at the Frankfurt Diet before the 1848 Revolution had been cordial because Prussia had recognized Austria's supremacy without reservation. After the revolution, and especially after Olmuetz, their relationship changed considerably. Vienna expected another Prussian attempt toward German unification and was determined not only to resist but to expand Austrian power and influence throughout the German Confederation. Austrian Prime Minister Schwarzenberg's plan was to unify Germany under Austrian leadership and to create a central European empire—*Mitteleuropa*. Berlin, on the other hand, was equally determined to achieve parity with Austria in the Confederation, and military and economic leadership in north Germany.[1]

In many ways Bismarck's appointment to Frankfurt constituted the fulfillment of his hopes and dreams; at the same time, he continued to long for the peaceful country life. "To be *Landrat* in Schoenhausen is still my ideal," he wrote to his friend Kleist-Retzow at the time. But when, after one year in Frankfurt he had to go to Vienna, he wrote to Johanna, "I long for Frankfurt as if it were Kniephof."[2]

When he came to Frankfurt he was exceedingly suspicious of Austrian aims and intentions. He was convinced that however Prussia might try, she could never appease Austria and that there was simply not enough room in Germany for the two powers to exist side by side. He believed Austria would use any means to subdue Prussia, including allying herself to France, Russia, Prussian liberals, or south German ultramontanes, or involving Germany in a foreign war, if these acts would maintain her supremacy in the Germanies. To forestall these possibilities, Bismarck felt that Prussia had to bring about a solution to the German question whenever the European situation was in her favor. The Prussian government was reluctant to face this issue squarely; while trying to assert itself north of the Main, it was, at the same time, afraid of offending Austria and her many sympathizers throughout the Germanies. Consequently Prussian policy toward Austria vacillated between defiance and compliance. At the Diet, Bismarck's role was a difficult one: preventing Berlin from showing weakness or compliance toward Austria, and simultaneously challenging Austria more forcefully than his instructions permitted. He tried to influence his government to consider the possibility of alliance with Russia and France against Austria, an act which would exert pressure on Austria from outside Germany. By strengthening Prussia's military and economic position through the Customs Union, railroad, postal, and banking agreements, and currency, trade, and military conventions with the lesser states, Bismarck hoped to make Prussia the center of the unity movement in Germany.

On July 15, 1851, Bismarck, who at the time of his appointment had been given the rank of counselor of legation (*geheimer Legationsrat*), became Prussia's minister of the Federal Diet. Von Rochow, who had instructed Bismarck in his new duties, left Frankfurt to return to his post at St. Petersburg, and from August 27 on, Bismarck was on his own. In his first encounter with Count Thun, the Austrian representative, Bismarck made a point of impressing on the count and the representatives of the other German states that, henceforth, Prussia was to be treated as Austria's equal. When Thun appeared in his shirtsleeves for a meeting, Bismarck took off his jacket; and when the Austrian, alone among the assembled diplomats, lit a cigar, Bismarck took one of his own and asked the surprised Thun for matches.[3] These were petty moves, but they stressed a point which was not lost on the representatives of the lesser states.

More serious were the discussions over the Prussian Customs Union and Austria's desire to join it. Because Austria's membership appealed to regional as well as national interests among the lesser states, Prussia could not oppose Austrian membership outright. Instead, the Prussian government decided to procrastinate. This decision was made easier by discussions within Austria. The industrialists demanded protective tariffs for their goods within the Customs Union, while the Austrian government aimed for free trade. Meanwhile, Prussia strengthened her position by concluding trade treaties outside the Customs Union with Hanover, Oldenburg, and Schaumburg-Lippe (September 7, 1851). At a conference in Vienna during January–February 1852, Austria tried unsuccessfully to persuade the lesser German states to support her inclusion in the Union. While these states opposed Prussian political pressure, their economic ties with and through the Customs Union were too strong to be broken.[4] In Frankfurt, Bismarck rejected all Austrian attempts to set up a competing central European Customs Union project and threatened Prussia's withdrawal from the Diet should Austria succeed. He also opposed Austria's intention to enact a stringent federal press law which would have banned all newspapers that advocated socialism, communism, or the overthrow of the monarchy. Bismarck's objections were not based on his belief in freedom of the press but on his opposition to the creation of a strong federal executive which would threaten the interests of Prussia.[5] And though a majority of delegates were in favor of the Austrian proposal, Bismarck was able to defeat it because a unanimous vote was needed to pass it.

At about the same time, Bismarck used the temporary absence of an Austrian representative—Thun was exchanging places with Prokesch, the Austrian minister in Berlin—to press for a revision of voting procedures at the Diet in favor of equality of members, more liberal access to the archives, and a more equitable administrative procedure which, until then, had heavily favored Austria and her allies. Prokesch, the new Austrian representative, a well-known historian and archeologist but a poor diplomat, was not able to stand up to Bismarck's reasonable and well-formulated arguments,[6] especially when they were supported by a majority of the delegates. As a result, a good number of Bismarck's proposals were adopted.[7]

Austria's acquiescent attitude did not signal a change of policy at the Diet so much as recognition of a change in the European diplomatic situation. The approaching Crimean War made it mandatory for Austria to keep the situation in Germany under control and to oppose Russian moves on the lower Danube, which threatened Austria's economic and political interests in this region. Austria was prepared to join Britain and France in their support of Turkey against Russia, and this in turn meant Russian enmity and the possibility of Russian-Prussian collaboration unless Prussia could be persuaded to support and follow Austria's policy.

Bismarck realized the implications of Austria's dilemma and wanted to keep Prussia and all the other German states free of any entanglements in the Balkans. This policy earned him Russia's gratitude, which could later be used against Austria. If, on the other hand, Prussia followed Austria's anti-Russian policy in this crisis, she should demand equality with Austria at the Diet. "No sentimental alliances," he wrote to Gerlach in February 1854, "which, secure in the knowledge of a good deed, find their reward in noble sacrifices." (*Nur keine sentimentalen Buendnisse, bei denen das Bewusstsein der guten Tat den Lohn edler Aufopferung zu bilden hat.*)[8] But Bismarck's advice went unheeded. Instead, partly to accommodate Austria, partly to exercise a restraining influence on her, Prussia concluded an alliance with her on April 20, 1854.[9] But Bismarck was able to thwart Austrian wishes when, in January 1855, she demanded that the German states order a partial mobilization of their troops to back her anti-Russian Crimean policy. Taking account of the lesser states' suspicion and their reluctance to oppose Austria openly and outright, Bismarck persuaded them to declare their armed neutrality against a general threat of war rather than against Russia alone, as Austria had demanded. His original goal had, in this way, been at least partially achieved, and his leadership in this maneuver was recognized in Vienna as well as in St. Petersburg. At the same time, he was aware that the German states had no intention of following Prussia's lead in solving the German question and that Austria was still the major power. These events convinced him that a solution to the German problem would only come about in the context of European political developments.[10]

During the summer of 1855, Bismarck visited Paris and the World's Fair, and to the chagrin of Leopold von Gerlach, made the acquaintance of Napoleon III and other French and English statesmen and politicians. Bismarck tried to calm his friend's fear by assuring him that an eager diplomat could not forever remain politically chaste. He also seems to have considered the possibility of cooperating with France and Russia and to have talked about the inevitability of an Austro-Prussian war. These speculations found no favor with Friedrich Wilhelm IV; he could not see how he, a king by the grace of God, could approach Napoleon III, the son of the revolution, to improve Prussia's position in Germany. But Bismarck refused to recognize this distinction; in a number of letters to Gerlach and Manteuffel, the prime minister, Bismarck tried to explain that eventually all regimes become legitimate and that, indeed, many territorial claims had revolutionary origins.[11]

At Frankfurt, meanwhile, Prokesch had been replaced by Count Rechberg, who would have liked to return to Metternich's policy of cooperation with Prussia; however, Buol, the Austrian prime minister, disagreed. Instead, he insisted that Rechberg, with the cooperation of the lesser states, obtain a majority at the Diet and outvote Prussia on all important issues. For Bismarck this became an intolerable situation. In a long and confidential conversation with Rechberg in June 1857, Bismarck explained that they, the representatives of the two major powers in Germany, should cease to pretend that the interests of Germany were constantly and foremost on their minds and, instead, openly admit and defend the interests of their own countries. He, Bismarck, would prefer an understanding between Prussia and Austria, but should this be impossible, Austria should know that Prussia would not hesitate to go to war against her. Rechberg was much taken aback by this unusual disclosure, but Bismarck's cool behavior toward him after his return from Paris, and his unusual friendliness toward the ministers of France, Russia, and Sardinia (all possible Austrian enemies) seemed to lend credence to his words. Actually, Bismarck was bluffing; the Prussian government was not supporting his tough policy, and an Austrian inquiry in Berlin would have cleared up the matter very quickly. But Bismarck gambled on Austrian reluctance to make such an inquiry and events proved him right.[12] When Austria continued to refuse to recognize Prussia's equality at the Diet, Bismarck started a war of nerves and used even the most insignificant details to assert Prussian rights. This, in turn, led to interminable procedural squabbles, prolonged conferences, and heated discussions. It was, in many ways, a fruitless undertaking which could only emphasize the uselessness of the Assembly and the Confederation. But Bismarck did not care; to him it was a matter of Prussian honor and power, and anything else was of little concern. Still, there was one major achievement to his credit during this period: Denmark's recognition of the Confederation's rights in Holstein and Lauenburg, a partial and temporary solution to the very complicated Schleswig-Holstein question.[13]

In the fall of 1858, Prince Wilhelm became regent of Prussia when his brother, King Friedrich Wilhelm IV, was pronounced insane.[14] Bismarck hoped to find the new ruler more sympathetic to his views, but this was not quite the case. In an earlier memorandum of March 1858, he had explained to Prince Wilhelm that Prussia could only succeed in her German policy if she ceased to court the lesser states, because Austria had more influence with them. Prussia's interests were identical with those of the people of the lesser states but not with those of their governments. Germany, Bismarck warned, was not synonymous with the Federal Diet, which was really an obstacle to Germany's future development.[15] Prussia's independence was being endangered by Austria, and Prussia's future could only be found outside the Confederation. The regent shared these views, but when Bismarck advocated an active and forceful policy of opposition toward Austria and declared that if the need arose, Prussia might even have to go to war against Austria, Wilhelm drew back. He was too much of a traditionalist to entertain such an idea, as his support of Austria during the Crimean War demonstrated. Wilhelm was determined to initiate better relations with Austria. Bismarck was obviously the wrong man for this in Frankfurt. Rumors of his differences with the regent had reached the Diet, where many of his colleagues would have been happy to see him replaced by a more congenial and pliable man, one who would recognize Austria's supremacy and be less of a troublemaker.

In January 1859, the government in Berlin decided on Bismarck's transfer to St. Petersburg. When he learned of it he was less than happy, though the post was considered among the most important in the Prussian diplomatic service. He hated to leave Frankfurt, especially when his policy was about to pay off. With the approach of the Austro-Sardinian War, Prussia's importance to Austria had increased significantly, and it was this moment, in the shifting balance of power, that Bismarck had planned to use to Prussia's advantage. Leaving now meant giving up eight years of hard work and watching his enemies triumph. Powerless, Bismarck was forced to watch Prussia and the Confederation agree to cooperate with Austria during her struggle in

Italy; this meant the end of his plans and his policy. On February 24, 1859, he attended the Diet for the last time, and on March 6 he left Frankfurt for St. Petersburg.[16]

Bismarck's reception in the Russian capital was extremely friendly. His pro-Russian policy during the Crimean War was well remembered, and he quickly established close ties with the czar's mother, Princess Charlotte, sister of the Prussian regent, as well as with the czar and his consort, Maria, a Hessian princess. As a result, the official atmosphere in St. Petersburg turned out to be a great improvement over Frankfurt, and Bismarck had a much easier life at his new post. At the same time, he was aware that his influence in Berlin had diminished considerably and felt that he had been "put on ice on the Neva."[17] But he was not willing to continue to play an inactive part.

Encouraged by the Austro-Sardinian War, Bismarck tried to convince Schleinitz, the new Prussian foreign minister, that the European political situation was uniquely favorable to Prussia. Austria should either agree to a more realistic relationship with Prussia at the Diet, or the Diet and the Confederation would have to be abolished. Prussia should then take over the leadership of a new German Federation, and with it, the leadership of the federal army. The Prussian army should then move into south Germany where there was considerable fear of a French invasion, and when crossing the border, the soldiers should put the frontier posts in their knapsacks and not put them down again until they reached Lake Constance or the southern limits of the Protestant faith.[18] While Schleinitz rejected these extreme views, he was sufficiently impressed by Bismarck's reports and letters to resist Austrian demands and Diet resolutions which would have dragged Prussia into the Austro-Sardinian War. He failed, however, to see the opportunities that the war presented—which Bismarck had pointed out to him—and declined to use Austria's predicament in favor of Prussia. The regent also shared Schleinitz's opinion; having grown up in the peaceful Metternich era, the prince meant to preserve peace. He considered Bismarck's opinions revolutionary and wanted no part of them. That these two men should ever find themselves in as close a relationship as they later did seemed impossible at the time.[19] Prussian public opinion regarding the Austro-Sardinian War was confused and divided. Some saw in Napoleon III's participation a parallel to Napoleon

I's campaign in Italy and wanted to help Austria prevent a repetition of familiar, though half-forgotten, events. Others saw in the defeat of Austria a possibility for Italian unification and a model for German unity. Before the Prussian government could make up its mind which policy to follow, Austria acknowledged her defeat by the combined French and Sardinian forces at Solferino and concluded an armistice at Villafranca on July 11, 1859, by whose terms she lost Lombardy but kept Venetia.

A month earlier Bismarck had contracted an illness which plagued him until the early part of the following year. (It was apparently caused by a neglected shinbone injury which developed into pneumonia, and at one point, brought him close to death.) He had left St. Petersburg for Berlin in July 1859, and although he had tried to return to his post (in October he participated at a meeting of the czar and the regent at Breslau), he was unable to do so because of a recurrent attack. He was forced to spend the winter on the von Below estate in Hohendorf near Elbing. In March 1860, he was finally well enough to go to Berlin, but his return to St. Petersburg was delayed partly because he needed to recuperate and partly because he was being considered as foreign minister to succeed Schleinitz.

Despite strong recommendations from many officials, Wilhelm could not be persuaded to accept Bismarck as foreign minister and asked Schleinitz to serve another term. Bismarck left for St. Petersburg at the end of May. There he won the confidence of Czar Alexander II and Gorchakov, the foreign minister, to such an extent that this relationship, strengthened by the family ties which bound the Romanovs and Hohenzollerns, formed the basis of Prussian-Russian friendship for decades to come. On the political level, this bond was also strengthened by Bismarck's support of the czar's anti-Polish policies during 1861. Bismarck realized, even then, that a liberal attitude toward the Poles by Russia would drive a wedge between Russia and Prussia because of Prussia's Polish minorities. Such an attitude would also strengthen Franco-Russian cooperation because France was a traditional champion of Polish independence. If these developments came to pass, Prussia would be isolated. Russia's anti-Polish policy, on the other hand, would deepen Russo-Prussian cooperation and isolate France. Russo-Prussian cooperation, then, was the key to Bismarck's future policy, best demonstrated by Russo-Prussian cooperation during the Polish revolt of 1863 and Russian neutrality during the Franco-Prussian war. Except for strengthening Russian-Prussian ties, Bismarck had no influence on Prussian policy during this period. He suffered in his honorable exile, as he called it, and chafed at the bit for lack of activity and excitement.[20]

In Berlin, meanwhile, reorganization of the Prussian army became a major issue between the regent and the Parliament. Wilhelm wanted to expand the regular army by reintroducing universal military service, while the deputies of the Prussian Diet favored retaining and strengthening the militia. The power of the crown in relation to that of the Parliament was at stake. Roon, minister of war and an old friend of Bismarck's, wanted to get Bismarck into the cabinet to strengthen the crown's case. He suggested appointing Bismarck, but Wilhelm was too suspicious of the "Pomeranian Junker" to agree. Bismarck and the king talked while Wilhelm was taking the cure in Baden-Baden, and during the conversation it became clear how far apart they were in their political views. Wilhelm was intent on safeguarding the principle of legitimacy everywhere and under all conditions, and had therefore supported Austria in the Crimean and Italian wars and had refused to recognize the illegitimate Kingdom of Italy. Bismarck, for his part, was interested only in what he considered to be the vital interests of Prussia. The end of the Italian mini-states and the overthrow of the Kingdom of Naples were matters of complete indifference to him. On the contrary, he considered the existence of a unified Italian kingdom an important asset for the successful development of Prussian policy. Still, Wilhelm valued Bismarck's judgment enough to ask his opinion about domestic policy, especially in connection with a new plan advocated by Roggenbach, a liberal Baden minister and a confidant of the Prussian crown prince.

Roggenbach's plan envisaged a reform of the German Confederation under the leadership of Prussia without, however, antagonizing Austria. It followed along the lines of the lesser German solution but provided for an alliance with Austria and mutual guarantees of each other's territories. Bismarck ignored the question of how to promote peace between Austria and Prussia and declared that it was rather a question of how to exert German power in Europe. The road to this goal was not by way of the Federal Diet, he said, but through Prussia's Customs Union. By giving the Customs Union members parliamentary representation, Prussia's national aims would be served as well. Not only would there be common trade and traffic legislation, but also a common army supported by Customs Union receipts. Bismarck's plan was carefully attuned to Wilhelm's views. He, too, had advocated a strengthening of the Customs Union, but in Bismarck's plan this was merely a point of departure; the Customs Union Parliament was the core of the matter, since it would assure Prussia's supremacy and Austria's exclusion. When presenting this plan, Bismarck avoided any references to the exercise of power or territorial conquests, but Wilhelm was not impressed and nothing came of it. Still, Bismarck continued to promote this plan while he accompanied the king to the coronation ceremonies at Koenigsberg (Friedrich Wilhelm IV had recently died, and Wilhelm was crowned king of Prussia on January 2, 1861) and back to Berlin.[21]

In the fall of 1861, the Prussian Conservative party published its program, which consisted of a strong endorsement of the principles of legitimacy and an equally strong condemnation of nationalism and popular sovereignty. Bismarck vigorously attacked it and was, in turn, branded as a revolutionary by the conservatives.[22] His old friends, the Gerlachs, Kleist-Retzows, Belows, and Blanckenburgs, were dismayed at his stand, and from then on a deepening rift developed between them.

When Bismarck returned to St. Petersburg toward the end of 1861, his future was not at all clear. There had been rumors of his reassignment to Paris or London, and during the winter when German domestic conditions took a turn for the worse (in connection with federal reforms and a renewal of the Schleswig-Holstein question), there was again talk of his entering the Cabinet. He returned to Berlin on May 10, 1862, but his audience with the king on May 13 brought no decision. Wilhelm still resisted and, possibly under the influence of Queen Augusta, finally decided against Bismarck's appointment. Instead, Bismarck was sent as minister to Paris and advised not to settle down at his new post but to keep himself available.

Paris was not a happy assignment. Bismarck went there alone, without his family and without his favorite mare, and this, combined with the uncertainty about his future, made him edgy and dissatisfied. His reception by Napoleon III was friendly enough, but Bismarck was bored with his duties, and after a few weeks, he went to London to visit the World's Fair. There he met Palmerston, Lord John Russell, and Disraeli; when asked by Disraeli what he planned to do should he become Prussian prime minister, Bismarck apparently replied that he would carry through the pending army reforms, with or without the consent of the Parliament, go to war with Austria, and unify Germany under Prussian leadership.[23] Disraeli was impressed, and years later when these ideas had become realities, he often remembered their conversation.

Upon his return to Paris, Bismarck felt the need to restore his health and asked and was granted leave to go to the south of France in July 1862. In Biarritz he met Nicolai and Kathy Orlow (Nicolai was Russian minister in Brussels), whom he had known in St. Petersburg. Bismarck spent several weeks in their company. He fell in love with Kathy Orlow, who was young, beautiful, and vivacious, played his favorite music, and went on long walks with him. He wrote his wife about the wonderful time he was having, and Johanna, secure in her love and knowledge of her husband, was pleased that he was happy. It was such a fine vacation that he overstayed his leave and did not return to Paris until September 16.

In Berlin, the constitutional conflict between the government and the Parliament had deepened to the point where even the king's conservative ministers advised him to make concessions. But Wilhelm refused; when the ministers would no longer support him, he declared that he would abdicate and called for the crown prince on September 17. On the same day, Roon sent an urgent telegram to Paris, asking Bismarck to come to Berlin, "There is danger in delay. Come at once." When he received the message, Bismarck took the train to Berlin on September 19 and arrived in the capital twenty-four hours later.[24]

Bismarck's Appointment and the Constitutional Conflict in Prussia

Arriving in Berlin on September 20, Bismarck saw Roon, who told him of the king's desire to abdicate. That evening the crown prince asked Bismarck for his views on the political situation. Bismarck evaded the issue, reluctant to discuss matters he thought should properly first be discussed with the king.[1] Roon saw the king the following day after church, and reported his feeling that the rift in the Cabinet could not be healed; appealing to the king's sense of duty, Roon urged him not to abdicate until all possible means of solving the conflict with Parliament had been exhausted. Alluding to Bismarck, Roon reminded the king that there was still one man who had not been called into the Cabinet who was willing to take on the responsibilities of office. Wilhelm hesitated. He still distrusted Bismarck and had mentioned his misgivings to the crown prince who, though he agreed with his father, had been at a loss to suggest an alternative.[2] Roon was insistent, the king evasive. "He [Bismarck] would not want to take over at this stage," he told Roon, "besides, he is not here and one could not discuss this with him." "He is here," Roon replied, "and will gladly follow Your Majesty's call."[3] The king yielded.

Bismarck's audience with the king in the castle and gardens of Babelsberg on September 22, 1862, was as decisive for the future of the two men as it was for the fate of Prussia-Germany. The king explained that he had been unable to find a minister who could resolve the impasse with Parliament, and that he intended to abdicate rather than accede to the delegates' demands. He then asked Bismarck what

CONSTITUTIONAL CONFLICT IN PRUSSIA

conditions he attached to his appointment and when Bismarck replied that he felt like a vassal toward his feudal lord and would support his king unconditionally, Wilhelm was much relieved. The king abandoned all thoughts of abdicating and decided instead to continue the fight against parliamentary opposition. Still, there was the question of how Bismarck intended to resolve the conflict. The king had prepared a lengthy memorandum on domestic and foreign policy, which was intended to hold the new appointee to a definite program. But the future chancellor and prime minister was not to be tied down so easily. He was as unwilling to divulge his plans as he was reluctant to make commitments regarding his future policy. It was, he told the king, a struggle for supremacy between royal government and parliamentary rule, and the parliament could be suppressed by a brief dictatorship, if need be.[4] To dispel any further doubts, Bismarck promised to submit willingly to all royal decisions as long as he was permitted to explain to the king any policies of his which conflicted with the king's commands. If, despite his explanations, the royal decision remained unchanged, Bismarck assured Wilhelm that he "would rather perish together with [him] than abandon [him] . . . in the fight against parliamentary domination."[5] The king was overwhelmed. He appointed Bismarck temporary chairman of the Cabinet, and two weeks later made him prime minister and foreign minister.

Johanna first learned about her husband's appointment through the newspapers. When Bismarck wrote her on September 24, he referred to his appointment, which he had sought and aspired to for over a quarter of a century, as "our misery" and asked her to submit to God's will.[6]

The constitutional conflict in Prussia, the principal reason for Bismarck's appointment, involved military reforms and the budgetary authorizations connected with these reforms. The problem was not whether the reforms were necessary, but how they should be carried out and, more important, whether the Lower House of the Prussian Parliament or the king had the authority to implement these reforms and to appropriate the necessary funds. The parties to this conflict were the king and the conservative delegates on one side and the liberal delegates, who held a majority in the Parliament, on the other. Implicit here was the liberal majority's desire to use the conflict as a test of the budgetary powers of the Lower House. As the struggle dragged on, it became increasingly clear that this was not merely a squabble over constitutional technicalities, but a fight which involved the very spirit and future character of the Prussian state.

General von Roon, minister of war since December 5, 1859, initiated the army reforms. His plan envisaged an increase in the call-up of annual recruits from 40,000 to 63,000 men (with three years of active service) and a corresponding increase of the standing army of 150,000 to 220,000 men. This would give the army an additional 39 infantry and 10 cavalry regiments. There would also be a change in the relationship between regular (line) troops and the militia (*Landwehr*). Under Roon's plan, the future wartime army would be composed entirely of regular troops, while the militia would be confined to garrison and fortress duties and to the supply services. The cost of these reforms was estimated to be about 9.5 million thaler annually.[7]

The value of the militia as a democratic force was a much debated issue. The militia's revolutionary spirit of 1813 had vanished by the 1850s, and its military value had been greatly diminished. The regular army, on the other hand, had become identified with the fatherland in the minds of the prince regent and the officer corps, especially after the shocking experience of the 1848 Revolution. Furthermore, it was believed that three years' service would make the recruits immune to the revolutionary *Zeitgeist* and convinced partisans of the monarchy.[8]

While the need for army reforms was generally recognized, questions over their scope and the authority for their implementation arose almost immediately. Both king and the Lower House of the Prussian Parliament claimed primary jurisdiction; although the king recognized the preeminence of the legislature in budgetary matters, he refused to share his exclusive rights and powers over the army. Wilhelm's position was based on the Prussian constitution of December 1848 and its revisions of January 1850, which left the army under the exclusive jurisdiction of the king. Soldiers swore allegiance to the king, not the constitution, while civil servants were required to uphold the constitution.[9] This was in line with conservative views formulated during the early nineteenth century Prussian reform movement, which advocated strict separation of civilian and military powers. The former could de-

CONSTITUTIONAL CONFLICT IN PRUSSIA

velop along liberal-constitutional lines, while the latter, based on autocratic concepts, belonged exclusively to the crown.[10]

Another point of dispute concerned the character of the future army. The organizational details of a large army based on universal military service could have been worked out between the government and the Lower House had the government been willing to use the army for national defense and to pursue a national German policy. What irked the liberals was the government's well-known intention of using the army to bring about conservative domestic reforms and to guard against future uprisings. The liberals wanted to preserve and expand General Boyen's reforms of 1814–15, which had started with the establishment of a national militia. Boyen's idea had been to replace an army of subjects (*Untertanen*) with an army of citizens—a national people's army.[11] But Wilhelm and his supporters saw in the militia an expression of the liberal national spirit. They wanted a more conservative, royalist army which would be a reliable tool against domestic disturbances. They wished to increase the term of service from two years to three to enhance the prestige of the military, curb civilian influence, and make the army independent of public opinion. Wilhelm and his followers believed that continuation of the shorter term of service would enlarge the status of the militia, further democratize the army, and hamper the government's freedom of decision. Wilhelm believed that the Lower House had the right and the duty to vote on expenditures, but only the king had the power over the army and its organization.[12]

The liberal majority favored army reforms but made them dependent on two conditions: a two-year term of service and the maintenance of the existing ratio between the regular army and the militia. On February 10, 1860, when the government submitted a bill on army reorganization which included an extension of service and a request for 9.5 million thaler, the committee of the Lower House rejected the request. Wilhelm (then prince regent) refused to authorize any of the changes in the bill which the committee had suggested. Instead, the government took the position that it really did not need the Parliament's authorization for a reorganization of the army because the army was under the exclusive jurisdiction of the crown. The government had approached the legislature in a spirit of cooperation, but once rebuffed, the crown invoked its executive powers. At the same time the government reintroduced the request for 9.5 million thaler for the period May 1, 1860 to June 30, 1861, as a provisional measure to increase the battle readiness of the troops. The minister of finance who submitted the request reaffirmed its provisional nature by assuring the delegates that unless funds were renewed, the entire measure could later be rescinded.[13] The delegates, believing they would still have the decisive voice regarding army reorganization and trusting the finance minister's assurances, approved the government's request on May 15, 1860, by a vote of 350 to 2. That same day the government dissolved thirty-six militia regiments; this and subsequent measures made it clear that far from considering these measures provisional, the government regarded them as permanent. During the following legislative session, the government introduced no army reorganization proposal, though the Lower House, by a considerably smaller majority, again approved the "provisional" appropriations. At the same time, it asked the government to submit proposals for army reorganization during the following year.[14]

The conservatives were badly beaten in the elections of 1861. Their number was reduced to 14, while 250 liberals were returned. (These were composed of 91 old liberals [*Altliberale*], 50 of the liberal center [*linkes Zentrum*], and 109 of the radical liberals [*radikale Linke*].)[15] In response to the request of the Lower House, the government submitted a draft for reorganization of the army. It was the same bill that the Lower House had rejected the previous year. Obviously, the government would neither change its policy nor be intimidated by the results of the election. The Lower House, on the other hand, was unwilling to extend the "provisional" army expenditures again, and to forestall any budgetary modifications by the government, a liberal delegate (Hagen) asked that the government submit a detailed budget for the then current fiscal year (1862). This the government was unwilling to do, and Wilhelm dissolved the Parliament on March 11, 1862. Liberal ministers in the government were dismissed and replaced with more conservative ones; the so-called liberal era was at an end.[16]

New elections in May 1862 continued the trend of the previous year and the conservatives were beaten once again. They lost 3 seats, retaining 11, while the liberals gained 35, for a total of 285 or 80 percent of the Lower House. Under these circumstances concessions by the Lower House were unlikely, and several ministers, including Roon, advised the king[17] to compromise with the liberal majority and to consider a two-year term of service for the army. But Wilhelm would not be persuaded. He was ready to govern without a budget, though his ministers advised him, on September 9, 1862, that this was illegal under the constitution. The liberals suggested a compromise: they would agree to create and pay for new regiments of line troops, if the government would agree to a two-year term of service. The king's ministers approved this compromise, but the king insisted on a three-year term. During a crown council on September 17, 1862, Wilhelm reaffirmed his views and expressed his readiness to relinquish the crown if the ministers insisted on a compromise with the Lower House.[18] That day Roon sent his telegram to Paris, asking Bismarck to return to Berlin at once.

It is easy to accuse both parties in this conflict of excessive stubbornness and of concentrating on apparently minor issues while the country was driven into a major constitutional crisis. But the fight over the length of army service was only the tip of the iceberg. Underneath lay the fundamental question of who should exercise power in the state: the Lower House or the crown. The liberals were determined to use the conflict and their control over the budget to attain power in the Parliament; this power could then be used to initiate a national German policy in Prussian foreign affairs. They also intended to achieve parliamentary government and to restrain the powers of the Prussian crown by popular representation. The Prussian liberals tried to achieve, in a legal way, the democratic-constitutional system which had been defeated by the counterrevolution of 1848–49.

It was precisely this effort that Wilhelm opposed with all the means and energy at his command. He was neither ready to permit the erosion of royal privileges nor willing to submit the traditional powers of the monarchy to a popular vote. Should either occur, he wrote to the grand duke of Baden, we would be "slaves of parliament." Wilhelm was convinced that the Prussian crown had been bestowed on the Hohenzollerns by the grace of God and that giving in to the demands of the Lower House of the Parliament would flout God's will and lead to a bourgeois monarchy. By assuming the final decision over army reorganization and length of service, Wilhelm felt that he was defending the royal prerogative as the indisputable basis of the constitution.[19]

The battle was joined. Bismarck's appointment appeared to contribute nothing to its solution. Most commentators of the time refused to take the appointment seriously and considered Bismarck quite unsuitable to lead the country out of this grave domestic crisis.[20] The liberals considered him an arch-conservative and "his appointment the desperate act of a distraught King."[21] The conservatives believed him too liberal, pragmatic, and unreliable. Bismarck himself was fully aware of the dangers and frustrations of his position. He realized that the queen was antagonistic to him and opposed to his policies and that many at Court and in influential positions were in sympathy with her. He owed his appointment to the king, not to any parliamentary or governmental faction; it was based entirely on Wilhelm's trust and confidence, and only Wilhelm could dismiss him. It had taken Wilhelm a long time to overcome his suspicion of Bismarck, and it had taken a major crisis to force Wilhelm to accept Bismarck's services. Bismarck's apparent submission to the king's views and his posture of a vassal accepting appointment from his feudal lord struck responsive cords and played a decisive part in Wilhelm's decision. And Bismarck was not totally insincere, for he believed deeply in this feudal relationship. His attachment to the king was reinforced by the realization that without the preservation of a strong Prussian monarchy there would be no possibility of solving the major problems which Prussia would have to face in the future. Bismarck was also concerned that Wilhelm's abdication would seriously weaken the royalist cause to which Bismarck was deeply attached. In his view, the majority in the Lower House was not truly representative of the Prussian people, but only of the Prussian bourgeoisie. Prussia was the creation of the Hohenzollern dynasty. It was not a nation, any more than its eastern and western parts could claim national identity. An effective Prussian policy was therefore only possible under strong monarchical leadership, and this required a powerful army under absolute royal control.[22]

Bismarck began his new career by attempting to conciliate the opposition. He offered cabinet posts to the liberal deputies Vincke, Simson,

CONSTITUTIONAL CONFLICT IN PRUSSIA

and Sybel, but was unable to grant the two-year army service on which the liberals insisted. Privately, Bismarck promised to persuade the king to adopt the two-year term (which Bismarck preferred because it would result in a greater number of trained reserves), but the prospects for this were remote and the liberals, unwilling to procrastinate on this issue, refused to enter the government.[23] Thus, the new prime minister had to look for new ways to resolve the conflict.

Following royal orders, he withdrew the budget for 1863 which had been submitted to the Lower House with the 1862 budget. By doing this, the government made any attempt by the opposition to eliminate funds for the army reorganization for the current year impossible. At the same time, Bismarck made it clear that if the Lower House refused military funds for 1862, he would govern without a budget. In his speech of September 30, 1862, he defended this policy by reminding the delegates that he had accepted his appointment from the king with the condition that he would, if need be, govern without a budget. The Prussian Parliament, he pointed out, had no exclusive power over appropriations. Instead, it was necessary for the Upper and Lower houses, together with the crown, to come to an agreement. Should one of these three reject a proposed budget, there would be a "tabula rasa"—a clean slate. In this event, which could be considered an emergency, the government had the right to govern without a budget, because the crown retained all those rights not expressly allocated to the Parliament by the constitution. This was Bismarck's famous theory of the "constitutional gap."[24]

Bismarck reminded his listeners that the German people looked to Prussia not for her liberalism but for her power. Several opportunities for Prussia to exert her leadership in Germany had already been missed. Prussia must concentrate her power; her frontiers, as fixed by the Congress of Vienna, were not suitable to healthy development. "Not through speeches and majority decisions will the great questions of the period be decided—those were the mistakes of 1848 and 1849— but through iron and blood."[25] This phrase (soon transposed to "blood and iron") became instantly famous. Its meaning has been debated endlessly. Contrary to many interpretations, the statement simply recognized existing political realities; it said nothing about Bismarck's plans for the unification of Germany. Bismarck realized earlier than most that Austria would not allow Prussia to attain equal status with her in Germany. Therefore, if Prussia wanted to play a leading role in Germany, as the liberals themselves desired, conferences and debates were useless and only force would achieve results.

But the Lower House was not impressed by Bismarck's speech. It accepted the budget for 1862, but deleted all military expenditures. The Upper House, however, accepted the government's budget, including the military items, thus complicating the constitutional conflict still further. As a result, Wilhelm dismissed both houses on October 13, 1862, proclaimed a state of emergency, and announced the government's intention of submitting a bill of indemnity to the Parliament once normal conditions had returned.[26]

The parliamentary session of 1863 was as futile as the previous one, except that Bismarck began a campaign against the liberals in the country at large by restricting the freedom of the press and by admonishing municipal councils not to engage in political (that is, antigovernment) activities. There was considerable popular protest against these measures and the crown prince openly disassociated himself from them.[27] Bismarck ignored the protests. The Parliament was dissolved once more and new elections called for October 28, 1863. An even larger liberal majority was elected. The deadlock continued. The government collected taxes and spent monies without parliamentary authorization; the people did not object.

When Johann Jacoby, a liberal deputy, suggested that the people should refuse to pay taxes, he was arrested for treasonable remarks. Ferdinand Lassalle, a well-known socialist and labor leader, commenting on the situation, compared conditions in England with those in Prussia:

> In England, wrote Lassalle, if the tax collector were to come to demand taxes not voted by parliament he would be thrown out of the house by the citizens. If the citizen were arrested and brought to court, he would be freed by the court and sent home with praise for having resisted illegal force. If the tax collector were to come with troops, the citizen would mobilize his friends and neighbors to oppose force with force. A battle would ensue with possible loss of life. The tax collector would then be haled into court on the charge of murder, and his defense that he acted "on orders" would be rejected by the British court since he had been engaged in "an illegal act." He would

be condemned to death. If the citizen and his friends had killed any soldiers, they would be released because they were resisting illegal force. "And because all the people know this would happen," wrote Lassalle, "everyone would refuse to pay the taxes—even those who are indifferent—in order not to be considered bad citizens. . . ."

In Prussia, Lassalle went on to say, it is different. If the Prussian citizen were to throw out the tax collector who came to collect taxes not approved by the diet he would be haled to court to receive a jail sentence for "resistance to lawful authority." If fighting and killing ensued, the soldiers would be protected from prosecution because they "obeyed orders," while the citizen who attempted to resist by force would be convicted and beheaded. "And because this is so and because from the start all the odds are against those who refuse to pay, the government will feel confident of any action it undertakes and all the officials will be loyal to it!"[28]

A major problem throughout the constitutional conflict was whether the overwhelming liberal majority of the Lower House of the Prussian Parliament accurately reflected the temper of the country at large.[29] Bismarck, who had a better understanding of political realities than most of his contemporaries, doubted that the majority of the Prussian population was as liberal as the delegates in the Lower House. The population, he believed, was for the most part rural and conservative, and the three-class system of voting gave the masses of people no adequate chance to make their voices heard. That was why Bismarck, to the horror of his old conservative friends, favored universal manhood suffrage. He believed, as did Ferdinand Lassalle, that an alliance between the nobility and the workers would defeat the middle class. But this was still in the future. The outcome of the election of 1863 would not have been materially altered by universal suffrage, nor would the deadlock between the government and the opposition have been less severe. Still, the liberals, despite their majority, felt less secure than would appear. They were uncertain of their support in the country and were unable to prevent the government from carrying on its business. Then too, trade and industry were prospering and the economic policies of the government were liberal and progressive.[30]

The Junkers, however, still believed they had inherent rights to leadership. They did not understand that industrial expansion would increase the value of their real estate and the demand for their agrarian products and that these, in turn, would transform the Junkers into upper-class capitalists and add greater political power to their newly acquired wealth.

The liberals seem not to have realized that these developments left them little time to achieve their aims. The liberals' failure to anticipate this shift in political power was due, perhaps, to their unwillingness to pursue radical measures and their lack of political acumen. Bismarck was the first to recognize the weakness of the liberals and the economic possibilities of the Junkers.[31]

By January 1864 both the government and the opposition, recognizing the hopelessness of the situation, looked to foreign affairs as a means of breaking the deadlock. There, in the tangled web of the Schleswig-Holstein question, the possibility of a compromise finally appeared.

Bismarck's
Three Wars

Despite his tough stand and show of confidence, Bismarck was unhappy about the constitutional conflict. He was mindful of public opinion and wanted popular support for government policies, not criticism and opposition. He particularly needed this support in foreign affairs, where, he believed, Prussian aims would have to be realized.

Two developments made his policies more difficult to pursue in 1863, at the height of the constitutional conflict: the Polish revolt against Russia, and Austria's attempt to join the Customs Union. The revolt in Poland in January 1863 provided Bismarck with an opportunity to establish closer ties with Russia, which he had contemplated since his stay as minister in St. Petersburg. When the Russians requested Prussian military assistance along the common border, the Prussian government, following the precedents of 1830–31 and 1848, mobilized half its army and closed its borders to Polish insurgents. General Alvensleben, the king's general adjutant, was sent to St. Petersburg to encourage further cooperation and "to strengthen the tsar's resistance to the pro-Polish party among his advisers."[1] An agreement which became known as the Alvensleben Convention was concluded on February 8, 1863: it stipulated cooperation and mutual assistance by the Russian and Prussian military commanders and permission for each to cross the border in pursuit of Polish revolutionaries. Although meant to be secret, the terms of the agreement became known in the major European capitals and led to a serious diplomatic crisis.[2] Napoleon III was particularly upset because he had pretended that the revolt was an internal Russian affair to avoid jeopardizing his country's friendly relations with Russia. Prussia's intervention made such an interpretation untenable. If a conservative power like Prussia could intervene to suppress the Poles, a liberal power like France should be able to assist them. Unwilling to challenge Russia directly, Napoleon put pressure on Prussia by suggesting that Bismarck's dismissal might ease the tension, and proposing that Britain and Austria present a joint protest in Berlin.

Strong liberal opposition to the Alvensleben Convention in the Prussian Parliament and general dissatisfaction with it throughout Germany were added to the diplomatic uproar.[3] There were rumors in Berlin of a ministerial crisis and Bismarck's resignation.[4] In an attempt to disarm his critics and forestall complications with France and Britian, Bismarck asked Gorchakov, the Russian foreign minister, to release Prussia from her commitments; the latter complied by declaring that the convention had never been in force.[5] Thus, Bismarck's first venture into foreign affairs was not exactly a resounding success (the czar called him a terrible blunderer), though Bismarck and scores of historians after him tried to present it as such.[6] Bismarck had intended to use the convention to earn Russian gratitude, suppress the uprising before the Western powers could intervene, and prevent a Franco-Russian alliance; instead, he was forced to back down in the face of determined domestic and foreign opposition.[7]

The second development in 1863 concerned Austro-Prussian rivalry for supremacy in Germany. The Austrian government realized that Prussia's humiliation at Olmuetz[8] had been only a temporary setback and that Prussia's economic leadership in the Customs Union was of more serious and more lasting consequence. Austria sought to join the Customs Union, hoping to assume leadership of a much larger free trade area in central Europe. This scheme became known as the *Mitteleuropa* plan. A good plan in theory, it foundered on the economic realities of the times. Prussia, whose economy was considerably stronger than Austria's, looked toward western Europe and the free trade opportunities of the Chevalier-Cobden treaty between Britain and France (January 23, 1860), rather than toward the protectionist system of the Austrian Empire. To this end Prussia, supported by the north German states, concluded a trade treaty with France in August 1862.[9] The Austrian government realized that the Franco-Prussian trade treaty strengthened Prussia's economic position in Germany and that Austria's chances for economic leadership in central Europe had been even further limited.

To recapture some of her lost prestige, Austria proposed a reorganization of the German Confederation which, if accepted, would have given her the preponderant influence in that body. It was a two-pronged plan. First, it called for a reorganization of the Diet at Frankfurt, by creating an assembly of delegates chosen by the state diets. Such an assembly would increase the votes of Austria and her allies to the detriment of Prussia. Bismarck countered this move with a proposal for a German parliament elected by universal suffrage. Without taking a stand on the Prussian proposal, the Diet voted on the Austrian plan and defeated it in January 1863. The second Austrian plan involved replacement of the Confederation by an assembly of princes, led by the Austrian emperor. The key to its success, as the Austrians fully realized, was Prussian cooperation. To achieve it, the Austrian emperor, Francis Joseph, personally invited King Wilhelm to an assembly of the German princes at Frankfurt. The king, flattered by the emperor's personal attention, was inclined to accept the invitation, but Bismarck was strongly opposed. In Bismarck's view, the Austrian plan, designed to attract liberal and greater German support, would impede Prussian policy and deny her a significant voice in German affairs. Wilhelm felt he could not refuse the invitation but Bismarck, after long arguments and threats of resignation, finally persuaded the king not to go. Prussia's abstention doomed the Austrian project, but a complete break between the two powers was avoided when Bismarck suggested a joint policy in the Schleswig-Holstein question.

The Danish War The Schleswig-Holstein question intruded upon the European diplomatic scene again in the spring of 1863, when King Frederick VII of Denmark announced, by royal decree, the incorporation of Schleswig and a new charter for Holstein.[10] This move violated the London Protocol of 1852, which provided for the inseparability of the duchies of Schleswig and Holstein and placed them in personal union with the Danish crown. King Frederick's proclamation was also a breach of the assurances Denmark had given Austria and Prussia in 1852, that the duchies would not be separated from each other or incorporated into Denmark. While the Danes were confident of British and Swedish support, the German Confederation (of which Holstein was a member) was much disturbed, and German public opinion was outraged. Prussia's inglorious campaign and the defeat of the Frankfurt National Assembly on the Danish question in 1848[11] had not been forgotten, and neither the Prussian government nor the people wanted a repetition of those unhappy events. Thus, when the Danish king died on November 15, 1863, German nationalists everywhere championed Duke Frederick of Augustenburg as the legitimate heir of the duchies, and urged their independence from Denmark. According to the London Protocol, however, Prince Christian was to succeed to the Danish crown and to the duchies.

For Bismarck the situation was still more complicated. On the one hand he felt that Prussia, in this instance, could not ignore German national aims if she aspired to leadership in Germany. On the other hand, supporting the duke of Augustenburg would violate the London Protocol and turn Britain, France, and Russia against Prussia. Then too, Bismarck believed that it was hardly in Prussia's interest to go to a great deal of trouble on behalf of German national aims if, in the end, he would be faced with another German state which would cast its vote against Prussia at the Diet. A better policy would be to incorporate the duchies into Prussia, by force if need be. Obviously, Bismarck could not announce these aims. Instead, he cautiously supported German public opinion without, however, endorsing the claims of the duke of Augustenburg. At the same time, he prodded Austria to join Prussia in whatever action might be appropriate against Denmark. (This was meant primarily to impress Britain, France, and Russia, to prevent Prussia's isolation, and to ensure military superiority in case of war.) The Austrians, opposed to warlike policies, would have been content if Denmark returned to the provisions of the London Protocol. King Wilhelm, on the other hand, was full of enthusiasm for the plan to wrest the duchies from Denmark and place them under the duke of Augustenburg.

When the Federal Diet voted in favor of military intervention in Denmark (October 1, 1863) and Hanoverian and Saxon troops invaded Holstein (December 24, 1863), the major powers were forced to reexamine their attitude toward the impending conflict. Britain, whose support of Denmark had been steadfast all along, was embarrassed by the Danish abrogation of the London Protocol and, after prolonged debates, decided that she could not go to war in defense of this Danish breach of an international treaty.[12] Russia, because of Bismarck's recent support during the Polish insurrection, was on Prussia's side, content to repay Britain and France for their anti-Russian role during the Polish uprising. Nor did France have any intention of coming to the aid of the Danes. Indeed, Napoleon III secretly encouraged Bismarck to annex the duchies, hinting that some territorial compensations along France's northeastern borders or along the Rhine would be quite welcome in exchange for his neutrality.

✳On January 16, 1864, Prussia and Austria concluded an alliance and sent an ultimatum to Denmark. They asked the Danes to revoke the constitution of November 1863, which had announced the incorporation of Schleswig with Denmark. When Denmark rejected the ultimatum, allied troops marched into Schleswig on February 1, announcing their intention of preventing the illegal union of Schleswig with the Danish crown and disclaiming any intent to destroy the Danish kingdom. Under these circumstances, the powers found it impossible to come to the aid of the Danes and proclaimed their neutrality.

The crisis created a serious dilemma for the Prussian liberals. While the moderates backed the claims of the duke of Augustenburg and urged the government to support his cause, the liberals vacillated between supporting outright annexation of the duchies and refusing to support the government in an aggressive war. It was the old problem of freedom versus power. The issue became urgent on December 9, 1863, when the government presented a bill to the Lower House asking for 9 million thaler to finance military operations against Denmark. This was a political maneuver to split the opposition, for the government did not actually need the money. Should the liberal majority in the Lower House refuse the authorization, public opinion would consider the liberals unpatriotic, and they would be discredited. For the liberals, the choice was both crucial and painful. Approving the funds meant acknowledging defeat in the constitutional conflict; rejecting them meant opposing the German unity movement and losing public support, which the liberals could ill afford.[13] After long debates the Lower House rejected the government's request by a vote of 275 to 51 (January 22, 1864). This, the liberals believed, would bring about Bismarck's resignation and resolve the constitutional conflict in their favor. But they were mistaken. Austro-Prussian military victory aroused German national enthusiasm, and for the first time Bismarck enjoyed popular support. An armistice with Denmark was arranged and the powers met in London on April 25, 1864 to conclude a settlement. When, in the course of the negotiations, Count Bernstorff, the representative of Austria, Prussia, and the lesser German states, declared the London Protocol of 1852 null and void, the powers protested but were unable to agree on a substitute. It was equally impossible to agree upon a solution for Schleswig, so the conference disbanded on June 25 and military operations were resumed the following day. This time the Danes were beaten decisively; at the preliminary peace of Vienna on August 1, they surrendered the duchies of Schleswig, Holstein, and Lauenburg to Austria and Prussia. The final settlement was signed in Vienna on October 30, 1864.

The allies' major problem was how to divide the spoils. At a conference in Schoenbrunn at the end of August, Rechberg, the Austrian foreign minister, suggested a trade-off: Prussia would take over the duchies and, in return, assist Austria in the recovery of Lombardy (lost by the Austrians to the Italians in 1859 at the end of the Austro-Sardinian war). This was an ill-considered suggestion, for it would have meant the dismemberment of recently united Italy and would also have aroused the enmity of a very suspicious Napoleon III, a price Prussia was not willing to pay. Without mentioning these considerations, Wilhelm and Bismarck evaded the Austrian offer and with many expressions of goodwill—and the major problem unresolved—the allies parted.

It had become clear to most observers in the Germanies that Prussia, under Bismarck's skillful leadership, had outmaneuvered Austria in the Schleswig-Holstein question. But what were his plans for the future? Determining Bismarck's policy toward Austria is crucial to an understanding of his long-range aims: it would establish whether or not he planned and wanted war with Austria, and would also reveal his attitude toward German unification. If this initial aim, as some historians believe,[14] was cooperation with Austria in return for Prussian hegemony in North Germany, then unification of all Germany under Prussian leadership was not a serious goal. If, on the other hand, Bismarck favored war with Austria, his avowed policy of Austro-German cooperation was only a pretext, and Prussian leadership in a united Germany was a definite aim.

There was, furthermore, the still unresolved constitutional conflict at home. It limited the government's freedom of action in domestic affairs and lowered Prussia's standing in the eyes of the other German states. If, however, a war with Austria could be used to distract the people's attention from domestic affairs, Bismarck believed that both crises might be solved simultaneously. The liberals' enthusiasm for a national cause would facilitate such a policy, and he hoped that the people in other German states would follow Prussia's lead, or at least be sympathetic to her aims.

After the Danish war, Austria and Prussia outwardly maintained a common front and unity of purpose, while the struggle for economic supremacy continued behind the scenes. Rechberg once again presented Austria's *Mitteleuropa* plan to the members of the German Confederation in the mistaken belief that Prussia had been dependent on Austrian support during the Danish war and needed the support of the lesser German states to get a renewal of the Prussian Customs Union. The Customs Union treaties were due to expire at the end of 1865, but Bismarck had already announced in December 1863 that their renewal was due in 1864, putting the member states under considerable pressure and causing confusion in their ranks. By concluding a trade treaty with Saxony in May 1864, Bismarck further strengthened Prussia's economic position and this, combined with Prussia's manifest leadership in the Danish war, made clear to the lesser states that they could not afford to leave the Customs Union. Politically and culturally most of the states preferred Austria to Prussia; economically, however, their bonds with Prussia were so strong that they simply could not afford a change. Thus it can be said that "the battle for the economic-political domination of Germany was decided when the continuation of the Prussian Customs Union . . . was signed in Berlin on June 28, 1864." [15]

The Austrian War Still, the problem of the division of the spoils of the Danish war remained unresolved. It proved a vexing matter. The joint Austro-Prussian administration of the duchies led to countless irritations and disputes on the local level which could easily become major political disagreements. While this may not have been Bismarck's original intention—especially at the time (October 1864) when Mensdorff replaced Rechberg as Austrian foreign minister—he was conscious of the possibility, and at the beginning of 1865 he informed Austria of Prussia's conditions for the establishment of a Schleswig-Holstein state.[16] For all practical purposes, Prussian demands amounted to complete Prussian domination, especially in communication matters and military affairs (soldiers of Schleswig-Holstein were to swear allegiance to the Prussian king). The question of a future ruler for the duchies was to be left open for the time being. The Austrian government rejected the Prussian note, as Bismarck had expected, basing its case on the incompatibility of the Prussian provisions with the constitution of the German Confederation, particularly the provision that the federation was an assembly of sovereign princes. The Prussian note also constituted a break with the duke of Augustenburg, whom Bismarck suspected of liberal leanings and of being in close touch with his enemies at Court.

A month later the Prussian government transferred its major naval establishment from Danzig to Kiel, a clear indication that it expected to annex the duchies permanently. At a Prussian crown council in May 1865, the king and Moltke (chief of the general staff) expressed themselves in favor of annexation, regardless of the consequences, while the crown prince strongly opposed it. Bismarck appeared undecided. Though he advocated further negotiations toward a peaceful settlement, he did not reject the possibility of war and warned (this was meant for the crown prince) that force could never be ruled out completely. Nor was this idle talk. In preparation for such an eventuality, Bismarck sounded out the French and Italian governments and received reassurances from both. Italy was anxious to get Venetia from Austria, and France, less specific in her territorial expectations, was forever looking for compensation along the Rhine. Napoleon's Mexican adventure was going badly and the possibility of an Austro-Prussian alliance in the center of Europe was not at all to his liking.

It is impossible to point to the exact moment when Bismarck decided to go to war against Austria.[17] As usual, he kept his options open and pursued several policies simultaneously. The European political situation was more favorable to an active Prussian foreign policy than it had been in the past, and Bismarck was aware of this. Using the moment to advantage, he bombarded the government in Vienna with complaints about the administration of the duchies, accusing Austrian officials, among other things, of supporting the revolutionary activities of the duke of Augustenburg, and threatening to take unilateral action unless the Austrians cooperated by removing the duke from the duchies.[18] The Austrians did not know how to deal with these provocations. They had just changed governments (Schmerling-Belcredi, July 1865), were in the midst of a financial and economic crisis, and had troubles with the Hungarians. They suggested direct negotiations; Bismarck agreed, and these led to the Convention of Gastein of August 14, 1865. Under its terms, the joint administration of the duchies was replaced by a "provisional" division: Austria was to administer Holstein, while Prussia assumed responsibility for Schleswig and acquired the rights to Lauenburg from Austria for 2.5 million thalers.

German public opinion was deeply shocked. Not only had the two powers disregarded what were considered the just claims of the duke of Augustenburg, they had violated the ideal for which the Germans believed they had fought the Danes in 1848 and 1864: the unity of the duchies. People in the lesser states were especially disappointed in Austria for having abdicated her leading role in German affairs, and for abandoning her conservative policy. Almost everywhere the Convention of Gastein was considered a victory for Prussia and a defeat for Austria.

Bismarck, however, considered it only a temporary settlement. To prepare for the next phase (and to see Kathy Orlow again), he traveled to Paris and Biarritz. The French had not taken kindly to the Austro-Prussian agreement and, in a circular note of August 29, 1865, had accused the two powers of basing their settlement on power and force.[19] Then too, the French government was suspicious of secret agreements from which it was excluded, and felt sure that Prussia must have given Austria additional compensation to obtain such a favorable settlement.[20] Bismarck went to France to reassure Napoleon III and to ask him for French friendship and understanding. He must have succeeded in his mission. Though he failed to meet Kathy Orlow (she had gone to Torquay and had not notified him of her change of plans) and missed her company, he returned to Berlin in high spirits. "We shall step on Austria's corns," he told Thiele, the undersecretary in the foreign office, "make an alliance with Italy, castrate the Augustenburger, and rape the [German] Confederation."[21]

The situation in the duchies did not improve following the Gastein agreement. The Austrian administration in Holstein was more relaxed than the Prussian in Schleswig, and the different attitudes of the occupying powers to the claims of the duke of Augustenburg contributed to the underlying friction between the powers and between them and the local population. Bismarck was not unhappy about this development. He was determined to keep these and other dissensions alive and, if need be, to exaggerate them. As before, he sent a constant stream of complaints to Vienna, accusing the Austrians of abandoning conservative policies agreed upon at Gastein, and threatening unilateral action in the future.[22] Bismarck's posture of the aggrieved and injured party was meant not only to put the Austrian government in the wrong, but also to stiffen the king's position. His ruse worked, for in the Prussian crown council of February 28, 1866, Wilhelm accused the Austrians of purposely alienating the local population in Schleswig-Holstein from the Prussian government.[23] During discussions of Austro-Prussian relations and the possibility of war, all participants except the crown prince agreed that war was unavoidable, and that it should neither be evaded nor initiated by Prussia. This latter proviso was necessary to make adequate diplomatic preparations and to negotiate with Italy. To this end the king, with Bismarck's prompting, agreed to send a mission to Florence. Moltke was confident of the readiness of the Prussian army, but he considered the diversionary effect of the Italian army essential for a military victory over Austria.

Bismarck's concern about Italian cooperation went back to the Gastein convention; he worried lest the Italians consider Austro-Prussian cooperation permanent and an Italian-Prussian alliance completely futile. This was exactly how the Italian government appraised the situation. Italians were suspicious of Prussian policy and would have preferred to reach a peaceful agreement with Austria on the acquisition of Venetia. But the Austrians, aware of Bismarck's intrigues in Paris and Florence and confident that they could beat the Prussians and Italians, could not make up their minds. Instead of allying themselves with either the Italians or the Prussians, they managed to antagonize both. One reason for their uncompromising attitude was Habsburg pride, which precluded their dealing with the Prussians on an equal basis, or recognizing the Italian government as legitimate.

When the Italians realized late in 1865 that the government in Vienna was not likely to come to an agreement over Venetia, they became more amenable to Prussian approaches. By the end of February 1866 the Italians were ready for a Prussian alliance against Austria and sent General Gavone to Berlin to work out the details.[24] (This made it unnecessary to send a Prussian mission to Florence.) How to reconcile Italian and Prussian aims was a major problem. Italy wanted a short, wartime alliance, expecting an early start of hostilities. Prussia needed more time to prepare and to create a suitable provocation to start a war.

At this point Bismarck seems to have realized that in the eyes of public opinion the question of the duchies would not be sufficient cause for war with Austria; he began to consider, instead, something more in line with common German national aspirations—a reorganization of the German Confederation or a realignment of the Federal Diet. Either would mean a postponement of the war, and this would make the Italians less anxious to enter into an alliance with the Prussians. The key to this alliance, both parties realized, was Napoleon III, and Bismarck took care to keep Benedetti, the French ambassador, fully informed of the progress of the negotiations. Benedetti, in turn, reassured the Italians, stressing especially Bismarck's determination for a war with Austria. The decisive turn came when Napoleon personally advised a special Italian emissary that Italy should sign the alliance with Prussia. The Italians accepted Napoleon's advice and on April 8, 1866, Gavone and Bismarck signed the treaty of alliance in Berlin. It was limited to three months and was in no way binding upon Prussia. If Prussia were to declare war on Austria within that period, Italy was to join, and the two powers agreed not to conclude a separate armistice or peace. In case of victory, Italy was to get Venetia, and Prussia some territory of similar size and population. There can be little doubt that with this treaty Prussia committed a grave breach of law against the provisions of the German Confederation, which forbade any member to ally itself with a foreign power against another member of the federation. Indeed, the king was uncomfortably aware of this breach and kept the treaty a well-guarded secret.

His foreign policy requirements well taken care of, Bismarck still had to find a solution to a very serious problem facing him at home:

how to finance the impending war. For even though taxes were collected without an authorized budget, the Parliament would not approve additional funds, nor would it "allow the government to sell state property without parliamentary approval."[25] In this difficult situation, Bismarck turned to his confidant and private banker, Gerson Bleichroeder.[26] It was Bleichroeder who had originally conceived of the sale of the Cologne-Minden Railroad, which the Parliament had vetoed in January 1866. Now, upon the request of the new minister of finance, August von der Heydt, Bleichroeder and his fellow banker and longtime friend, Hansemann, formed a consortium to buy the government's shares of the Cologne-Minden Railroad and thus provided Bismarck with the necessary funds to prepare for war.[27]

The Austrians, meanwhile, informed of the Italian-Prussian negotiations, hoped that Wilhelm's traditional conservatism would rule out any firm and binding commitments between Italy and Prussia. When this proved futile, the Austrians started negotiations with the French and on June 12, 1866, concluded a secret convention with them. By its terms the Austrians agreed, in return for French neutrality, to cede Venitia to the Italians if the Austrian armies were victorious in Germany. But even if the Austrians were to beat the Italians, Venetia would still be turned over to Italy. As compensation Austria could acquire territory in the Germanies, as long as this did not upset the balance of power in Europe. An oral agreement between Vienna and Paris envisaged territorial gains for Saxony, Wuerttemberg, and Bavaria and—shades of the Rhenish Confederation—the creation of an independent German state west of the Rhine.[28] This would have been a thinly disguised French satellite meant to compensate Napoleon III for his troubles in these negotiations. The Austro-French convention illustrates the shortsightedness of Austrian foreign policy well. Pursuing dynastic policies and cabinet diplomacy, the Austrian statesmen were either unaware of public opinion or of German national aspirations or were undisturbed by them.

Exploiting the German question, Bismarck informed the governments of the lesser states in March 1866[29] of his intention to suggest reforms of the Confederation. At the same time, he asked what their attitude would be in case of a conflict with Austria. Two weeks later he submitted his plan for reform to the Diet.[30] It consisted, essentially, of a national parliament, based on universal suffrage, which was to establish a federal constitution and was much like the plan he had proposed three years earlier.[31]

It had no chance of being accepted, nor had Bismarck intended that it should be. His aim was to gain the support of national liberal forces throughout Germany and to discredit Austrian policy. To the king and the Prussian conservatives it was a revolutionary plan, but to Bismarck the alliance with German nationalism seemed the only way of preserving the powers of the Prussian monarchy in the modern age. Ever since the Revolution of 1848 he had believed that the masses were essentially conservative and that universal suffrage, far from aiding the liberals, would provide a solid basis of support for the existing government in Prussia.

But the support that Bismarck expected from the German people in the spring and summer of 1866 was not forthcoming. Outside Prussia, many people were either indifferent or opposed to Bismarck's aims. Particularism was widespread in the lesser states; though a number of Germans favored Prussian leadership, many were suspicious of her policies, especially in light of the constitutional conflict. The governments also hesitated, but they finally referred Bismarck's proposal for reform to a commission, thus rendering it ineffective for the time being.

Abroad, Bismarck's proposal for a reorganization of the Confederation encountered mixed reactions. The czar opposed it, seeing in it the dread threat of revolution. Napoleon, though flattered that Bismarck should adopt his own methods of universal suffrage, worried lest it lead to a strong and united Germany. In England, public opinion was divided. Some refused to take Bismarck seriously; others considered him a genius.[32] The Austrian government decided in March, despite serious economic difficulties, to strengthen its military forces in Bohemia, the area most exposed to Prussian invasion. It did so for two reasons. First, the army's communication system and its technical services were so poor that mobilization of its forces would require several weeks, much longer than similar Prussian preparations. Then too, Bismarck's bellicose statements had so alarmed the Austrian general staff that it was able to prevail upon the emperor to authorize these measures over the objections of the foreign minister. To Bismarck this was a most welcome development and he used it to convince King Wilhelm of the perfidy of Austrian policy and to induce him to order partial mobilization of the border forces. The immediate threat of war was averted, however, by an Austrian declaration assuring the European powers of her peaceful intentions and by English attempts, through the royal court, to impress upon Wilhelm the inherent dangers of Bismarck's policy. A military confrontation was averted for the time being but could not be avoided for long.

On April 8, Bismarck concluded the alliance with Italy and the Italians, heartened by this alliance, began to prepare for war. When this became known in Vienna on April 21, Austrian troops were mobilized along the southern border. Unlike the earlier military measures in Bohemia, this was a more serious development. The Italians, encouraged by Bismarck, heightened the crisis and, in a wave of patriotic enthusiasm, the Italian parliament voted the necessary war credits and the government informed the European powers that the Italian forces were being mobilized for the defense of their country.[33] While this enabled Bismarck to forego military demobilization in the wake of British mediation attempts, it threatened his carefully laid diplomatic plans. The possibility of an Austrian attack on Italy had not been considered in drafting the Italian-Prussian treaty and the danger of such an attack led to Italian inquiries in Berlin regarding the government's attitude. Bismarck, on the king's orders, had to tell the Italians that the Prussian government would adhere strictly to the treaty's provisions. Rumors of Napoleon's mediation attempts were circulating and Bismarck feared that this, combined with his rejection of the Italians, would lead to their defection from the alliance.

Napoleon's intervention at the beginning of May was indeed a serious threat to Bismarck's plans. The emperor informed the Italian envoy on May 5 that Austria, in exchange for a free hand in Germany, was willing to cede Venetia to France, which would transfer it, unconditionally, to Italy. It was now up to Italy to decide whether there should be peace or war. Clearly, the Italians were on the spot. To them it was primarily a matter of pride. To acquire Venetia without a struggle would not only be degrading, it would also give Napoleon a voice in Italian affairs, and with Italian memories of Plombières and the Austro-Sardinian war[34] still fresh, they rejected such a settlement forth-

with. Meanwhile, Bismarck had persuaded the king to order the mobilization of the eastern army corps, thus reassuring the Italians that
they could, after all, count on Prussian assistance.[35]

In the midst of full military mobilization by all sides, there now occurred a curious episode that seemed once more to enhance the
chances for a peaceful solution: the Gablenz mission. The Gablenz
brothers, coming from an old family of imperial knights, seemed especially suited for this mediation attempt. Anton was a former Saxon
chamberlain and Prussian deputy; his brother Ludwig was a general in
the Austrian army and governor of Holstein. To them, as to many in
Germany, the possibility of an Austro-Prussian conflict carried the
specter of a fratricidal war and they were determined to prevent it.
The authorities in Berlin and Vienna received them and heard their
proposals, which entailed, in essence, creation of an independent
Schleswig-Holstein state under a Prussian prince, Prussian sovereignty, special rights in the port of Kiel, a 30 million thaler indemnity for
Austria, and the division of German military command along the Main
between Austria and Prussia. The Austrians accepted the plan in principle, but asked for one concession: a Prussian military commitment
against Italy. Bismarck rejected this out of hand. His counterproposal
was to give the Prussian king more power as federal commander in
chief in Germany. This the Austrians could not accept. They felt they
could not, once again, betray what little trust they might have among
the lesser states; they also felt they must have some security against
Italy. On May 28, 1866, the Austrian government formally rejected
the Gablenz plan.[36]

Failure of the Gablenz mission brought about a scramble for the allegiance of the lesser states. Most were pro-Austrian to begin with,
and all Bismarck could do was to threaten and cajole them. He did not
succeed. On June 1, the Austrians, in defiance of the Convention of
Gastein, placed the future fate of the duchies in the hands of the Federal Diet. The die was cast. On the ninth, Prussian troops marched into
Holstein, but much to Bismarck's chagrin, they failed to encounter
Austrian resistance. Two days later the Austrians asked the Diet to
mobilize all federal troops and on the fourteenth, the Diet voted the
request by nine to five. On the following day Prussia sent ultimatums,
which were rejected, to Saxony, Hanover, and Kassel. That night

Prussian troops started to move and on June 21 they crossed the border into Bohemia.

The military developments were as swift as they were decisive. The Austrians defeated the Italians at Custozza (June 24) and Lissa (July 20). But the Prussians defeated the Hanoverians at Langensalza (June 27–29) and the Austrians at Koeniggraetz/Sadowa (July 3). This was the decisive battle. The victory should be credited to Moltke's superior strategic leadership, utilization of railroads for rapid mobilization and the movement of troops, and to the new breach-loading needle gun, which was faster and more effective than the Austrian muzzleloader.[37]

Prussia's lightning campaign and decisive military victory caught Napoleon completely off guard. He had hoped for a long, drawn-out war and had planned either to intervene or mediate a peace and, at the end, obtain suitable compensations. On July 5 the Austrians had asked for the emperor's mediation and from then on French intervention was a possibility which Bismarck had to consider. He was prepared to counter it in two ways. First, he held out the possibility of territorial compensation on the left bank of the Rhine to the French, and simultaneously threatened to incite a national uprising in Germany against France, if French demands were too high. To counteract the possibility of French military intervention and to defeat Austria more quickly, he was prepared to support a Hungarian and Serbian uprising against the Habsburg monarchy.[38] The victory at Koeniggraetz/Sadowa made it unnecessary to use either plan.

The threat of French intervention, a cholera epidemic in the Prussian army, and the arrival of Austrian reinforcements from Italy persuaded Bismarck to press not only for a quick preliminary peace but also for lenient terms for the Austrians. This was particularly irritating to King Wilhelm who, full of righteous indignation, wanted to punish the Austrians, march into Vienna, and dictate a punitive peace in Schoenbrunn palace. He had the generals on his side and Bismarck, mindful of possible foreign intervention, finally persuaded the king, with the help of the crown prince, to agree to more sensible terms. On July 26, 1866, a preliminary peace was signed at Nikolsburg; the Austrians were required to give Venetia to the Italians and pay an indemnity. Austria's greatest loss was one of prestige: she was forced out of the German Confederation. These terms were confirmed in the final Treaty of Prague on August 23. Prussia's lack of territorial gains from Austria was amply compensated for by generous acquisitions from Austria's allies in north Germany. There, Hanover, electoral Hesse, Nassau, and the city of Frankfurt[39] were incorporated into Prussia, uniting Prussian territory into one contiguous unit for the first time. The deposing of the Hanoverian dynasty, in violation of the monarchical principle, was a severe shock to the czar, who, scandalized by these revolutionary measures and Bismarck's blatant disregard of monarchical solidarity, called for a European congress to discuss these radical changes. But Bismarck angrily rejected such outside interference in German affairs. He threatened to support Polish nationalism against Russia and let it be known in St. Petersburg that "should there be revolution, we would rather make it, than suffer it."[40]

With Austria's elimination from Germany and Prussia's territorial acquisitions, the German Confederation had been destroyed. The states north of the Main now formed the North German Federation under Prussian leadership, while those south of the river were free to form their own union. While bargaining over compensations with France, Bismarck used his talks with Benedetti to impress upon the south German states the continued threat of French aggression and, as a result, concluded secret defense treaties with Baden, Wuerttemberg, and Bavaria which were later incorporated into the peace treaties. The most significant provision in these defense treaties was the king of Prussia's assumption of supreme military command over the forces of the south German states in case of war with France.

The territorial enlargement of Prussia made her the largest and most powerful state in Germany. Her military alliances with the south German states and her economic predominance in the Customs Union made the unification of Germany under Prussian leadership, that is, along lesser German lines, a likely possibility. One major obstacle remained: the settlement of the constitutional conflict. Here, the victory over Austria played a decisive role. Popular enthusiasm knew no bounds; it was accompanied by a massive shift of votes from the liberals to the conservatives. The election of July 3, 1866—the day of the battle of Koeniggraetz/Sadowa—gave the conservatives 136 mandates (up from 35) and the liberals and progressives 148 (from 247). In combination with the old liberals (24 mandates, up from 9), the conservatives now controlled the Lower House of the Prussian Parliament.[41] The election's outcome made it possible for Bismarck to offer the liberals a compromise. He proposed a bill of indemnity which, though acknowledging no wrongdoing by the government, asked the Lower House to approve, retroactively, the government's unauthorized expenditures of past years. After he had won the king's approval—over the strenuous objections of the old conservatives—Bismarck submitted the bill to the Lower House on August 14, 1866. After considerable debate it passed, 230 to 75, on September 3.[42]

The outcome of the war greatly increased Bismarck's power and prestige, but caused considerable upheaval among the major political parties. Both liberals and conservatives split and sought new alignments. The liberals divided into the Progressive and the National Liberal parties; the former contained the core of those Prussian liberals who had opposed Bismarck's domestic policies all along. The latter were mostly those from the newly acquired territories who welcomed and supported Bismarck's economic and national goals.[43] Among conservatives the shock and confusion over Bismarck's policies were, if anything, greater than the frustrations experienced by the liberal camp. Bismarck's advocacy of universal suffrage and a national parliament, his support of Italy, and his dispossession of the legitimate rulers of Hanover, Hesse-Kassel, and Nassau, left the conservatives utterly bewildered. A small group, which grew steadily as time passed, stayed with Bismarck and the government and formed the Free Conservative party. This was composed of civil servants, professional people, industrialists, and big businessmen. Most of the old nobility, the large Prussian landowners, the Lutheran clergy, and some army officers, stayed loyal to the Old Conservative party.

The massive swing to Bismarck was reflected throughout Germany. Prussia's victory of 1866 seemed to convince many of the advantages of the realpolitik of the 1860s over the idealism of the 1840s. People wearied of supporting the unsuccessful policies of Austria and were frustrated by the seemingly unattainable goals of liberalism and constitutionalism. But beyond that, the unification of the country under Prussian leadership now seemed within reach. German nationalism drew its strongest support from the fear of foreign, especially French, aggression. There was a general desire to end German weakness and disunity and to prevent foreign intervention in German affairs such as had occurred in the Danish crisis of 1848 and the Olmuetz confrontation of 1850. The example of the recent unification of Italy also played an important part.[44] To most Germans it became simply a matter of priorities. If the country could be united first, constitutionalism could be achieved later.[45]

Foreign reaction to the formation of the North German Confederation was relatively mild. Bismarck's genius was everywhere admired and recognized; as long as Prussian domination did not extend beyond the Main, the European powers were not especially concerned.

The North German Confederation　Treaties between Prussia and the lesser north German states on August 18, 1866, laid the foundation of the North German Confederation. In these treaties, the governments agreed to elect a parliament by universal suffrage which would draft a federal constitution. The outline for this constitution was based on Bismarck's draft of December 1, 1866—based in turn on the famous Putbus dictations of October 30 and November 19—which, after a number of corrections and additions by various assistants and government agencies, was circulated to the governments of the North German states on December 15.[46] In spite of much adding and redrafting, the North German constitution was very much Bismarck's handiwork. Inasmuch as this constitution became, with minor changes, the constitution of the German Reich in 1871 and lasted in this form until 1918, the significance of Bismarck's work was inestimable.

From the time it was drafted, opinions have varied as to the constitution's intent and meaning: whether it established a German national state or whether it was merely a decoy for an enlarged Prussia, perpetuating Prussian hegemony in Germany. It is impossible to divine Bismarck's true intentions, but it can reasonably be assumed that he wanted to continue his and Prussia's control in any future national government. "The essence of the Bismarckian constitution was its conservation, by the use of revolutionary means, of the Prussian aristocratic-monarchical order in a century of increasingly dynamic economic and social change."[47]

Bismarck's draft and the version that was finally adopted provided for an Upper House, the Federal Council (*Bundesrat*), which was an assembly of representatives from the North German states in which Prussia, because of its size and population, had seventeen out of a total of forty-three votes. Prussia was also given the federal presidency (*Bundespraesidium*), which gave her authority over foreign representation and the conduct of foreign affairs. The Prussian king was made commander in chief of the Confederation's armed forces and executor of federal legislation, and he was given authority to declare war. Thus Prussia's hegemony in the federation was assured.[48] The Lower House (*Reichstag*) was composed of delegates elected for a three year period by universal male and direct suffrage. There was no provision for a supreme court, nor was there a bill of rights.

The most important debates in parliament on the proposed constitution revolved around ministerial responsibility and the Reichstag's budgetary powers. In Bismarck's draft there were no provisions for a federal government or a federal administration. The only parliamentary responsibility within the federation was between the state governments and their local diets and the instructions they issued to their representatives on the Federal Council. The National Liberal majority strongly objected to this "oversight" and asked for a ministry responsible to the Reichstag. Bismarck, who suspected quite rightly that this plan would lead to Reichstag approval of ministerial appointments, declared his firm opposition to such a measure and threatened to dissolve the assembly. Two proposals recommending ministerial responsibility were submitted by Bennigsen on March 26–27, 1867; both were defeated. A compromise establishing *one* responsible minister, without specifying the exact nature of his responsibility, was accepted.[49] The compromise was accepted by the liberals in the hope that they might later attain their goal of full ministerial responsibility.

In Bismarck's original draft, the chairman of the Federal Council was to be a federal chancellor (modeled after the Austrian representative to the Frankfurt Diet). He would be subordinate to the Prussian foreign minister, and would be an undersecretary for German affairs in the Foreign Ministry. He would be chairman at meetings, and would also act as executive secretary to the Federal Council.[50] In the course of the debates it soon became clear that the federal chancellorship would have to be combined with the office of Prussian minister-president and foreign minister; this position was, in effect, created for and around Bismarck. The responsibility of the future chancellor was not spelled out. Whom he would be responsible to and how this responsibility was to be implemented was not stipulated. The chancellor's responsibility was, at best, political or moral, not legal.[51]

By accepting "responsibility," the position of the chancellor had changed considerably from what Bismarck had originally intended it to be. The chancellor now became the chief federal minister. His government could now develop independently of Prussia and establish its own administration. Herein lay the principle that the chancellor was the responsible official for the direction of federal as well as Reich administration. At the same time, the chancellor's office stood between the Federal Council and the Reichstag and thus assumed governmental functions toward the latter as well. This greatly enhanced the position of the chancellor and gave the crown its most powerful weapon: the right to appoint and dismiss the chancellor and with him the leading administrative officials of the Confederation and later of the Reich.

On the question of budgetary powers, the delegates were able to obtain authority over a yearly civilian budget, but control over the military budget eluded them once again. A compromise was found by which the expenditures for the army were fixed by a quota system—1 percent of the population at 225 thaler per soldier—which was to remain unchanged until the end of 1871. (This became known as the "iron budget.") After that, the Reichstag was to have authority over military expenditures as well. (This was not achieved automatically, however, and another parliamentary struggle ensued in 1874 which resulted in a compromise—the *Septennat*, a law which gave the Reichstag the right to vote on the military budget only at intervals of seven years.)

On April 16, 1867, the parliamentary assembly accepted the constitution by a vote of 230 to 53. In opposition were the Progressives, the Poles, the Catholics, and August Bebel, the only socialist. To Bebel the whole Reichstag was "a mere figleaf to cover the nakedness of absolutism."[52] "Unity over freedom and power over law—this was the constellation under which the German Reich was born."[53]

The National Liberals overestimated the effects of their compromise on future constitutional developments, because Bismarck resisted all further attempts toward the creation of a parliamentary government for the rest of his term of office. Thus the dream of German liberals, to create a system modeled after that of Great Britain, was never achieved. Instead, a government of mixed powers was established and fundamental constitutional problems—the budgetary power and ministerial responsibility—were not resolved until half a century later, after a lost war and in the midst of a popular uprising.[54]

The Hohenzollern Candidature to the Spanish Throne and the War with France   After the Austro-Prussian war, the movement toward German unification was in complete disarray. The establishment of the North German Confederation, with the Main River line dividing the north from the south, seemed to make this division permanent and appeared to give Austria, as well as France, more influence in southern Germany than before. At the same time it became clear that both Britain and Russia would probably oppose any military action by the North German Confederation which would force the southern states into a union with the north. An evolutionary development toward unification was unlikely in the predictable future, inasmuch as anti-Prussian and particularist sentiments were widespread in the south. Even in Baden, a traditionally liberal state which favored unification, the pronational, liberal forces were badly divided.[55] Lack of popular support for Prussia was also apparent in the results of the 1868 elections to the Customs Union Parliament, when anti-Prussian forces received overwhelming majorities in Bavaria and Wuerttemberg, and were only narrowly defeated in Baden.

At the beginning of 1870 it seemed that Bismarck's policy toward unification along lesser German lines was not only blocked, but that opposition to his policy was gaining strength. The morale of Bismarck's supporters was correspondingly low, and to raise their morale and, at the same time, to get the national movement going again, the National Liberals suggested that Baden join the North German Confederation.[56] Bismarck, however, refused. This plan would have meant exposing Baden to economic retaliation and placing undue pressure on Bavaria and Wuerttemberg. Baden was the chief exponent of union with the north; if she joined the North German Confederation, the southern unification movement would lose its leader. The French would undoubtedly have been alarmed to see Baden a part of Bismarck's new state. Bismarck also realized that the other southern states would interpret such a move as aggression by the North, thus rendering the anti-French military assistance clauses between the Confederation and the south German states inoperative. This last consideration—that there had to be a clear case of French aggression to put the military alliance between the North and South German states into effect—became Bismarck's foremost concern. This was also essential domestically, to overcome the reluctance of the opposition parties, and equally crucial for foreign policy, to prevent Austria, Britain, or Russia from coming to the aid of France.

Of the three powers, only Austria could really have assisted France. In the aftermath of Koeniggraetz, France and Austria drew closer together, Austria reluctant to accept her exclusion from the Germanies, France concerned about losing her influence in southern Germany. When Napoleon visited the emperor in Salzburg in August 1867 to express his condolences over the death of Maximilian of Mexico, Francis Joseph's brother, the ministers of the two powers began negotiations aimed toward a future alliance. The talks were complicated and drawn out. Napoleon wanted Austrian assistance in maintaining south German independence and some commitments from Vienna in case of war with Prussia. This the Austrians refused. They realized that giving in to French demands would not only alienate Austria's German population, but it would also antagonize the Hungarians, who had recently achieved an equal voice in the affairs of the empire. (The Compromise of 1867.)

A break in the deadlocked Franco-Austrian negotiations occurred when the Italians indicated that they wanted to join a future Austro-French alliance, hoping in this way to gain Tyrol, Rome, and possibly Nice. Taking advantage of the Italian offer, the French circulated a draft treaty in March 1869 which substituted a few clauses stressing security and the peaceful intentions of the participating powers for the anti-Prussian tone of their original draft. The new draft provided for French neutrality in case of a Russo-Prussian war and Austrian neutrality in case of a Franco-Prussian war. Only if Russia or Prussia were to come to each other's aid would France or Austria enter the war. Italy would furnish 200,000 men in either case. But the Austrians were not willing to give up their neutrality under any circumstances and the Italians asked for French evacuation of Rome before they were willing to commit themselves. This Napoleon could not do because of pressure from the French clerics; for these reasons the grand scheme of a triple alliance against Prussia miscarried. France now stood alone.[57]

In the summer of 1866 the Eastern question came alive once more when a revolt in Crete against Turkish rule again brought the plight of Christian minorities to the attention of the powers. Russia, recovered from the Crimean War, hoped to reestablish her prestige among the Balkan peoples. She tried to persuade Britain and France to remind the Turkish government of its responsibilities for reforms promised to its subjects after 1823. But the two western powers were reluctant to get involved in the East at a time when the Luxembourg question focused their attention on the Rhine. Once the Luxembourg crisis was over, Czar Alexander and Gorchakov visited Paris, hoping to gain the diplomatic support that had eluded them earlier. But this visit was a failure; Napoleon III was unwilling to enter into serious commitments and an assassination attempt against the czar spoiled the Russians' stay.[58] French-Russian relations, which had suffered a setback during the Polish insurrection of 1863, reached an even lower ebb. Denied French support at the Straits, Gorchakov saw no reason for backing France on the Rhine. With Britain seemingly disinterested, and Austria openly competitive with Russia in the Balkans, Russia turned to Prussia.[59]

At the beginning of March 1868, Alexander proposed to the North German ambassador that the two countries support each other if one of them were involved in a war. Russia would put 100,000 troops on Austria's eastern frontier to keep her quiet if France attacked Prussia; in return, Alexander expected similar help from Prussia if Russia were involved with Austria in the Balkans. Bismarck welcomed the Russian initiative but was not willing to make any written commitments; instead, he persuaded the Russians to be satisfied with a mutual understanding of common aims and policies. For Bismarck and Prussia, the benefits of such an understanding were substantial and apparent in a little over two years.[60]

Bismarck, and with him German public opinion, was aware that Napoleon's domestic position had been so weakened by the diplomatic setbacks of the Austro-Prussian war, the Luxembourg question, the military debacle in Mexico, and the political developments in Italy,[61] that he could not possibly survive another diplomatic or military defeat. Following Prussia's victory over Austria, French public opinion began to realize that the country's prestige had suffered considerably. As a result, Napoleon III tried to recapture some of his former glory by looking toward France's northeastern border as a suitable area for expansion. Luxembourg seemed an especially suitable area for compensation. Louis Napoleon hoped to purchase the duchy from the king of the Netherlands and, because it was part of the German Customs Union (and a previous member of the German Confederation), he started negotiations with Bismarck to gain his approval of the scheme. Bismarck indicated that he would acquiesce as long as the arrangements were done quickly and quietly and without involving him in any way. The French, however, mismanaged the affair. News of the impending purchase was made known prematurely, the king of the Netherlands changed his mind when negotiations were almost completed, and Bismarck was asked in the Reichstag about the details involved. The Reichstag inquiry came from Bennigsen, and it is generally assumed that Bennigsen's tone, which was belligerently nationalistic—expressing the utmost determination to stop any and all attempts aimed at ceding ancient German territory from the fatherland—was drafted by Bismarck. Bismarck's reply, however, was cautious and calm, though it was clear that he would not resist popular opinion. The French, needless to say, were outraged and felt betrayed by these goings on.[62] It was equally clear that any move of Bismarck's that challenged, or even appeared to challenge, the position or prestige of France would elicit a violent response from Paris. Given these circumstances, all that was needed to excite French national feelings was a plausible excuse. Bismarck found this in the issue of the Hohenzollern candidature to the Spanish throne.

Contrary to long-cherished opinion, Bismarck was not suddenly inspired in the spring of 1870 to champion Prince Leopold, of the Sigmaringen and Catholic branch of the Hohenzollern family, as the candidate for the Spanish throne.[63] Bismarck apparently considered the situation as early as the fall of 1868, shortly after the Spanish queen's flight. In March 1870, when Salazar, the Spanish envoy, made a formal offer of the crown to Prince Leopold, Leopold accepted subject to the approval of King Wilhelm, head of the Hohenzollern family. Wilhelm was initially reluctant, but finally gave his blessings (June 19, 1870) at Bismarck's urging. Wilhelm was persuaded by the very favorable report of Bucher and Versen, who had been sent to Madrid to report on conditions in Spain. It seems certain now that these "reports" were prepared in Berlin, and probably under Bismarck's supervision.[64] The climate in Spain, contrary to the reports, was most unfavorable for a Hohenzollern prince.

In Spain, Parliament adjourned before it could vote on Prince Leopold's candidature; rumors of the Hohenzollern candidature reached Paris, where French opposition was predictably strong. When asked, Bismarck adopted a most innocent demeanor and insisted that this was entirely a Hohenzollern family affair and that he knew no more than was printed in the newspapers. In the second week of July, Benedetti, the French ambassador, had an audience with King Wilhelm at Ems and expressed his government's grave concern. He asked that the candidacy of Prince Leopold be withdrawn. Wilhelm, entirely unaware of Bismarck's machinations and not in favor of Leopold's candidacy to begin with, told Benedetti that it was up to Leopold, or his father Charles Anthon, to make up their minds in this matter. Privately, Wilhelm wrote to Leopold, advising him to withdraw his name, and on July 12, Charles Anthon did so on behalf of his son.[65]

Bismarck, who had spent several days on his estate at Varzin to demonstrate his lack of involvement in these affairs, was furious at the turn of events. He became still more enraged when he learned that the French government, not satisfied with Leopold's formal renunciation, had requested another interview with King Wilhelm on the following day (July 13). On this occasion Benedetti asked Wilhelm for a written guarantee of Leopold's refusal and a promise not to revive the candidacy in the future. The king refused these requests, politely but firmly, and when Benedetti asked to see him once more, Wilhelm declined to receive him. Wilhelm sent a telegraphic account of this encounter to Bismarck who, upon receiving it, edited it in such a way that it appeared to be a personal affront to Benedetti and a slur on the honor of France.[66] The French, already enraged over the affair, accepted the challenge and, predictably, declared war on Prussia on July 19, 1870.

The course of these events has long been known; what fascinates historians to this day, however, is the extent of Bismarck's involvement and his underlying motives.[67] It now seems fairly certain, on the basis of newly discovered documents and a reinterpretation of old ones, that Bismarck planned a war from the very beginning. In this aim he had much of public opinion and the influential business community solidly behind him.

The center of controversy in the North German Confederation was the constitutional stalemate over the military question. This and the high level of armaments among the major European powers had a deadening effect on business and trade. As the Prussian crown prince noted to Lord Acton, "the persons who had most urged on the war at Berlin, [sic] had been the bankers, who had declared that another six months of armed uncertainty would ruin Germany."[68]

The compromise over the military budget which ended the constitutional conflict in 1866 had led to the adoption of the "iron budget,"[69] which was to be effective until 1871. There are indications that Bismarck, when accepting this compromise, counted on a war with France before 1871 to solve his parliamentary problems as the war with Austria had solved similar problems in 1866. The 1871 session of the North German Parliament would have to deal once again with the explosive issue of the right of Parliament to control military expenditures. For Bismarck the problem could be solved only along the lines of monarchical principles and Prussian militarism, and to this end a victorious war with France was necessary. At the same time, it had to be a war in defense of legitimate German and Prussian interests, so that the secret defense treaties with the South German states would be put into effect, and to achieve the benefit of European and German public opinion.

France's reaction to Prussia's victory in 1866 and her frustration in the Luxembourg crisis made it more than likely that she would react violently to the Spanish crisis. France's susceptibility was common knowledge, and to believe that Bismarck was unable to foresee the consequences, "requires an act of faith."[70] Whether or not Bismarck really aimed at a preventive war with France, particularly after Gramont became foreign minister, has not been established; the answer must await further research and clarification of French foreign policy. But Bismarck's determination to bring about a war "seems to be the predominant trait in his policy toward the Spanish Candidature."[71]

Thus, when France declared war, an irresistible patriotic wave swept Germany, and north and south united to defeat the French aggressor.

Victory by the combined armies of North and South Germany was made possible by the superior military leadership of Helmuth von Moltke, the chief of staff of the Prussian army, and by the organizational talent of Albrecht von Roon, the Prussian war minister. In a rapid campaign reminiscent of the one against Austria, the German armies defeated the French at Woerth and Weissenburg. The decisive victory occurred at Sedan on September 1, 1870. The French army capitulated and Napoleon III was captured. This should have been the end of the war, for Bismarck was ready to enter into peace negotiations with the emperor. But for the French people, and especially the Parisians, the war was not yet over. They proclaimed a republic (September 4), established a government of national defense, and vowed to continue the war until the Germans were defeated and driven out of the country. Their military prowess, however, was not equal to their patriotic fervor. The German armies, sweeping all resistance aside, advanced rapidly and by September 19 had reached the outskirts of Paris. The long siege of the city began.[72]

This unexpected prolongation of the war created serious strains in the Prussian military-political leadership and led to an open break between Bismarck and Moltke. Moltke, with his narrow military outlook, wanted all political and diplomatic negotiations suspended while military operations were in progress, while Bismarck, with a much wider view, was aware of the constant interaction between political and military strategy. Bismarck was willing to explore the possibilities of a Bonapartist regency during the siege of Sedan, while Moltke worried that the negotiations would deprive the army of a well-earned victory. During the siege of Paris a similar dispute regarding the bombardment of the city and negotiations with the provisional French government finally led to a break between the two men, and Moltke denied Bismarck all access to military intelligence and planning. Considering that Bismarck had fought some bitter parliamentary battles not so long ago to preserve the power of the Prussian military establishment, Moltke's opposition to the chancellor seemed especially ironic. It was only through the king's intervention on Bismarck's behalf that unity was restored at the highest level of Prussian leadership. At the heart of the conflict lay the question of timing and methods regarding peace negotiations while military operations were still in progress; though Bismarck eventually gained the upper hand, Moltke's prolonged and stubborn opposition established an important precedent which was to have disastrous results under less able civilian leadership during the First World War.[73]

Diplomatic Negotiations with France for an Armistice and with the South German States for the Establishment of a New Reich Bismarck's negotiations with Jules Favre, the acting foreign minister, began at Ferrièrs, outside Paris, on September 18. From the very beginning the territorial issue dominated the negotiations. The foremost German war aim was the demand for Alsace-Lorraine. It was met by equally determined French resistance. "Not an inch of our territory or stone of our fortresses,"[74] Favre told Bismarck, and the negotiations were broken off. French defiance was based on its newly organized armies and on an appeal for assistance to the other powers. They were to be disappointed on both counts. The armies were defeated and Thiers's mission to London, Vienna, and St. Petersburg proved futile.[75] Russia's attitude, which was decisive for the French, was influenced by Bismarck's pro-Russian policy in Poland and by the czar's concern over the revolutionary government in Paris. Still, Bismarck wanted to end hostilities before a change in the European diplomatic constellation led to intervention by the powers.

An opportunity to renew the negotiations presented itself at the end of January 1871, when worsening conditions in Paris (there was only enough bread for two more days) led Favre to ask for a meeting with Bismarck on January 23. These negotiations led to an armistice by which the French surrendered the Parisian forts and agreed to pay an indemnity of 200 million francs, but insisted that the Germans not occupy Paris or take Belfort. The armistice was set for 21 days (it was later extended several times) during which elections for a national assembly were to be held to form a new French government.[76]

After the elections, Thiers, who had been elected head of the government, came to Versailles for further negotiations with Bismarck; after long and arduous conferences, a preliminary peace was signed on February 26, 1871. It provided for German annexation of Alsace and part of Lorraine, a French indemnity of 5 billion francs, and German occupation of northern France to ensure payment. Thiers managed to retain Belfort for France but had to allow the Germans to enter Paris. A definite treaty was to be signed later on.[77]

Even while the battles in northern France continued, the problem of the future shape of a united Germany became a major issue. The attitude of the four South German states, Baden, Hesse, Wuerttemburg, and Bavaria, was crucial to this question. The attitude of each toward the new Reich and the conditions under which they were willing to join differed considerably. Baden was willing to recognize the constitution of the North German Confederation and to join unconditionally. Hesse, because of its geographic position, wedged between Baden and the western provinces of Prussia, had little choice but to follow Baden's example. Wuerttemberg, however, fought for special rights and a change in the North German constitution, though she was, in principle, ready to enter the new Reich. Only Bavaria refused outright. Bavaria, along with Saxony, wanted a redrafting of the North German constitution and the founding of a new federation. Their aim was to break Prussian hegemony and create a looser federal organization in which each state retained a wider margin of sovereignty. This Bismarck opposed energetically. He realized that Prussia's dominant position in the new Germany was at stake, and while he was willing to make certain concessions to the sovereign rights and particularist feelings of the southern states, he was not ready to sacrifice substantial power to them. He insisted that the southern states give up their right to an independent foreign policy to the new federal state.

Bismarck's concept of the new Reich was based on the established North German Confederation and union between it and the south German states. The new Reich government would have authority over the army and navy, and its own source of income through tariffs, consumer taxes, and shipping duties. There would be a uniform system of weights and measures, a common currency, and a common law to promote trade and industry. Legislative powers would be exercised through a federal assembly and a parliament (the Reichstag), and the executive powers through the Prussian king, who would also be commander in chief of the army and navy.[78]

Bavaria held the key to the new Reich. If her opposition could be overcome, the other southern states would follow suit. If she stayed out, the Reich would be weakened and susceptible to Austrian and French influence. At the same time Bismarck realized that undue pressure on Bavaria had to be avoided so as not to complicate future developments. After the victory at Sedan, Bavaria reconsidered her position and entered into negotiations with Bismarck. Bavaria demanded the right to send and receive diplomatic representatives, to conclude treaties (so long as they were not contrary to federal interests) and, in time of peace, to maintain her own army, railroad, post and telegraph system, and her own legislative, administrative, and financial powers. The real stumbling block was her refusal to enter the new Reich under the existing North German constitution. The Bavarian negotiators demanded a reorganization of the federal union on a new and less centralized basis which would give Bavaria a special position.

Concurrently, Bismarck held private talks with Bavarian representatives involving the payment of a subsidy to King Ludwig of Bavaria in return for his offering the imperial crown to King Wilhelm.[79] There were, furthermore, negotiations with Baden, Hesse, and Wuerttemberg aimed at isolating Bavaria, and when these were unsuccessful, Bismarck threatened to bypass an assembly of German princes, which was to approve the peace treaty with France and the constitution of the new Reich, and go directly to the people. As he had done so often in the past, he played two tunes simultaneously, the liberal and the conservative. When the latter failed, he turned to German public opinion which, anxious for unification, was kept in a state of excitement by a well-directed press campaign and by the prospect of participating in the final decisions. In the face of these well-orchestrated proceedings, Baden and Hesse signed a treaty with the North German Confederation on November 15, Bavaria joined on November

23, and Wuerttemberg on November 25, 1870. Aside from some minor changes in the North German constitution and certain privileges granted to Bavaria, the new Reich was but an extension of the North German Confederation.[80]

The final ceremony in the great hall of mirrors at Versailles on January 18, 1871, was entirely in character with the course the unification of Germany had taken. Kings and princes of the German states and generals and officers of the victorious armies attended, and, of course, Bismarck. Only the representatives of the German people were missing.[81]

The
New Reich

"Now that we have achieved the most cherished dream of our lives, what is there left to live for?" Heinrich von Sybel exclaimed after the unification.[1] Most of his contemporaries, liberals and nationalists alike, expressed similar sentiments. Those who had doubted after the Revolution of 1848 that their country would ever be unified now rejoiced. It had all come true, because of the genius of Bismarck, and praise of his accomplishments echoed across the land. The future looked brilliant, and the first years after unification fulfilled the highest expectations. Then, suddenly, a severe economic and financial crisis led to bitter disillusionment. In the midst of this crisis, Bismarck began his fight with the Catholic church—the *Kulturkampf*—and then, in the late 1870s, his anti-Socialist crusade. These two domestic struggles caused widespread dissatisfaction among Catholics and workers who, through their political parties—the Center party and the Social Democratic party—formed the core of the government's opposition. These dissidents were joined by the French from Alsace-Lorraine, the Guelphs from Hanover, the Danes from Schleswig-Holstein, and the Poles from East and West Prussia. Taken together they made a formidable group whose diversity and size are an index of Bismarck's failure in domestic affairs.

It seems ironic that a man who was able, despite three wars, to convince the European powers of his peaceful intentions was unable to achieve a similar success at home. Bismarck apparently never fully understood the forces that transformed central Europe from an agrarian to an industrial economy and from a rural to an urban society, nor did he appreciate the consequences of these changes for German political life. His aim was to preserve the monarchy and the established social order, based on the nobility, the bureaucracy, and the army. While he was willing to make concessions in economic matters, he refused to do so in political affairs. With foreign wars no longer a necessity after the unification, Bismarck transferred the struggle to the domestic scene; his fight against Catholics and Socialists can be considered a device to divert popular attention from unresolved social and constitutional problems.

Bismarck's personal style of conducting affairs of state brooked no outside interference; he was intolerant of colleagues, and forever suspicious of real or imaginary rivals such as Arnim and Stosch.[2] Nor were his assistants as devoted and loyal as earlier historians have believed. Bismarck was an exacting taskmaster, but he was also a capricious superior. "He disdained stupidity and rebuffed independence. He wanted intelligent servants without private judgment or ambition, well-wrought tools for his master hands."[3] He never quite knew how to deal with party politicians; in Windthorst, for example, Bismarck could only see the defeated Hanoverian minister bent on revenge, never the leader of the Center party.[4] Bismarck was unable to tolerate opposing points of view, however sincere, and always considered opposition to his policies as personal attacks, motivated by selfish or group interests.[5] According to Holstein, one of the chancellor's closest and most faithful subordinates, Bismarck was a cynic in his relationships with his fellowmen, using or dropping people whenever it suited his purpose.[6] Contrary to his methods in foreign affairs, he tended to exaggerate domestic conflicts, declaring open warfare on his opponents instead of working toward peaceful solutions. These attitudes and policies were ill suited to healthy political development, nor were they designed to attract able men to politics.

> The achievements of 1871 had been extraordinary, and an age that glorified heroes rather than analyzed anonymous social and economic forces attributed them to Bismarck's genius. He had forged institutions that would promote Germany's power by providing for common commercial and foreign policies and that would guarantee Germany's survival by a common military establishment under thinly disguised Prussian hegemony. By creating a national parliament, Bismarck had inserted democratic and popular elements into the structure of the Reich without materially weakening the preceding monarchical-conservative order. By making concessions to modernity, the old order prolonged its life. The new Reich facilitated the immense expansion of material power—though the attendant social transformation undermined Bismarck's political structure. Bismarck was slow to appreciate the danger from that quarter. He was more attuned to

foreign dangers. For the great Bismarck was at home abroad, and estranged at home.

He devoted his best efforts to shielding Germany from foreign wars. His greatest accomplishment after 1871 was his assimilation of Germany into the European state system; he persuaded a suspicious Europe that Germany had become a satiated power—and by the time Europe fully believed him, he was dismissed from office, and Germany ceased being satiated.[7]

Thus, his achievements, while remarkable, were mixed and altogether not solid enough to last more than seventy-five years.

The Annexation of Alsace-Lorraine The final peace treaty with France, signed at Frankfurt on May 10, 1871,[8] contained two provisions which caused major problems in the development of the Reich: the acquisition of Alsace-Lorraine and the French war indemnity of five billion francs. The former became a constant and sometimes major irritant to Franco-German relations and was a contributing factor to the outbreak of World War I, while the latter was one of the more important causes of the economic depression of 1873 which had a major impact on German economic and political affairs.

In retrospect it is easy to see that the annexation of Alsace-Lorraine was a tragic mistake, though it was clear even at the time that France would not suffer the loss of her provinces with equanimity. In view of Bismarck's lenient terms for Austria in 1866 and his avowed desire for peaceful relations with France after the war, his insistence on acquiring this territory (the mineral wealth of which was not known at the time) is difficult to understand. The usual explanation has been that he reluctantly gave in to overwhelming military pressure; the general staff considered the provinces of the utmost importance for the next war against France. But the problem was more complicated than that. In 1870–71, the annexation of Alsace-Lorraine was, for German public opinion, an expression of the popular, national spirit of the unification movement. The acquisition of the French provinces was not the result of old-fashioned power or cabinet diplomacy. This popular aspect was further supported by memories of French invasions of German territory in the revolutionary and Napoleonic wars. Strasbourg, especially, had been a bone of contention between Germany and France for several hundred years, changing rulers whenever the fortunes of war favored one side. Thus, the vast majority of Germans looked upon the acquisition of Alsace-Lorraine as a legitimate and even necessary part of the peace treaty.[9]

There were, however, other considerations, such as the self-determination of the local population, which was overwhelmingly French in the case of Lorraine, and at least partly so in the case of Alsace, and the constitutional problem of the status of the annexed provinces within the Reich. The annexation of Alsace-Lorraine also diminished the chances of a lasting settlement with France within the framework of a new European alignment, and affected Germany's future role among the great powers. Popular demand for annexation appeared shortly after the start of the Franco-Prussian War, first in South Germany and then in the North. These claims appear to have arisen spontaneously: there is no sign of governmental influence on the press. A few liberal papers, such as the *Frankfurter Zeitung*, opposed annexation on the grounds that it would make the war appear to have been aggressive rather than defensive, and to have been directed against the French people rather than Napoleon III and his government, as many Germans believed it to have been. The nationalistic press dismissed these arguments as sentimental drivel. The preference of the local population would soon be changed under German rule, according to these papers, and the principle of self-determination should be secondary to the demands of German nationalism. Or, as a Wuerttemberg liberal expressed it during the first month of the Franco-Prussian War, "the opposition of the population [in Alsace-Lorraine] cannot be taken into account; we are neither sentimental politicians nor doctrinaire fools. Nationalism [that is, pro-Germanism in Alsace-Lorraine] will come to the fore in due time. Until then, the country can be kept in check and governed militarily."[10] At about the same time a majority of Germans became convinced that the French nation, and not Napoleon III, was the real enemy, and that under these circumstances demands for annexation were valid.

Bismarck's own attitude did not follow public opinion. He seems to have decided on annexation at an early stage, though it is impossible to determine exactly when he made up his mind. It is known that during the Revolution of 1848 he asked that Strasbourg be again incorporated into the Reich. He believed that France would hate Germany and seek revenge in any case, and meanwhile Alsace-Lorraine would provide much-needed security for southern Germany. Then too, Bismarck strongly believed in realpolitik,[11] and this called for annexation of territory after a victorious war. (The example of 1866 did not contradict this principle, because Prussia's failure to acquire Austrian territory was compensated for by Prussian annexations in central Germany.) This concept of power politics demanded that France be weakened territorially, militarily, and economically. France, prior to the war, was vastly superior to Germany in military and economic strength and Bismarck, the leader of a relatively minor power, could not have foreseen that Germany would eclipse France in the following decades.

While German public opinion was overwhelmingly in favor of annexation, this was not a decisive factor for Bismarck. He could have led public opinion toward a negotiated peace after Sedan, but he chose instead to emphasize the dangers of foreign intervention and the stubborn resistance of the French. He was neither the exponent nor the opponent of German national opinion. He considered the problem as an aspect of foreign policy, and was not concerned with its future domestic implications—the form of the territory's integration into the new Reich—and, as it turned out, his policy was shortsighted and mistaken on both counts.

Political and Economic Reversals   The five billion franc indemnity that France was forced to pay as part of the peace treaty created an unprecedented economic boom in Germany. Industrial expansion, building construction, and land and stock market speculation reached new heights, and people believed that an age of continuous prosperity had finally arrived.[12] When, in 1873, the bubble burst because of overexpansion, overproduction, and manipulation of the stock market, the consequences were far-reaching.[13] Industrialists and businessmen demanded protective tariffs to strengthen home industries, alleviate unemployment, and avert the threat of socialism. During the War-in-Sight crisis of 1875,[14] they also advocated a strong industrial base to bolster Germany's military strength.[15] Artisans and shopkeepers asked for state protection, curtailment of free trade, and the end of economic individualism. Farmers and peasants united in demanding cheap credit, lower taxes, higher prices for their products, and protection against exploitation by middlemen. And the workers began to organize themselves under the pressure of unemployment and industrial dislocation.[16]

The way out of the economic crisis appeared increasingly to be protective tariffs. At the same time, the need for tax reforms to make the Reich financially independent of the states, the promulgation of a new army budget, and the reorganization of Reich ministries combined to create a deadlock between Bismarck and the liberal majority in the Reichstag. Bismarck's proposal for a fixed and permanent army budget was rejected by the liberals who, for the first time since the unification, opposed the government.[17] Under pressure from public opinion, a compromise was reached and army expenditures were fixed by law for a seven-year period; this law became known as the *Septennat*. Still, the liberals were none too happy. On the question of tax reforms and reorganization of Reich ministries, they wanted ministers of the government to be responsible to the Reichstag, a demand which Bismarck refused.[18]

By 1875–76 Bismarck's domestic policy of moderate liberalism appeared to have failed[19] and his foreign policy of isolating France had proved unsuccessful.[20] A change of allies and policies, both domestic and foreign, seemed clearly in order.[21] At home, Bismarck looked for and found support among leaders of heavy industry and high finance, and by sacrificing Delbrueck, head of the Reich Chancery and the chief proponent of free trade (who resigned Aprii 25, 1876), the chancellor's shift toward protectionism was firmly initiated. In the wake of a severe agricultural depression at the end of 1875, protectionism gained additional support from agrarian interests. As a result of the depression Germany turned from a wheat-exporting to a wheat-importing country, and unrestricted overseas and Russian imports severely endangered German, and especially Prussian, agriculture. Thus agrarian and industrial interests, both traditionally strong supporters of the Church and the monarchy, combined in their demands for protective tariffs.[22] They would also be able to provide solid conservative support for Bismarck, should he ever choose to abandon the liberals.

The economic depression had discredited liberal policies all along the line, and had "laid bare the foundations of *soi-disant* liberalism in the Germano-Prussian state."[23] The 1877 Reichstag election resulted in a conservative majority and a decline in liberal strength. Protectionists, largely with the help of the Center party, also increased their power.[24] This conservative-protectionist alliance in the Reichstag enabled Bismarck to carry through his tax reforms and the reorganization of the Reich administration. These developments meant an increase in the chancellor's authority and a defeat for the liberals; they strengthened the conservative forces and preserved the leading position of the Prussian nobility, the army, the bureaucracy, and the foreign service. This conservative-agrarian-industrial alliance, which became characteristic of the political-economic structure of the Reich, endured long after Bismarck. In domestic affairs, the alliance of conservative interests contributed to Germany's failure to solve her social problems, led to the anti-Socialist struggle, and was also a factor in her pursuit of colonial acquisition and world policy. Thus, 1877–79 can be considered more decisive for the future development of Germany than 1870–71, the years of Germany's unification.[25]

The political-economic reversal from a liberal to a conservative policy and from free trade to protectionism was a major, though not the only, consequential development in Germany in the 1870s. Two significant conflicts—the Prussian government's fight against the Catholic church (the *Kulturkampf*), and the Reich government's campaign against the Socialists—took up most of the two decades of Bismarck's chancellorship.

The Kulturkampf   In the new Reichstag which opened in Berlin on March 21, 1871, the fifty-eight delegates of the Center party were second in number only to the National Liberals. The Center party was founded in Prussia in 1870 to represent the interests of the Roman Catholic minority in the Prussian Parliament and, after the unification of Germany, it expanded its organization in the hope of attracting non-Catholics to its ranks. In this it was only partially successful. A few Poles and Guelphs joined the party and supported its opposition to Bismarck, but the overwhelming majority was made up of Catholics from Bavaria, Silesia, the Rhineland, and Westphalia. It was composed of peasants, workers, shopkeepers, and intellectuals. Suspicious of any forces not under his control, and forever looking for conspiracies directed against his person as well as his policies, Bismarck believed that the Center party constituted a major threat to the new Reich. He habitually equated his person with the state, so that an attack on one invariably was seen as an attack on the other. To Bismarck, the Center party was particularly suspicious because of its connection with the papacy, its support of the papal dogma of infallibility,[26] and more recently, its stand in favor of federalism and against the centralizing tendencies within the new Reich.

"Thinking himself far more infallible than the Pope," Lord Russell, the British minister in Berlin, wrote to the Foreign Office, Bismarck could not "tolerate two infallibles in Europe and fancies he can select and appoint the next Pontiff as he could a Prussian general who will carry out his orders to the Catholic clergy in Germany and elsewhere."[27] Bismarck also believed that a Catholic conspiracy, involving Austria, Italy, France, his domestic enemies, and possibly the Empress Augusta, existed.[28]

Politically, the struggle began over two issues: the right of the Catholic church to regulate its own affairs as guaranteed by the Prussian constitution of 1850, and the Center party's support of certain fundamental rights in the Reich constitution. Joining in this struggle for fundamental rights were the Reichstag delegates from Alsace-Lorraine, Schleswig-Holstein, and those of the Polish minorities and other splinter groups, which made the Center party the leader of the opposition.[29] Outside the Reichstag a controversy erupted over the Catholic church's teaching of the dogma of papal infallibility, which the government considered unwarranted interference in its domain. The liberals, who wanted to secularize the schools and rid the Church of its medieval superstitions, vigorously supported the government's stand against the Church. To the liberals, the *Kulturkampf* signified a struggle between modernity and medievalism; the essence of German culture (hence the term *Kulturkampf* or cultural struggle) was at stake. Just as the Holy See defended the powers of the Church against the encroachments of the state and of modern science, the government and the liberals meant to extend the knowledge of science for the improvement of mankind, the recent discoveries of Darwin being a special case in point.

The first incident in the *Kulturkampf* occurred when state-employed Catholic theologians and religious instructors refused to teach the dogma of papal infallibility. When their superior, Bishop Krementz, suspended them from all future teaching, the Prussian minister of culture refused to recognize the bishop's decision and, after extended altercation, terminated all state subsidies to the bishop on September 25, 1870.[30] The following summer the Catholic section of the Prussian ministry of culture was dissolved because its officials had allegedly supported Polish and Catholic, rather than German, interests in Prussia's eastern provinces. This action was followed, in March 1872, by a new school law which substituted state supervision for ecclesiastical supervision in the schools. That summer the Jesuits were expelled from Germany (June 1872) and their Society was dissolved. In May 1873 the Falk Laws, named after Adalbert Falk, the Prussian minister of education and ecclesiastical affairs, restricted the training and employment of priests, limited the disciplinary powers of the Church, made civil marriage obligatory, and made it easier for Prussians to leave the Catholic church.[31]

These measures aroused the unanimous and determined opposition of Catholic bishops, the lower clergy, and the laity. If the struggle's aim had been the destruction of the Center party, the results were disappointing. The party, as well as other Catholic organizations, emerged stronger and more resolute in its opposition to the government. Taking advantage of the freedom of the press, the Center party almost doubled its voting strength in the election of 1874 and received nearly 28 percent of the total popular vote. The effects of the government's measures and the clergy's opposition to them created hardships for Prussia's Catholic population. Young theologians refused to take the prescribed stated examinations, and the closing of seminaries and the refusal of bishops to fill existing vacancies led to a severe shortage of parish priests and to a crisis in the religious welfare of many Catholic communities. By 1876 most of Prussia's Catholic bishops had either been arrested or fled abroad.

The overall effects of the *Kulturkampf* on Prussia and Germany are difficult to assess. For Bismarck and the liberals it was a struggle for the supremacy of the state over the Church. In this struggle, the liberals soon found themselves in a very awkward position. While they were for the separation of church and state and for state education and opposed to the federalistic and particularistic tendencies of the Center party, they were forced, in support of the *Kulturkampf*, to agree to a series of coercive measures that were not at all to their liking. The liberals took this stand believing that it would strengthen their powers and those of the Reichstag against the chancellor's semiautocratic policies in other fields. The liberals were not successful in enlarging their powers or that of the Reichstag; they overestimated their powers and political skills compared to those of Bismarck. As the future was to show, Bismarck did not need their support, and by the end of the decade he abandoned them without further ado and switched to the conservatives.

The conservatives, especially the Protestants among them, were also in a dilemma. Many were anti-Catholic; if they did not actively support the *Kulturkampf*, they tacitly approved of it. But while they opposed papal infallibility and were glad to be rid of the Jesuits, they were also opposed to the separation of church and state, the government's educational policies, the provisions for civil marriage, and the limitation of ecclesiastical independence. A relatively small group of Old Conservatives, led by Ludwig von Gerlach, opposed Bismarck outright. They considered his struggle with the Roman Catholic church an attack on Christian religion and Christian principles. In their view, Prussia was a Christian state which had received its original mandate from the Church through the Teutonic Knights; Bismarck's policy was, therefore, against true Prussian interests and tradition.

Caught in the crossfire of conflicting religious emotions and state policies, Emperor Wilhelm probably suffered a great deal. His basic sympathies and loyalties were often—though not always—with the Old Prussian Conservatives, an attitude which was shared by the queen.[32] But the chancellor, by persuasion, tact, persistence, and sheer force of personality, was able to convince the king of the reasonableness and the necessity of the *Kulturkampf*.

Bismarck, like many observers at the time, was unaware that federalist and particularist tendencies, as represented by the Center party and its allies, were still very much in evidence despite unification. Considering that the actual powers of the Reich—as distinct from those of Prussia—were few in number and limited in scope, Bismarck attempted to strengthen the state's position over the Church just at the time when the Church, through the decisions of the Vatican Council, was trying to redress the imbalance that had existed for centuries in Germany. The fight was not initially directed exclusively against the Catholic church—though it quickly became so because of the Catholic church's strong centralized organization and resistance—but against the Protestant church as well. Thus, Bismarck wanted to abolish the position of *summus episcopus* (ranking bishop; that is, highest church office of the German Protestant territorial princes), to take over the administration of schools, Protestant or Catholic, at least at the secondary level and if possible at the elementary level as well, and to limit the Church to religious instruction. The chancellor also wanted to ensure the state's right to approve all ecclesiastical appointments and to move the administration of religious affairs from the Ministry of Culture to the Ministry of Justice.

Foreign reaction to the *Kulturkampf*, including the pastoral letters of the French bishops in support of German Catholics, and Pius IX's encyclical of November 21, 1873, protesting the *Kulturkampf*, reinforced Bismarck's suspicion that there was an international Catholic conspiracy against Germany; these developments made him more determined than ever to curb the powers of the Church.[33] But the struggle dragged on, the resistance of the Church remained unbroken, and the strength of the Center party even increased. The resistance of the Old Conservatives and of the orthodox wing of the Protestant clergy against the *Kulturkampf* also stiffened, and the government began to lose popular support just at the time when the adverse effects of the economic depression were being felt throughout the country. By the end of the decade, Bismarck had grown tired of the struggle and was ready to seek some form of accommodation. At about the same time, the leadership of the Center party also appeared willing to come to terms with the government. In political outlook, social composition, and geographic distribution, the Center party was particularly well suited to represent the Reich's new economic interests. Since the beginning of the *Kulturkampf* a considerable number of industrialists and landowners who favored higher tariffs and were opposed to liberalism and laissez faire had joined the Center party, and the party was now ready to use its influence for political ends, especially to press for the termination of the *Kulturkampf*.[34] Bismarck's aim had never been the destruction of the Church, nor had he intended to break with the Old Conservatives. The death of Pope Pius IX, in 1878, presented an opportunity to end this futile struggle. Pius's successor, Leo XIII, was more amenable to compromise and negotiations between Prussia and the Holy See started in September 1879.[35] In June of the following year Falk resigned as Prussian minister for education and ecclesiastical affairs, and his resignation made it easier for Bismarck to change his policy toward the Catholic church in Prussia.

Negotiations with the Holy See and a change in Prussian ecclesiastical legislation led to a gradual easing of tension. Eventually, diplomatic relations with the Vatican were restored (1882) and some of the more stringent anti-Catholic laws were repealed (1882–87).[36] The *Kulturkampf* was not a glorious episode in Bismarck's career. He saw it as part of the age-old struggle between church and state, a relationship which had to be redefined periodically. To him it was essentially a political, and not a philosophical, struggle; but in his quest for state supremacy, he was unable to confine it to the political arena. When the *Kulturkampf* spilled over into the religious field, the results were disastrous for the new Reich.[37]

A Change in Political Alignment and the Anti-Socialist Crusade

Bismarck's dislike for and suspicion of parties and organizations with international connections were not limited to the Catholic church. They extended to the Socialist movement as well, particularly since the Socialists had attracted a considerable number of voters and had increased their delegates in the Reichstag from two in 1871 to twelve in 1877. Bismarck's attempts to suppress the Socialists, combined with the economic depression, tended to strengthen rather than weaken the workers' movement. The two existing workers' organizations, Ferdinand Lassalle's General German Workers' Movement (*Allgemeiner Deutscher Arbeiterverein*), founded in Leipzig on May 23, 1863, and August Bebel and Wilhelm Liebknecht's Social Democratic Labor Party, organized in Eisenach on August 7, 1869, were drawn closer together as a result of Bismarck's anti-Socialist policy. From the beginning there had been considerable rivalry and friction between the two parties. Lassalle's faction was more concerned with immediate and practical achievements, while the Bebel-Liebknecht wing was more ideologically inclined and, at least theoretically, more faithful to the teachings of Marx and Engels. On May 22, 1875, at Gotha, the two parties united to form the Social Democratic Labor Party of Germany (*Sozialdemokratische Deutsche Arbeiter Partei*, SDP).

Bismarck's halfhearted attempts to suppress the Socialist movement in the early 1870s had failed,[38] but when, in 1878, two attempts were made on the emperor's life, Bismarck took advantage of the public outrage and used these incidents to launch an anti-Socialist crusade. The underlying motives for this campaign are difficult to fathom, particularly since the end of the *Kulturkampf* was nowhere in sight and it was not Bismarck's habit to fight two major campaigns simultaneously. He preferred to destroy his enemies one at a time, after having made certain that they were isolated and without friends and allies. In this case he clearly misjudged the situation. He may have believed that with public feeling so strong he would be able to destroy the Social Democratic party in a short time and with little effort. The chancellor considered the party's growth dangerous to the monarchy and to the social and religious makeup of the state; and in foreign affairs, he was concerned that the SDP, like the Catholic Center party, would use its international connections to ally with Germany's enemies. In the aftermath of the economic recession of 1873 and the general antiliberal trend throughout the country, the time seemed propitious for an anti-Socialist campaign. This tendency in Bismarck's thinking was reinforced by his desire to rely on political support from the conservatives rather than the liberals and to abandon the Reich's free trade stance.[39]

With the help of the conservatives, he hoped to get an "exceptional law" (*Ausnahmegesetz*) through the Reichstag which would outlaw the Social Democratic party. The occasion came after the May 11, 1878, attempt to assassinate the emperor. But the bill failed to pass because the conservatives, though eager to fight the Socialists, were afraid of the precedent such a law would create. The following week, however, a second assassination attempt seriously wounded Wilhelm I. Bismarck blamed this act on the Socialists, though their responsibility was never proven, and used the incident as an excuse to dissolve the Reichstag and call for new elections.[40] The chancellor hoped that public outrage would cause the Social Democrats to lose heavily at the polls. His expectations were not fulfilled, for the party only lost three deputies overall; it actually gained strength in Berlin and other major cities. In the same election the liberal parties lost heavily, and in general there was a distinct shift to the right. (The number of National Liberal delegates declined from 127 to 99 and the Progressives lost 9 seats, while the number of Conservatives rose from 40 to 59, the Free Conservatives gained 19 seats, and the Center added 6 deputies to its ranks.)[41]

When the exceptional law came up before the new Reichstag, the Conservatives, Free Conservatives, and National Liberals supported it, while the Progressives and the Center opposed it. (The Center, still suffering under *Kulturkampf* legislation, refused to sanction any repressive bill.) On October 19, however, the Reichstag passed the anti-Socialist bill by a vote of 221 to 149. The measure was not quite as severe as Bismarck had hoped it would be. While it "empowered state and local governments to abolish societies with 'social-democratic, socialistic, or communist' tendencies . . . and to prohibit the publication and distribution of Social Democratic newspapers, periodicals, and books . . . and to impose a Minor State of Siege (*Kleiner Belagerungszustand*) providing the means to expel the most dangerous persons,"[42] it did not prohibit party members from running for elective office. It had simply not occurred to anyone that a party whose publications had been prohibited and whose organization had been shattered could elect anyone to a seat in the Reichstag. Paradoxically, the anti-Socialist law united and strengthened the SDP and ensured its survival.

Bismarck took advantage of the election of 1878 to realign the political balance in the Prussian Parliament and in the Reichstag, and to launch the anti-Socialist crusade. The chancellor had become increasingly unhappy about the influence of the liberals in the Reichstag, and by 1878, the government and the liberals had reached a constitutional impasse.[43] The origins of the crisis can be traced to the elections of 1874, when the National Liberals had gained a key position in the Reichstag which enabled them to choose an opposition policy with the Left, or a policy of cooperation with the Right. They decided to cooperate with the Left and to push for legislation which would lead to constitutional guarantees in financial matters. In particular, the liberals wanted the finance minister to be responsible to the Reichstag.

THE NEW REICH

This development frightened the conservatives, who saw it as a threat to the established order and a move toward liberalization of the government which could lead to parliamentary control. Though the conservatives saw this act as a "red revolt," it was actually no more than a move toward constitutionalism by the liberals, who would have preferred to achieve this goal with the consent of the chancellor rather than in opposition to him. The liberals failed, however, to take Bismarck's attitude into account. They also overlooked the dissension in their own ranks and misjudged the temper of public opinion. (They could not, of course, have foreseen that the assassination attempts on the emperor would spoil whatever chances they may have had.)

Bismarck's tax reform proposals to stabilize Reich finances became the key issue between the liberals and the government. His plan entailed raising the indirect taxes on beer and petroleum, instituting a state monopoly of tobacco and sugar, and placing higher taxes on taverns. These sources would give the Reich an adequate independent income—which it had not had heretofore—and, at the same time, avoid direct taxation. Since the Reichstag had a voice in matters of direct taxation, Bismarck's tax proposals, combined with his moves toward protectionism, were a clear indication of his intention to reduce the political powers of the Reichstag. If his proposals failed, and many signs pointed in that direction, Bismarck appeared to be ready to dispense with the Reichstag and govern without it. The two assassination attempts provided the necessary pretext and the chancellor's first reaction was to dissolve the Reichstag.[44] Remembering the March days of 1848, he was prepared to proclaim a state of emergency and even inquired whether the Berlin garrison was ready to meet an armed rebellion. For a time Bismarck hesitated, unsure whether to submit his tax reform program to the old Reichstag in the hope that the delegates would be sufficiently intimidated to pass it, or to dissolve the Reichstag and call new elections in the expectation that the shock of events would cause the electorate to return a conservative majority. Bismarck decided to dissolve the Reichstag, and the federal states were so informed and asked to give their approval. When some of the southern states expressed reluctance, State Secretary Buelow hinted at the involvement of Socialist agitators and informed the states that a state of emergency might be declared. He also pointed out the dangers of opposing Prussian policy. The threat was unmistakable. The states could choose either to comply voluntarily or do so under the threat of Prussian military force.[45] Not since 1866 had there been such a confrontation between North and South. In a special directive to Baden, Buelow added that if Prussia's proposals failed to receive a majority in the Federal Council, it would be an indication of the inadequacy of the Reich constitution and a revision of the constitution would have to be considered. This was the first time that a legal dissolution of the Reich and its reorganization under Prussian control was seriously contemplated.

Bismarck apparently considered the threat to Prussia's dominant position in the Reich great enough to warrant the most radical solution. "If I don't make a coup d'état," he told the Wuerttemberg envoy, "I won't get anything done."[46] In the end, Bismarck did not have to carry out his threat. The Federal Council voted unanimously in favor of the Prussian proposal. The rattling of Prussian sabers had been effective and had shown the South Germans just how much influence they had on Reich policy. The dissolution of the Reichstag in 1878 marked the end of the liberal era.

The dissolution of the Reichstag was followed by the government's successful anti-Socialist and antiliberal campaign, and resulted in an election victory for the conservatives. Bismarck had broken the domination of the liberals in the Prussian Parliament and in the Reichstag. The constitutional crisis was at an end. But this was only a temporary solution which failed to solve the underlying constitutional problems. In a rapidly growing urban and industrial society, Bismarck tried to preserve the ancient privileges of the ruling classes without making any concessions to the new forces. A coalition based on the interests of heavy industry and large landowners now formed the parliamentary base for the chancellor's antiliberal policy; this coalition favored the economic interests of these two classes to the disadvantage of the liberals. The landowners and industrialists, in turn, were satisfied with the existing system and grateful to have a strong government representing their interests and supporting law and order.

The new Reichstag was more conservative and less likely to challenge Bismarck's policies than the old one had been. His tariff and tax reform proposals had, however, not been acted on, and until they were, his policy against the Socialists—and this meant against liberalism, free trade, and parliamentarianism as well—was bound to fail. In an effort to achieve a solid majority for his program, Bismarck tried various coalitions of parties, as well as foreign diversions.[47] None of these arrangements worked for very long, and the threat of a revolution from above remained. There was no solution to the contradictions of the German constitutional system. Just as the outcome of the Prussian constitutional conflict had failed to resolve the inherent contradiction between the Prussian monarchy and constitutional government, so, too, Bismarck's Reich failed to reconcile royal power and parliamentary responsibility. The only means of maintaining the existing order against the new and rising forces of the Left was the threat of a coup d'état from above.[48]

For Bismarck, the Socialist movement was not only a grave peril to the newly created state—its international aspects made its members *ipso facto Reichsfeinde* [enemies of the Reich]—but socialism was also an ungodly philosophy and an immoral movement which sought to change the God-given order of society. In his eyes this was rebellion, and rebellion had to be crushed.[49] Bismarck's attitude toward socialism and the labor movement had probably undergone little change since the March days of 1848 when, outraged at the successful uprisings in Berlin, he wanted to crush them singlehandedly. If anything, his convictions had deepened. He was, like most Germans, confirmed in his conservative beliefs by the republican developments in France and especially by the uprising of the Paris Commune in 1870–71. The very one-sided press reports of these events, which exaggerated the "red peril" but were silent about the excesses perpetrated by the French troops, frightened the public and made the labor movement appear a deadly threat to the state and to society. The declaration of the German workers' movement, expressing solidarity with the Commune, greatly enhanced these fears.[50]

It is curious that Bismarck, like Napoleon III, recognized and used the emerging industrial masses for political purposes and that both men also feared them. Like Napoleon, he believed he could control them by introducing universal suffrage and giving them a voice in the Reichstag. Convinced of the righteousness of his cause and the reasonableness of his policy, Bismarck attempted to deal with the workers in two ways: repressive measures to destroy the workers' organizations and turn them away from the antireligious, materialistic teachings of Marx and Engels, and governmental social measures which would, at the same time, bind them to the state. "He wanted to satisfy their physical needs so as to dull their spirit and break their will."[51] Bismarck's sincerity toward social measures is open to question, inasmuch as his legislative proposals were somewhat lopsided. He approached the problem from the employer's point of view, and never believed that the social question could or would be solved by protective legislation. Though his sickness, accident, and old-age insurance laws failed to protect children and women workers and did not shorten the work day or seven-day week, they were a progressive and pioneering series of measures and became the model for similar laws in many other countries.[52]

The social laws presented the Social Democratic Party with a very serious dilemma. These laws, combined with certain proposals for nationalization and monopolization of certain industries, were the clearest examples of state socialism in Germany. State socialism forced the party to decide whether democratic-political principles or socialistic-economic ideas should prevail in its program. If democratic-political principles were to dominate, Bismarck's policies would have to be opposed, but if socialistic-economic ideas were paramount, accommodation with the government was possible. Thus, when the accident, sickness, and invalid insurance laws were presented to the Reichstag in November 1881, and the proposals for a state tobacco monopoly the following year, the party was faced with a serious crisis. Accepting the insurance program meant giving up opposition to the government in the Reichstag; at the same time, however, the party could not completely reject the government's program on political grounds, having demanded similar improvements for the workers for so long. The course the Social Democratic party finally adopted was to approve the program in principle but to declare that it did not go far enough and to demand many more benefits for the workers.[53] "Since their [the Party's] amendments were never incorporated into the final bills, they could always vote against the welfare legislation on the ground that it was wholly inadequate and therefore fraudulent."[54]

THE NEW REICH

After 1882, increasing urbanization and steady improvement in economic conditions led to a strengthening of the party and the trade union movement. The success of the SDP in the election of 1884 clearly demonstrated the failure of Bismarck's anti-Socialist policies: the party gained 13 delegates and over 100,000 votes.[55] The government parties failed to achieve an absolute majority, which further enhanced the importance of the SDP's Reichstag position. But Bismarck was not ready to give up the fight. The strengthening of the labor movement in Germany and throughout Europe led to an increase of trade union activity, and an increasing number of demonstrations and strikes. By 1886, when the anti-Socialist legislation came up for renewal, the chancellor could argue that labor's revolutionary activities had to be curbed and that there were signs that anarchists had penetrated the Socialist movement. His arguments, coupled with disunity within the opposition parties—the Center and the SDP—enabled the government to achieve its aim; the anti-Socialist laws were passed for another two-year term by a 173 to 146 margin.[56] The government used this victory in a further attempt to destroy the labor movement and cripple the party. By forbidding strikes, closing meetings, and expelling and arresting party officials, it almost succeeded in its aims. But the leadership of the party continued its fight for social and political reforms in the Reichstag, and by using all legal and some illegal means, the party succeeded in keeping its organizational structure intact. During the November 1886 parliamentary session it opposed Bismarck's seven-year army bill, the *Septennat*, and helped to bring about its defeat (January 14, 1887). As a result, Bismarck dissolved the Reichstag and called for new elections. The outcome was a slight increase of the SDP's share of the popular vote (from 9.7 percent in 1884 to 10.1 percent in 1887), but a decline in its parliamentary strength, from 24 to 11 deputies, caused primarily by the government's failure to reapportion the growing urban districts. During this period the party overcame most of its internal differences. August Bebel assumed the party leadership, which diminished the strength of the moderate wing; Marxism, as interpreted by Karl Kautsky, became the official party creed. Kautsky and his followers stressed the economic and revolutionary aspects of Marxism and downgraded political action, except when it affected economic developments. This suited the party's parliamentary faction, which drew increasingly closer to the liberal parties in its actions and outlook.

The beginning of 1890 saw the final defeat of Bismarck's anti-Socialist crusade. The Reichstag's refusal to renew the anti-Socialist laws (January 25), and the party's victory at the polls (to 35 seats from 11), played an important part in the crisis of Bismarck's dismissal. A coal miners' strike in the Ruhr in May 1889 had brought young Kaiser Wilhelm II (who succeeded to the throne at the time of his father's death in 1888) face to face with the plight of the German workers and had impressed upon him the need for more extensive labor legislation. This attitude deepened the emperor's conflict with the chancellor and contributed materially to the latter's dismissal. At the same time Wilhelm's openly expressed concern for the workers lent respectability to the party. The party's impressive electoral victory, confined largely to the North German, Protestant areas, can be explained to some extent by the growing alienation of the workers from German bourgeois society, with its emphasis on education and property (*Besitz und Bildung*).[57]

German Society and Culture   The impact of the bitter and prolonged struggles against the Catholics and Socialists on German society was deep and long lasting. The immediate effect on German political life was to create a large though unorganized mass of disaffected citizens, composed of minorities—Poles, Danes, French, and Guelphs—and Catholics and workers. The fact that this opposition was disorganized made it easier for the nobility, the army, and the bureaucracy to maintain their hold on the government and the country, and made governmental or constitutional reforms seem superfluous. This situation was reinforced by the middle class's exaggerated emphasis on culture and learning and its disdainful attitude toward politics. This belief was expressed in the slogan, "the Buerger is meant to work, not rule, and a statesman's primary task is to rule,"[58] an attitude which led to the so-called apolitical German. In fact, the apolitical German bourgeois was afraid of the masses, suspicious of democratic government, and consistent in its support of conservative policies.[59] The bourgeois ideal was the scholar, immersed in learning and completely disinterested in daily affairs or practical knowledge. Unlike his English or French counterpart, the German university professor had no connection with the business community or the cosmopolitan world of the aristocracy. Separated from contact with the petite bourgeoisie and the artisans, the German academic remained isolated and developed an exaggerated faith in education and equally strong dislike of practical affairs. Education had traditionally been the only way for members of the German middle class to improve their position, and since the eighteenth century many had chosen this route to enter the civil service and the universities.

The prestige of a German university degree before 1890 surpassed that attached to any similar degree anywhere else. Economically and socially, German university professors ranked with the highest state and church officials and were considered the intellectual leaders of the nation. Practical politics were considered beneath their dignity and, "in this sense . . . the German intellectual was and considered himself apolitical: he had an aversion for the practical aspect of the political process."[60] This attitude was further reinforced after 1870 when the political parties openly competed for the vote of the masses. Many feared that under democracy the victorious mobs would sweep away "the aristocracy of birth, the aristocracy of money, and finally the aristocracy of education," as they had allegedly done in France.[61]

Thus, a majority of German professors, themselves conservatives, approved the antiliberal and anti-Socialist measures of successive governments and opposed any trend toward political or social reform. By the late 1880s they were concerned about the general decline of German culture and learning, and blamed the developments on industrialization and rising materialism. They felt powerless and confused, though their social prestige continued to remain high well into the twentieth century.

To the bourgeoisie's general and widespread disinterest and disdainful attitude toward practical politics was added the belief that the threat to liberty was greater and more serious from below than from above. These beliefs, combined with Bismarck's inability to attract new talent into government service, stifled a healthy and meaningful political life.

As one perceptive observer noted,

It is a common enough error among newcomers and superficial observers in Berlin to take for real the parliamentary system as it exists
here; with more experience and reflection, one quickly recognizes that
Germany is endowed with a fine and beautiful facade, remarkably
embellished on the surface, faithfully representing a picture of a parliamentary and constitutional system; the rules are correctly applied,
the customs observed, the external prerogatives respected; the play
of parties, turmoil in the corridors, lively debate, stormy sessions,
defeats inflicted on the government and even on the powerful Chancellor (only in matters of course that he considers of secondary importance), in short everything is done that can give the illusion and
make one believe in the gravity of the debates or the importance of
the votes; but behind this scenery, at the back of the stage, interven-
ing always at the decisive hour and having their way, appear Emperor and Chancellor, supported by the vital forces of the nation—the
army dedicated to the point of fanaticism, the bureaucracy disciplined
by the master's hand, the bench [*magistrature*] no less obedient, and
the population, sceptical occasionally of their judgments, quick to crit-
icize, quicker still to bow to the supreme will.[62]

After the depression of 1873–79 the bureaucracy, under Bismarck's
leadership, heeded the call for increased state intervention in economic
and social matters and effectively bypassed the Reichstag and the
political parties by issuing administrative rules and regulations. Thus
the political system began to resemble Bonapartism, with its monarchical trappings, bureaucratic tradition, constitutional compromises, universal manhood suffrage, and pseudo-parliamentarianism.
It was able to deal effectively with trade and economic problems, taxes
and the codification of laws, and was supported by large segments of
the middle class and the aristocracy because it prevented the take-
over of the state by the Socialists.[63]

The conservative coalition of the nobility and the upper and middle
bourgeoisie, "knitted together by common fears and common interests
. . . and the institutions they dominated, formed an almost irresistible
barrier to substantial social and political reform."[64]

In the social and cultural spheres, the consequences of the anti-Catholic and anti-Socialist struggles are difficult to assess. In combination
with the disillusionment which followed the *Gruenderzeit* (the period
of excessive building and speculation after the Franco-Prussian War)
and the subsequent economic slump, these internecine struggles contributed to the general mood of frustration and dissatisfaction. The

new Reich, despite its military trappings and efficient organization, failed to create its own ideology. Attempts to define and expand on the "ideas of 1871" proved an abysmal failure.[65] The hope that military victory in war would result in a triumph for German culture abroad was not borne out, though popular writers and patriotic historians continued to equate power with culture. There were, of course, exceptions. Nietzsche expressed the fear as early as 1873 that German culture (*Geist*) was being sacrificed to unification. Others noted that the new and widespread fashion of imitating army slang and behavior did little for the improvement of German culture and society. Love for imitations and fakes characterized the period—cardboard for wood, glass for onyx, gypsum for marble. Useless copper kettles, pewter jugs, and medieval swords graced fake beams, and imitation oak furniture was the fashion of the day. The paintings of Hans Makart and the operas of Richard Wagner were representative of German civilization in the latter part of the nineteenth century; the contrast between this period and the neoclassical age of German culture of the eighteenth and early nineteenth centuries was startling.

There was, on the other hand, a decided advance in the historical sciences. Schliemann's excavations of Troy and Mycenae, Ranke's *World History*, Mommsen's *History of Roman Law*, and Treitschke's *German History* were the foremost examples. But the greatest advances were in the natural and technical sciences. There Bunsen, Helmholtz, Virchow, Koch, Siemens, Daimler, Benz, Bayer, and Hertz combined to give Germany a preponderant lead.

Thus two divergent moods dominated popular consciousness. On the one hand, technological and scientific achievements and confidence in the political and economic potential of the newly established empire created considerable pride and optimism. No task seemed too difficult, no goal too distant. A mixture of romantic idealism, belief in Germany's world mission, and an increasingly aggressive nationalism, "rejecting the pacifistic tendencies of the western world," led to imperialism and world policy.[66] On the other hand, the gross materialism of the period underscored the widening gap between material achievement and moral and artistic development, producing a pessimistic world outlook (*Kulturpessimismus*).[67] This widespread pessimism, based on unfulfilled hopes and the realization of the discrepancies between idealism and reality, led to a rejection of many aspects of modern life. The squalor of urban living, the unemployed masses, poor living conditions, and false values, industrialization and its ravages, the decay of small towns and the decline of peasant holdings, all symptoms of a changing society (which were present then, as they are present now), led many to look into the past and to long for a better and simpler life. These people found what they were looking for in an idealization of the agrarian, feudal society of the Middle Ages, when there were few large towns and everyone knew his place in society.

From this longing the Volkish movement emerged, a mixture of conservatism and nationalism. It rejected modernism, liberalism, and western democracy. As in neoromanticism, the Volkish movement stressed feelings and emotions over reason and intellect, sought simple solutions, and longed for the simple life. The peasant, rooted in the soil, became the Volkish ideal; both rural and primitive society were glorified. Its emphasis on the simple virtues contrasted favorably with the complexity and rootlessness of contemporary society, whose uprooted workers and "alien" Jews became the favorite targets of Volkish propaganda. Volkish ideology, disseminated in the writings of Paul de Lagarde and Julius Langbehn, was elaborated into a Germanic faith.[68]

The Volkish movement attracted an increasingly large following in Germany in the last decades of the nineteenth and the early years of the twentieth centuries and appealed to two totally different groups. On the one hand it attracted those who opposed science and modernism and dreamed of the Middle Ages and the glories of the Germanic tribes. On the other hand, a considerable segment of the Volkish movement followed Ernst Haeckel, the foremost popularizer of Social Darwinism in Germany and a recognized and reputable zoologist and biologist.

"The form which Social Darwinism took in Germany was a pseudo-scientific religion of nature worship and nature mysticism combined with notions of racism. It was based on both the social Darwinian ideas of Haeckel and the ideology of Volkism which was related to and largely inspired by his writings."[69] Haeckel made Volkish ideas respectable, and through him large segments of the academic community, including university students and primary and secondary school teachers, were attracted to the movement.

Haeckel's study of evolution and the works of Darwin led him to see man as an integral part of nature and of his environment, and he developed this view of man and society into a new philosophy, Monism. His stress on the animal origin and nature of man opposed the traditional views of western civilization, which looked upon man as an individual, separate from and above his animal ancestors. Stressing the Darwinian concepts of the "struggle for existence" and the "survival of the fittest," the Monists blamed the false humanitarianism and misleading individualism of western society for the general decline and degeneration of the major European states. Rather than believing in the equality of mankind, the Monists emphasized racial differences, which included differences in color and intelligence. Among the various races, they believed that only the Germanic race had any value.

The racial nationalism of the Monists set the racial and Volkish community and the state above the individual citizen. Instead of individual and natural rights, they stressed community and the mutual obligations of the individual to society. They opposed civil rights, constitutionalism, and the supremacy of the individual, and believed that Monism would free Germany from the shackles of western civilization and might lead to a regeneration of her social and political life. At home the Monists advocated abolition of political parties and the establishment of a corporative state. Abroad they supported German colonial expansion and the construction of a powerful navy. They were especially active in the Pan German League and the various colonial and naval organizations.

The impact of Haeckel's interpretation of Social Darwinism and of his monistic philosophy in Germany was considerable. He had popularized his views in his best-selling work *Die Weltraethsel* (published in London in 1900 as *The Riddle of the Universe at the Close of the Nineteenth Century*), which, because of its readable style and the scientific reputation of its author, was read avidly by the literate and semiliterate masses. Thus, while others—such as H. S. Chamberlain and Ludwig Scheman, the founder of the Gobineau Society—also contributed and spread racial nationalism throughout Germany, Haeckel added scientific authority and academic respectability to this movement.[70]

Anti-Semitism had roots other than Haeckel's Social Darwinist and racial theories, however. The anti-Semitic movement had received its greatest impetus during the *Gruenderzeit* and the subsequent economic crash. Its leaders, Konstantin Frantz, Rudolf Meyer, and Paul de Lagarde, were conservative intellectuals, opposed to liberalism and concerned with the Jewish question mainly from an economic and religious aspect. By the middle 1870s, the *Kruezzeitung* and other conservative publications blamed the Jews not only for the depression but also for the *Kulturkampf*. In January 1878, Adolf Stoecker, the Berlin Court preacher, founded the Christian Social Workers' Party and started anti-Semitism as a mass movement. His greatest success was not among the workers (he dropped "Worker" from his party's name in 1881) but among small shopkeepers, artisans, businessmen, and officials. Still, Stoecker's anti-Semitism was based on religious grounds while others, such as Bernhard Foerster, Max Liebermann von Sonnenberg, and Ernst Henrici, began to propagate racism and the elimination of Jews.[71]

Bismarck's attitude toward Jews had undergone a change since his Landtag speech in 1847.[72] When he said in 1871 that he favored "the joining of a gentile stallion with a Jewish mare [because] the money had to get into circulation once more and the resulting race would not be so bad either," he probably meant it.[73] His banker, Bleichroeder, his physician, Cohen, and his lawyer, Philip, were all Jews, and his good relationship with all of them was well known, much to the annoyance of his conservative friends.

While Stoecker's anti-Semitic agitation continued, however,

> the government's refusal to take an unequivocal stand . . . lent further respectability to the agitation and foreshadowed later prevarication and concealed discrimination on the part of the government. In the 1880s the Bismarck regime began a policy of covert discrimination against Jews . . . and Bismarck's own role in setting this policy was far more decisive than has previously been noted.
>
> Bismarck's moral insouciance hid a more complicated opportunism. Anti-Semitism was no part of his creed; he had come to discover the usefulness of Jews to the state and to himself. There was, moreover,

THE NEW REICH

a presumption against extreme demagoguery, partly because of concern over foreign reaction. On the other hand, Bismarck lacked the principles that would automatically shield him from the temptation of political anti-Semitism. He had no basic commitment to what we call civil rights; he had no attachment to any kind of equality; the very idea affronted him. At best he had come to accept the civic equality of Jews.[74]

At the same time that anti-Semitism was increasing, German society took on an exaggeratedly militaristic aspect. The Prussian officers' corps had always been a narrow, self-sufficient organization composed almost entirely of East Elbian Junkers. The expansion of the army after 1871 did not change this pattern appreciably. Admittance of commoners was discouraged and training at the War Academy and service schools was restricted to specialized military subjects; general knowledge, especially politics and economics, was discouraged. In this way the officers' corps was immunized against the evils of the times, but it was also incapable even of understanding the political realities of the period. Thus, the nonpolitical soldier, who believed that war was exclusively a matter for the military and that politics had to be set aside during wartime, came into being. This attitude became apparent before and during the First World War and continued in the *Reichswehr* during the interwar years. The narrow base of the officers' corps and its antidemocratic and reactionary outlook contributed to the widening gap between the army and society, and especially between soldiers and workers.[75] The prestige of the military was enhanced by the father figure of Emperor Wilhelm I and even by Bismarck who, though no militarist, wore the uniform at all official functions.

The adoption by civilians of military slang and barracks behavior became characteristic of German society in the last quarter of the nineteenth century. The highest ambition of the petite bourgeoisie was to attain the rank of lieutenant in the reserve. Contrary to developments in western Europe, universal military service in Germany did not lead to a "civilizing" of the military establishment, but rather to a militarization of civilian life. The widespread view that in Germany the human being started with the officer became more than just a *bon mot*.[76]

7

Bismarck's
Foreign
Policy

Bismarck's fame has always rested on his achievements in diplomacy. His handling of the Schleswig-Holstein question, his struggle for supremacy in Germany, and the treatment of the Hohenzollern candidature were great successes in foreign policy, achieved against considerable odds. And though each of these crucial events in German history caused war, they were limited wars which led, in the end, to the unification of Germany. As a unified major power in the center of the continent, Germany changed the balance of power in Europe. Bismarck had fought three victorious wars in a very short time and the question was whether he would continue a belligerent, expansionist policy or would follow a more peaceful course. Bismarck decided for peace, not only for Germany, but for Europe. He recognized Germany's limitations and realized that localized wars were no longer possible in Europe, since all the major powers would be drawn into any larger war, no matter where it started. As far as Bismarck was concerned, Germany was satiated; what had been accomplished could not be risked for the sake of any conquest, no matter how tempting. His successors, less restrained toward war and convinced that Germany's power was overwhelming, willingly risked her position and reputation; in so doing they brought about her eventual defeat and ruin.[1]

The attitude of the powers toward Germany in the aftermath of the Franco-Prussian War was restrained and suspicious. France, thinking of revenge, looked to Russia and Austria as possible allies in case of future war with Germany. Austria, still smarting from her defeat at Koeniggraetz, was jealous of Germany's newly acquired big power status and kept her reserve toward Germany. Russia, though worried about the revolutionary developments in France, was disturbed by Prussia's vastly increased power and by the emergence of a unified Germany. Britain alone seemed unconcerned.

BISMARCK'S FOREIGN POLICY

In this situation, preserving Germany's newly won position of pre-eminence was difficult. Ideally Bismarck thought Germany should seek no further territorial conquests; instead, all the powers except France should vie with each other in an attempt to gain Germany's friendship. At the same time, the tension among the powers would be great enough so that they would not combine against the Reich.[2] Bismarck's system was an extremely complicated one, requiring a continuous assessment of the relationship among all the possible combinations of powers to see that the ideal balance was maintained. Bismarck's policies after the Congress of Berlin toward Austria, Russia, Britain, France, and Italy were attempts to achieve this ideal condition.

After 1871, Bismarck consistently supported a republican regime in France, for he believed that no monarchical government in Europe would enter into an alliance with a republic out of fear of revolutionary intrigues.[3] He concentrated his initial efforts at alliance on Austria and Russia. An alliance with Russia and Austria accomplished both of Bismarck's goals: it isolated France, and at the same time gave him a majority of three among the five great powers of Europe. Bismarck also used alliances to restrain his alliance partners—he compared alliances to a rider and a horse—and he endeavored at all times to be the rider. This tactic was particularly successful in his alliance with Austria.

Bismarck's success in foreign policy was based on three factors. He had a realistic appreciation of the international scene and the interests and relationships of the powers involved. He kept his ultimate aims in mind and always considered several methods of achieving them. Most importantly, his close relationship with Wilhelm I enabled him to carry out his policies. In addition, a combination of circumstances enabled Bismarck to unfold his diplomatic talents to their fullest extent. The age of the masses and the impact of public opinion on foreign affairs had barely emerged in the latter part of the nineteenth century in Europe; while public opinion was a factor that could not be ignored, it was a relatively minor irritant and could be manipulated, as Bismarck had shown prior to the Danish and French wars. Foreign policy could still be conducted on the cabinet level. Diplomacy had accepted rules, a restricted area (Europe), a fixed number of players (the five great powers), and more or less limited aims. Under these conditions Bismarck performed brilliantly. He was the last of the great diplomats, in the tradition of Richelieu, Kaunitz, and Metternich. At the same time, Bismarck's understanding and manipulation of public opinion in the conduct of foreign affairs rivaled that of Napoleon III, whom Bismarck surpassed in methods as well as achievements.[4]

Following the 1871 peace treaty with France, Bismarck set out to repair relations with Austria. The Austrians, prodded by their Hungarian partners, were willing to come to terms with their powerful neighbor.[5] The Austrian and German emperors and their foreign ministers met at Ischl and Salzburg during August and September 1871 to clear up past misunderstandings and lay the foundation for a future alliance. A year later the two emperors and Alexander II of Russia met in Berlin and in a series of informal conversations agreed to maintain the status quo in Europe. Formal negotiations which resulted in military agreements were concluded between Germany and Russia on the occasion of Wilhelm and Bismarck's visit to St. Petersburg in May 1873; similar negotiations between Austria and Russia took place at Schoenbrunn, outside Vienna, in June of the same year. The outcome of these negotiations was the Three Emperors' League, whose purpose was to demonstrate monarchical solidarity and preserve the status quo. For Bismarck, the League meant support against France and was a means of preventing a possible Austro-Russian conflict over the Balkans.[6]

A crisis in German-French relations, initiated by the fall of Thiers, was soon to test the strength of this newly formed Emperors' League.[7] French economic recovery had been faster and more thorough than had been expected and the French government was able to pay off the five billion franc war indemnity ahead of schedule, which resulted in the complete evacuation of French territory by German troops in September 1873. This, combined with the reorganization and strengthening of the French army, caused the German general staff considerable anxiety. After the defeat of 1870, the French army had reorganized its training and organizational structure, adding a fourth battalion to each regiment early in 1875. At the same time, rumors of extensive French purchases of horses and fodder alarmed the German military command and led Moltke, chief of the general staff, to advocate a preventive war against France.[8]

BISMARCK'S FOREIGN POLICY

Bismarck's concern over these developments in France was heightened by his fear of a Catholic conspiracy, involving France, the papacy, and Belgium. He believed that such a conspiracy might actively support German Catholics in their struggle against him and the *Kulturkampf*. The French, on the other hand, were alarmed by Radowitz's mission to St. Petersburg in February 1875; they believed that Radowitz, then German minister in Athens, had been sent by Bismarck to secure Russian support for a preventive war against France. It seems highly unlikely, however, that Bismarck actually contemplated war. Whatever his motives, whether to frighten the French or to mollify the German general staff, a front-page article under the banner headline, "Is War In Sight?" appeared on April 8 in the Berlin *Post*. It had been written on Bismarck's instructions and was followed by a similar piece in the *Norddeutsche Allgemeine Zeitung*.[9] The two articles created a sensation and a war scare throughout Europe. French apprehensions were increased when, at a dinner on April 21, Radowitz told the French ambassador that it was logical for the Germans to consider a preventive war in such circumstances. At this point Decazes, the French foreign minister, appealed to Britain and Russia for support; at the same time, he placed an anonymous article in the London *Times*,[10] accusing Germany of planning an invasion of France. For once Bismarck was on the defensive. The British and Russian governments asked Bismarck to refrain from warlike measures, the former by a letter from Queen Victoria, the latter through Gorchakov, the foreign minister who was then in Berlin with the czar. Bismarck was intensely annoyed, and protested that it had all been a misunderstanding and a false alarm. The crisis blew over. Its significance, not lost on Bismarck, was that for the first time Britain and Russia were willing to come to the aid of France. It did not mean that the two powers intended to restore France to her pre-1870 status, but neither were they willing to tolerate further German aggression. They were satisfied with the status quo and, for that matter, so was Bismarck.

The weakness of the Three Emperors' League in this crisis forced Bismarck to reexamine Germany's relationship to her two partners. This became even more urgent when, in July 1875, an insurrection against Turkish rule broke out in the Balkans. Any trouble in the Balkans, where Austrian and Russian interests clashed, was potentially threatening to Germany and the peace of Europe. Reconciling Austro-Russian differences became Bismarck's most pressing task, second only to the French problem. Recognizing the potential explosiveness of the situation, Bismarck realized—as some of his successors did not—that Germany's attitude toward the two eastern powers was of crucial importance. Only an evenhanded and disinterested Balkan policy had any chance of success. As far as he was concerned, active German participation in Balkan affairs "was not worth the healthy bones of a single Pomeranian grenadier."[11]

Except for the years of struggle leading to unification, Prussia, and after 1871, Germany, had maintained close and friendly relations with Austria as well as with Russia. Germany had a common bond of language and culture with Austria, and although the struggle for supremacy had left some unhappy memories, the feelings of kinship and understanding between Germany and Austria outweighed any lingering resentments. Germany's relationship with Russia was somewhat more complicated. There were close dynastic ties between the Hohenzollerns and the Romanovs—Nicholas I had married a sister of Wilhelm I—in addition to memories of the united struggle against Napoleon I and their common policy toward Poland. The dynastic influence was apparent at the end of the Franco-Prussian War, when the Russians agreed that Germany should take Alsace-Lorraine. According to Bismarck, this was the result not of official Russian policy, but of the personal policy of Alexander II.[12]

The impressions Bismarck had gathered during his ambassadorship in St. Petersburg in 1859–62 played an important part in his Russian diplomacy. He had noted the decline of pro-German sentiments and the rise of prorevolutionary and prowestern sympathies among the ruling classes, and had seen the beginning of the Pan-Slav movement.[13] Prior to the Russo-Turkish war of 1877, Bismarck encouraged Russia to pursue her own policy, regardless of the approval or disapproval of the other European powers, because in such circumstances the Russians would be more grateful for German assistance, however limited. Bismarck's Russian policy proceeded along two tracks. On the one hand he had the emperor write personal letters to the czar, expressing his and Prussia's eternal gratitude for Russia's benevolent neutrality in

1866 and 1870–71 and indicating his government's readiness to support Russia unconditionally. The emperor, Bismarck, and most Russian diplomats realized that these letters were only expressions of good will to influence and reassure the czar, not firm policy commitments. On the other hand, Bismarck's official policy was designed to keep Russia friendly to Germany and out of the French orbit; Germany needed both Russia and Austria, and could therefore not afford to become involved in the Near East or the Balkans.[14]

Austro-Russian relations, strained since the Crimean War (1854–56), threatened to deteriorate further as Austrian interests in the Balkans increased. Austria's defeat at Koeniggraetz, her losses in Italy, and her subsequent exclusion from Germany made her turn East in an attempt to regain her lost prestige and territories. For the Austrians, this was neither a new role nor an unknown region. The Habsburg Empire had expanded toward the southeast ever since the defeat of the Turks at the gates of Vienna in 1683. There, along the Danube, the Austrian drive toward the Black Sea clashed with Russia's centuries-old push south toward Constantinople and the Straits. The economic-strategic competition between the two powers was further complicated by the religious and nationalistic struggle of the Balkan peoples. The majority of them were southern Slavs under Turkish sovereignty who belonged to the Eastern Orthodox Church. They looked to Russia for national as well as religious protection. Since the end of the Napoleonic wars, nationalistic revolts had loosened the ties between the sultan and some of his non-Turkish subjects and the independence movements during the last quarter of the nineteenth century threatened the very existence of the Ottoman Empire. Due to the rise of Pan-Slavism, the Russian government frequently supported these movements, thereby coming into open conflict with Turkey. The Austrians, though not averse to partitioning the Turkish Empire in Europe, opposed Russian support of nationalistic and revolutionary movements in the Balkans, fearful that these movements, once set in motion, would disrupt the Habsburg Empire. "Once the Balkan Slavs were astir, the Russian government dared not let them fail; Austria-Hungary dared not let them succeed."[15]

Thus, the Austro-Russian struggle for the domination of the Balkans became one of the major problems of European diplomacy. That Bismarck was able to contain it even temporarily was one of his great achievements. It was not an easy task. For the longest time he maintained a policy of strict neutrality but when, in October 1876, the Russians wanted to know what Germany's position would be if the difficulties in the Balkans led to a Russo-Austrian war, Bismarck had to take sides. He expressed the hope that peace would be preserved, but let it be known that if war did occur, Germany would not allow Austria's position to be weakened nor the balance of power to be upset.[16]

The insurrection, which had started in Bosnia and Herzegovina in July 1875, spread to Bulgaria in May of the following year, where it was bloodily suppressed by the Turks. When Serbia, later joined by Montenegro, declared war on Turkey on June 30, 1876, she was decisively defeated by the Turkish army at Alexinatz on September 1, 1876. Now it was Russia's turn. She wanted to aid her Serbian "brothers" and occupy Constantinople and the Straits, but not if this meant fighting the European powers. To avoid this and before going to war with Turkey, Russia had to prevent the resurrection of the Crimean coalition of Britain, France, and Austria. In a loosely worded agreement concluded at Reichstadt on July 8, 1876, and confirmed at Budapest on January 15, 1877, Andrassy and Gorchakov, the foreign ministers of Austria and Russia, agreed on Austrian neutrality in case of a Russo-Turkish war, on Austria's claim to the occupation of Bosnia and Herzegovina, and on Russia's right to regain Bessarabia. Assured of Austria's benevolent neutrality, Russia joined France and Britain at a conference at Constantinople in December 1876 for a settlement of the Balkan problem. It was agreed, with Turkey assenting, that Bulgaria would be divided into an eastern and western part, that Bosnia and Herzegovina would be united into one province, that there would be reforms in the Turkish Empire, and that the powers would supervise these reforms and, if necessary, enforce them. These terms were confirmed when Ignatiev, then Russian ambassador in Constantinople, toured the major European capitals during February and March 1877 and a protocol (with slightly less favorable terms for Russia) was signed in London on March 31, 1877.[17]

Thus, the Russians believed that they had obtained a free hand from the powers to carry out their mandate should the Turkish government fail to live up to its commitments. If Russia could do so quickly and decisively, she had a good chance to impose her will upon Turkey without outside interference. Her opportunity came when the sultan rejected the London Protocol on April 9. On April 24, Russia declared war on Turkey. Despite Russia's military superiority and her initial successes, the Turks were able to halt the Russian advance at Plevna. When the fortress finally fell on December 10, the Russian troops were too exhausted to capture Constantinople and an armistice was arranged on January 31, 1878, with the Russian army camped just outside the city limits. A treaty between the two belligerents was signed at San Stefano on March 3. The provisions of the treaty were quite severe for Turkey. Serbia, Montenegro, and Rumania would become independent, Bulgaria would be autonomous, considerably enlarged by the inclusion of Macedonia and an outlet to the Aegean Sea, and occupied by Russian troops for two years. Russia was to receive Kars, Batum, and Bessarabia, in addition to a large indemnity.[18]

The powers, especially Britain, were alarmed at these sweeping Russian terms. A European congress was called to redress the balance of power in the Balkans and to settle existing differences. Britain, anxious to keep the Russians out of Constantinople and to bolster Turkey, demanded that the size of Bulgaria be reduced. Britain wanted Bulgaria to be divided into a northern part, Bulgaria proper, and a southern part, Eastern Rumelia, with Macedonia excluded from the new Bulgarian state. The Russians, in no condition to resist, signed a secret agreement with Britain along these lines on May 30, 1878. Turkey, after obtaining British guarantees, signed an agreement on June 4, handing Cyprus to Britain in appreciation for her services. An Austro-British agreement on June 6—in which Britain supported Austria's claims to Bosnia and Herzegovina, and Austria supported Britain's settlement of the Bulgarian frontiers—completed the arrangements. The stage was set for the Congress of Berlin.

That the Congress met at Berlin (June 13, 1878) was an indication of Germany's preponderance in Europe and of Bismarck's eminence among her statesmen.[19] The chancellor had been reluctant to assume the presidency of the Congress, which met in a time of domestic crisis (the two assassination attempts on the emperor of May 11 and June 2, and the dissolution of the Reichstag on June 11). Bismarck's role at the Congress was not so much that of "honest broker" as it has been traditionally described and as he himself characterized it (in a speech to the Reichstag of February 19, 1878),[20] but rather that of umpire. His major interests were to safeguard the peace, to support Britain and her agreements with Austria and Russia, and to make the settlement palatable to the Russians. For the Balkan people he showed no concern whatever.[21] The settlement agreed upon at the Congress was based on the military balance of power—Russia's inability to take Constantinople—and on the agreements concluded by Britain, Austria, and Russia. It meant, essentially, a lesser Bulgaria (divided into two parts and without an outlet to the Aegean Sea) and a considerable loss of prestige for Russia. Though they lost no territory, the Russians were furious and blamed Bismarck for their diplomatic "defeat."

The Three Emperors' League was, for all practical purposes, dead. It was not a great loss. Its effectiveness had been marginal at best, and the Russo-Turkish war had exposed the underlying rivalry between the Habsburg and the Romanov empires. Bismarck took this rivalry seriously and considered it a potential threat to the European balance of power. With the Russians sulking, Bismarck turned to Austria.

The alliance with Austria, the Dual Alliance of October 1879, marks a change in Bismarck's foreign policy from a policy of a free hand to one of firm and definite commitments. It was the beginning of a complicated system of alliances by which Bismarck maintained Germany's predominant position and peace in Europe. The reasons for this drastic change are complex and not altogether clear.[22] Initially Bismarck seems to have favored the renewal of the Three Emperors' League, but Russian dissatisfaction with the outcome of the Congress of Berlin, for which Bismarck was blamed, made it unlikely that Gorchakov or the czar would agree to such a step. After the Congress there were numerous incidents which contributed to further Russo-German estrangement. German representatives at the various commissions set up by the Congress generally voted with Austria and often against Russian interests. The Austro-German agreement on the abrogation of Article 5 of the Treaty of Prague (August 1866), requiring a plebiscite in North Schleswig (made public February 4, 1879, signed on February 13, 1878, but postdated to October 11, 1878) was considered by the Russians as Austria's payment to Germany for services rendered at the Congress. Finally, an outbreak of the plague on the lower Volga

BISMARCK'S FOREIGN POLICY

at the end of 1878 produced swift German and Austrian countermea-
sures and inspired articles in the press, which the Russians resented.
This, combined with higher German tariffs on Russian grain which
greatly reduced Russian exports, severely limited her earnings of
foreign exchange, and slowed down her economic expansion, resulted
in bitter and widespread anti-German feeling within the Russian government.[23] On the German side, the expansion of the Russian rail net-
work on Germany's eastern border and an increase of Russian troops
in the same area caused considerable anxiety in Berlin.[24]

At the same time, Bismarck had to deal with the Rumanian question. This involved the recognition of Rumanian independence by the
powers as soon as Rumania emancipated her Jewish citizens, as stipulated by the Congress of Berlin; a settlement of German claims in connection with the construction of Rumanian railroads was also involved.[25] Thus, while Bismarck might have preferred to maintain his
independent position in foreign affairs, the Russian and Rumanian
problems were too complicated to continue a policy of the free hand. To
cope with the Russian difficulties, he began to rely increasingly on
Austria and to look to the British and French for assistance with
Rumanian problems. In this way his foreign policy, which had earlier
concentrated on the isolation of France, became more and more complex.[26]

At times the threat (whether it was real or imagined does not really
matter) of an unfriendly coalition—Austro-Russian, French-Russian,
or even Austro-French-Russian, the old Kaunitz alliance—seems to
have overwhelmed him and spurred him on to more frenzied activities.
This may have been the case just prior to the conclusion of the alliance
with Austria. The announcement of Andrassy's impending resignation
as Austria's foreign minister caused Bismarck to press for the conclusion of an alliance.[27] Andrassy and Bismarck drafted the terms in
Vienna on September 24, and signed the alliance on October 7, 1879.[28]

From a domestic point of view, an alliance with Austria would be
popular with large segments of the German population, especially
among liberals and Catholics; East Elbian agricultural interests, which
favored protective tariffs, would be glad to see the elimination of
duty-free imports of Russian grain. Only Emperor Wilhelm strongly
opposed his chancellor's proposals. For Wilhelm, brought up in the old

Hohenzollern tradition of friendship with Russia, a break in this age-old pattern was utterly inconceivable. Bismarck had to use his most persuasive arguments, fabricate some unlikely threats and, finally, submit his and the Prussian cabinet's resignation, before Wilhelm relented.[29]

The Dual Alliance which formed the cornerstone of Bismarck's alliance system lasted until November 1918. As long as he was in power, his restraining influence—and prevailing international conditions—kept the peace, and the Austrian alliance was a major factor in this achievement. Bismarck did not intend the Dual Alliance to be anti-Russian. On the contrary, he expected that Russia would come around and, possibly to frighten her into making up her mind, he approached Britain, inquiring about her attitude in case of a Russo-German war.[30] The British reply was noncommittal, promising only that Britain would keep France quiet.

In January 1880 Saburov, now Russian ambassador in Berlin, suggested reviving the Three Emperors' League; Bismarck showed considerable interest, but the Austrians refused. They would have preferred an alliance with Britain, with Austria dominating the Balkans, Britain Asia Minor, Germany supporting both, and Russia left out altogether. But Gladstone's victory in the general election of April 1880 changed British foreign policy and put an end to Austria's plans for an alliance. By September the Austrians were ready to join the League, and after extensive negotiations the Three Emperors' Alliance, as it became known, was signed on June 18, 1881. "The basis of agreement was the Austrian belief that Germany would automatically support her and the Russian belief that she would not."[31]

The alliance had little in common with its predecessor, the Three Emperors' League of 1873. Instead of vague generalities regarding conservative principles of solidarity, it contained specific clauses, the most important of which stipulated neutrality of the partners should one of them go to war with a fourth power. This meant Russian neutrality in case of a Franco-German war, and German neutrality in case of a Russo-British war. As to the Balkans, the Russians recognized Austria's right to annex Bosnia and Herzegovina, while Austria and Germany agreed not to object to the union of Bulgaria with Eastern Rumelia. The main beneficiary of the Alliance was Russia, which achieved a certain security against British encroachment toward the Straits; it also brought Russia out of the isolation she had suffered since the Congress of Berlin. For Bismarck, the Alliance meant that he did not have to choose between his two incompatible allies.[32]

But Bismarck's pleasure with the Russians was short lived. The rise of Pan-Slavism, together with attempts in St. Petersburg to revive interest in a Franco-Russian alliance, culminated in the Skobelev affair, which alarmed Bismarck and led him to seek additional safeguards against Russia and France.[33] By including Italy in the Austro-German alliance, Bismarck believed that he had found his safeguard. Emerging empty-handed from the Congress of Berlin, Italy felt isolated and deceived. Having lost Tunis to France (the Treaty of Bardo of May 12, 1881, established a French protectorate over this territory), and faced with a renewed conflict with the papacy, Italy was looking for security and assistance. Thus, despite Austrian reluctance—mainly because of Italian irredentist activities in South Tyrol and Istria—Bismarck was able to conclude the negotiations which led to the Triple Alliance, signed on May 20, 1882. Germany and Austria promised the Italians their assistance in case of war with France, and Italy was to reciprocate in case of a Franco-German war. Italy was to be neutral in an Austro-Russian war, but would come to the aid of her allies if they had to fight a Russo-French combination. For the rest, the partners assured each other of the maintenance of the status quo in their respective countries. This clause was designed to reassure Italy that no power would interfere in her internal affairs as France had done. The alliance looked good on paper, but its actual worth was debatable. Italy probably gained the most, having obtained assistance against France and great power status through her association with Germany and Austria.

Two more alliances were concluded in this period to round out the Bismarckian system, the Austrian alliance with Serbia of June 28, 1881, which consolidated Austria's hold of the region and made Serbia a satellite of the Habsburg monarchy, and the Rumanian alliance of October 30, 1883, with Austria. The Rumanian alliance resulted from Austrian and Rumanian concern over alleged Russian designs on Rumania and was meant to be a pact of mutual assistance against Russia. Germany later joined the Austro-Rumanian alliance.[34]

The Three Emperors' Alliance was renewed in 1884, but before another year had passed, trouble in the Balkans tested it once again. Austria and Russia had been peacefully extending their economic interests in the Balkans by building railroads.[35] The Austrians were pushing a line through Serbia, Montenegro, and the Sandjak of Novi Pazar which would connect Vienna with Salonika. The Russians, going through Rumania and Bulgaria, hoped to build a line to Constantinople. But Russia's economic situation was such that she could not compete with the other powers even in Bulgaria where she enjoyed a predominant position. To overcome this disadvantage, Russia invested in large railroad concessions which were guaranteed by the Bulgarian government. This enabled her to put pressure on Bulgarian officials to obtain preferential treatment.[36] At the same time, it contributed to Russian unpopularity, and when a revolt broke out in Eastern Rumelia against Turkish rule in September 1885, Alexander of Battenberg (who had been installed by the Russians as prince of Bulgaria following the Congress of Berlin) followed a Bulgarian national policy and was openly anti-Russian. The revolutionaries demanded the union of Eastern Rumelia and Bulgaria, the greater Bulgaria which Russia had demanded in the Treaty of San Stefano and which the powers had opposed at the Congress of Berlin. In a complete reversal of roles, Russia, angry at Alexander for pursuing an anti-Russian policy, refused to support the union, while the British favored it.

Inevitably, Germany and Austria were drawn into this conflict, the more so since Serbia, unwilling to see Bulgarian power increased, declared war on Bulgaria on November 13, 1885. The Serbs were decisively defeated by the Bulgarians, and only Austrian intervention saved them from complete annihilation. A compromise among the powers was finally worked out and Alexander of Battenberg was made governor of Eastern Rumelia, which established, in effect, a greater Bulgaria. The Russians rejected this settlement and Alexander, after being kidnapped and held for a week by Russian officers, resigned on September 7. The struggle over a successor led to increased Austro-Russian tension because neither country was prepared to accept the other's candidate for the Bulgarian throne. Bismarck tried in vain to persuade the two powers to divide the Balkans into two spheres of influence, Russia taking the eastern half with Bulgaria, and Austria the western half with Serbia. When the Austrians asked for German assistance, Bismarck reminded them of the defensive nature of the Dual Alliance and of Germany's disinterested policy in the Balkans. Instead, he suggested that Austria approach Great Britain. The British wanted to keep the Russians away from Constantinople and the Straits, but they were afraid to escalate their already serious conflict with Russia any further.[37] When the Austrians suggested cooperation, Great Britain refused. A solution to the dilemma was found by shifting the focus from the Balkans to the Mediterranean and by including Italy in the arrangements. (The inclusion of Italy bolstered Britain's position against France in Egypt, while Italy gained support in her tariff war with France and her territorial aspirations in North Africa.) In an exchange of notes—to bypass Parliament—Britain and Italy agreed on February 12, 1887, to maintain the status quo in the Mediterranean, the Adriatic, the Aegean, and the Black Sea. Austria joined the agreement on March 24, and Spain on May 4. This First Mediterranean Agreement, as it became known, was strongly supported by Bismarck, particularly because it strengthened Austria against Russia without directly involving Germany.

Bismarck's concern over Russia continued, not only because of Austro-Russian tension in the Balkans but also because of renewed nationalistic agitation in France. There, Paul Deroulède and his League of Patriots preached revenge against Germany and alliance with Russia. General Boulanger, minister of war (and the prototype of the "man on horseback"), became the symbol and the rallying point of this movement. The pro-Russian and anti-German agitation in France was paralleled in Russia by Katkov's Pan-Slav activities and by increasing demands for an alliance with France.

Giers, Gorchakov's successor in the Russian foreign ministry, wanted to renew the Three Emperors' Alliance but the czar, many of his advisors, and public opinion were anti-Austrian and strongly opposed to such a course.[38] At the same time Bismarck pressured the Russian government to conclude a separate German-Russian agreement, and the Russians finally agreed. This secret treaty (known as the Reinsurance Treaty), in which the two powers agreed to stay neutral should one go to war with a third power, was signed on June 18, 1887. The agreement was not to apply in case of aggressive war by

Germany against France or by Russia against Austria. A special clause recognized Russia's preponderent influence in Bulgaria and Germany's moral and diplomatic support of Russia in her quest for an outlet to the high seas through the Straits.

Bismarck's motive in supporting this rather risky undertaking was his desire to keep Russia away from France and to tie her to Germany as closely as possible. When the terms of the Reinsurance Treaty became known after Bismarck's dismissal, it was called "a protective immunization for the Czar against a French infection," "political bigamy," "the finest example of diplomatic duplicity," and much more.[39] These epithets usually referred to the treaty's apparent incompatibility with Germany's alliance with Austria. Actually, the Reinsurance Treaty conflicted more with the Second Mediterranean Agreement (December 1887) than with the Dual Alliance. The agreement, also known as the Near Eastern Entente, between Britain, Austria, and Italy, reaffirmed the status quo in the Near East and the independence of Turkey. Bismarck, who had been instrumental in its formation, refused to join it, preferring to let Britain and Austria emerge as the defenders of Turkish independence. Thus, while he pledged his support for Russia's drive toward the Straits in the Reinsurance Treaty, he knew that Britain, Austria, and Italy were bound by the Second Mediterranean Agreement to halt such a drive.[40]

The benefits as well as the effects of the Reinsurance Treaty have been exaggerated. The relationship between Russia and Germany actually deteriorated during this period, mainly because of Bismarck's directive of November 10, 1887, which forbade the placing of Russian loans and the acceptance of Russian securities (*Lombardverbot*) in Germany.[41] The effects of this move were immediate and far-reaching. Having been denied access to the German capital market, the Russians turned to France, whose bankers and politicians were only too happy to accommodate them. A year later, in November 1888, France granted Russia a 500 million franc loan and agreed to supply the Russian army with 500,000 rifles.[42] Other economic and financial agreements followed, and in August 1891 France and Russia concluded a political agreement, followed by a draft for a military convention in 1892. There were, of course, other reasons for the conclusion of the Franco-Russian alliance[43] but whether it would have come so soon and

developed so rapidly without Bismarck's interference seems highly unlikely. Thus, the question of Bismarck's motivation and his awareness
of the consequences of his actions is of considerable importance.

There were several reasons for Bismarck's action. By the fall of 1887
many army leaders, Moltke and Waldersee among them, were convinced that a conflict with Russia was inevitable; they urged preventive war.[44] They were especially disturbed by the extensive Russian
construction on Germany's eastern border and charged that German
loans to Russia had financed these undertakings. Some German industrialists supported the military leaders by pointing out that these
funds could be better invested at home, where they would lower the
interest rates and help German industry to overcome the Russian tariff
barrier. Because of high Russian tariffs against German industrial
goods, German exports to Russia had declined while Russian imports
to Germany had increased; so had British imports to Russia, while
Russian industrial production had expanded to satisfy the greater demands of her home markets.[45] In Germany, large landowners and
wealthy agrarians also complained about the scarcity of capital and the
exorbitant interest rates. They objected to sending money to Russia to
build railroads which facilitated Russian grain exports.

Though strongly opposed to preventive war himself, Bismarck's de-
nial of funds to Russia appeased those who advocated it, and this move
also strengthened the agrarian and industrial interests whose political
support he needed. At the same time, there was a general feeling that
Russia was about to disintegrate and that in such a case, or in case of
war, German loans would be lost. Government officials were dissatisfied with German policy and believed that Russia had for too long accepted German economic and political favors without giving much in
return. If her loans were stopped, Russia would realize that she was
dependent on Germany and, according to Herbert Bismarck, the chancellor's son, would see that without German help she could do very little in the field of European power politics.[46]

So much for Bismarck's motives; but what about his ability to
foresee the consequences of his action? In general he was quite capable
of evaluating economic factors correctly, though he apparently believed that politics and economics could be neatly separated. In Germany's relationships with Austria and Russia he always stressed polit-

ical considerations, monarchical solidarity, and common interests to the exclusion of economic factors. In the case of denying loans to Russia he may have underestimated the economic consequences, misjudged the readiness of French financial institutions to accept Russian securities, and overlooked the political consequences of Franco-Russian financial cooperation. Nor was this a momentary misconception. Bismarck continued to refuse the acceptance of Russian loans and securities in Germany and would not allow German banks to subscribe to the Russian loan of 1888.[47]

For Russia the cutting off of German funds in addition to the curtailment of Russian grain imports (German agrarian tariffs reached their highest point in 1887) created severe economic hardship. German investment capital and the earnings from the sale of grain were the major sources for Russian industrial expansion, which was at a crucial stage at the end of the 1880s. To maintain the pace of its industrialization Russia had to look for an alternate source of capital; this could only come from France. Ironically, shifting to France strengthened Russian finances and thus, Bismarck's ill-conceived move hastened, rather than retarded, the possibility of a future Russo-German conflict and with it the specter of a two-front war.[48]

Bismarck's colonial policy, initiated in the 1880s, was as complicated as his Russian policy. Why Bismarck decided to acquire colonies, and whether he was an imperialist or not, is an interesting question. Bismarck's foreign policy had been peaceful from 1870 on; he had carefully avoided unnecessary friction and potential conflicts. He told the explorer Eugen Wolff, "Your map of Africa is very pretty; but mine is here in Europe. Here is Russia, and here is France, and we are in the middle; that is my map of Africa."[49] He also maintained that, "so long as I am Chancellor, we shan't pursue a colonial policy."[50] He considered colonies a temporary European folly and wanted no part of them. He admired Britain's informal mid-Victorian empire and was horrified by the prospects of installing an extensive administration, bureaucracy, and military garrison overseas.[51] To Bismarck, colonial possessions were "a source of weakness rather than strength," as he wrote to Wilhelm I in 1873.[52] If business and other interests were clamoring for overseas possessions, let them go ahead on their own and administer and exploit them through private syndicates and chartered companies. Government support would have involved the Reichstag, because "colonial administration would be an extension of Parliament's parade ground," and giving the Reichstag more power was the last thing Bismarck wanted.[53] At the same time, he believed that there was not enough popular support for an active colonial policy. He seems to have been right about this, for the majority of the Reichstag refused to extend government guarantees to an old established German trading company in Samoa that had run into financial difficulties in 1880.[54]

But public opinion was slowly changing, and in December 1882 Prince Hohenlohe-Langenburg and Johannes Miquel founded the German Colonial Society in Frankfurt. German economic and financial interests, like those of other countries, began to look toward overseas trade and investments as a new and possibly profitable activity. This colonial interest coincided with a period of economic fluctuation when, after a short recovery from the great depression of 1873–79, another recession in 1882 rekindled earlier fears and brought renewed demands for economic and political changes. There was widespread fear of social unrest and talk of a "red peril"; though this may have been exaggerated, it was not completely unfounded.

After the 1873–79 depression, Bismarck had abandoned free trade and had adopted a moderate protective tariff policy in 1879. But the changes in economic policy that higher tariffs entailed neither satisfied the business community nor alleviated the consequences of the recession of the early 1880s. At the same time, as the pressure for colonies increased, Bismarck responded to it.[55] He did so for several reasons. He hoped that by winning foreign markets, economic prosperity and stability would be achieved at home and social tradition would remain undisturbed.

The acquisition of foreign markets, however, required a national commitment, because individual German traders could no longer compete with nationally subsidized British and French colonial enterprises. There were ample German precedents for state-subsidized undertakings, such as steamship lines, railroad companies, and financial institutions. As Bismarck told the French ambassador in the fall of 1884, "The aim of German policy was the expansion of unrestricted trade and not the territorial expansion of German colonial

possessions."[56] There were also other considerations. Colonial acquisitions could be used to divert public opinion from the divisive domestic
struggle against the Catholics and Socialists. From 1884 on, Bismarck
used the colonial issue to stir up national sentiment; the press attacks
against Britain in connection with the establishment of a German settlement in Angra Pequena in Southwest Africa are an example of this
tactic. Colonies also provided a much-needed rallying point—an
ideological substitute as it were—on which the dissident elements at
home could agree. Bismarck also used the colonial issue for electoral
and parliamentary maneuvers, and to enhance his own position and
prestige. This was successful in the election of 1884, when the conservatives won a decisive victory and the progressives were badly beat-
en.[57] But Bismarck never used colonial policy as a basis for Germany's
claim to status as a world power, nor did he believe in the superiority
of the German race or in her "mission" in the world. And though
others, extreme nationalists and Pan-Germans, did later believe in a
German "mission," Bismarck's aims were far more restricted. He
wanted to alleviate economic hardships and preserve the social and
political status quo. By 1889 he was "sick and tired of colonies," but
by then it was too late to change course.[58]

Germany's major colonial activity was concentrated within a short
two-year period from 1883 to 1885 and was led by merchants and
explorers. In 1883 the Bremen merchant Adolf Luederitz acquired
Angra Pequena, which later became German Southwest Africa. The
explorer Gustav Nachtigal became German *Reichskommissar* for
Cameroon and Togo, on the west coast of Africa, in July 1884, after
several Hamburg merchants had established trading posts on the Gulf
of Guinea in 1882. The explorer Carl Peters (who had founded the Society for German Colonization in 1884) concluded several treaties with
native chiefs on the east coast of Africa in 1884 and obtained an imperial charter in February 1885 for the territory which became German
East Africa in the following year. This led to friction with neighboring
British colonial interests, which was settled by the Anglo-German colonial agreement of July 1, 1890. Under the terms of this treaty, Germany obtained Helgoland from Britain in exchange for territory in
East Africa. In the Pacific, the New Guinea Company, under the leadership of the Berlin banker Adolf von Hansemann, obtained a protec-

torate over territories on the north coast of New Guinea and adjacent islands which became, in 1885, the colony of Emperor Wilhelm Land and the Bismarck Archipelago.

The German colonial empire came into being during a period of intense imperial rivalries among the European powers, such as the Anglo-Russian competition in Asia and the Anglo-French struggle in Egypt and the Sudan. Bismarck used these rivalries in a way that avoided major confrontations and shifted his support first to one, then to another power, always keeping in mind that colonial issues were second to Germany's prime interests, which were in Europe.[59]

Bismarck's Dismissal

The colonial enthusiasm of the early 1880s gave way to disillusionment at the end of the decade. The exaggerated hopes and promises had not been fulfilled; disappointment in colonial affairs was thus added to the discontent caused by the *Kulturkampf* and the anti-Socialist campaign. On March 9, 1888, Emperor Wilhelm I died and his son, Friedrich III, who succeeded him, died three months later (June 15) of cancer of the throat. Wilhelm II became emperor at age twenty-nine; he was unlike his father or grandfather in behavior or outlook. Wilhelm II was of medium height, fair complexion, and restless temperament. He was sensitive all his life about his withered left arm, which had been crippled at birth. His main interest was the army, but instead of concentrating on military affairs, he occupied himself with the trappings and trivia of military life and wore a uniform at all times. (He is said to have appeared in the full dress uniform of an admiral at a performance of *The Flying Dutchman*.) He admired and tried to emulate his grandfather, Wilhelm I, but he was closer to his granduncle, Friedrich Wilhelm IV, in his indecision, bombastic and deceptive oratory, and narrow view of royal prerogatives.[1]

Apart from these characteristics, the difference in age between the new emperor and the chancellor, now seventy-three, would have made it difficult even under the most favorable conditions to continue the close cooperation that had existed between Bismarck and Wilhelm I. For Bismarck such cooperation was crucial because his office and power were based exclusively on the confidence of the emperor. Inasmuch as the Reichstag in Germany (and the Parliament in Prussia) lacked the power to choose a government, the Reich chancellor and Prussian prime minister were appointed by the German emperor and king of Prussia (combined in the person of Wilhelm II) and served at his pleasure. It is well to remember that it was Bismarck himself who, during his entire term in office, vigorously opposed all attempts to

BISMARCK'S DISMISSAL

strengthen parliamentary powers and to bring about a constitutional monarchy in Germany. And though public opinion and the Reichstag delegates played an increasingly important role in governmental affairs, the right of appointing and dismissing ministers was still exclusively the crown's.

Wilhelm II had already indicated, at an early date, his intention either to curtail the chancellor's duties or to dismiss him altogether. He had told Adolf von Scholz, the finance minister, in December 1887 that "Prince Bismarck was, of course, very much needed for a few more years, but then his functions would be distributed and some of them taken over by the Emperor." And according to Court Chaplain Stoecker, the emperor had said, "we'll give the old man a six months' breather, then I shall govern myself."[2]

But there were other, more substantive issues that precipitated a major crisis between the two men. An increasingly difficult domestic situation seemed to indicate the failure of Bismarck's mixed system of government by the end of the 1880s. The combined pressure of liberals and Socialists for political recognition and for a more responsible parliamentary government could no longer be resisted; the manipulation of parliamentary majorities, threats of foreign wars, and colonial adventures were no longer producing the desired results. Two issues needed almost immediate attention: the extension of the anti-Socialist laws and the adoption of a new army budget. It was generally assumed that neither one would get Reichstag approval.[3]

Aware of the emperor's desire to dismiss him and determined to stay in office, Bismarck decided that he could survive only in a political situation so utterly chaotic that he would be asked to remain as his country's savior. Since no such situation was likely to occur in time to save him, he set about creating one. To begin with, he worked behind the scenes against the government's coalition parties. The *Kartell*, as the coalition was called, was composed of the National Liberals, Free Conservatives, and the moderate, or national, wing of the Conservative party. Through Bismarck's secret machinations, these parties suffered heavy losses in the election of February 1890, while the opposition parties, the Social Democrats and the Center, and the ultra Conservatives made considerable gains. (Heretofore Bismarck's dismissal has been linked to the outcome of this election, with the implication that the political parties, and with them the Reichstag, had played an important role in this crisis. It was not known that Bismarck was actually behind these activities, nor that the Reichstag or the parties had nothing to do with these developments.)[4] The outcome of the election was a great disappointment to the emperor, who had supported the *Kartell*, and especially to the National Liberals, whom Bismarck had disagreed with as early as 1889. The program of the National Liberals called for colonial expansion, an anti-Russian stance, more social welfare legislation, and tax reforms, all measures which Bismarck opposed. Had Bismarck supported the *Kartell* parties, he would have been following the emperor's lead, thereby surrendering his unique position as political leader of the Reich. Backing the Center and the extreme Conservatives meant defeat of the government's coalition, which would deprive Wilhelm II of much of his political support.

The liberal and moderate conservative elements saw the Center party's victory as a major threat to the established order, and feared that, as a result, Catholic Bavaria would henceforth replace Protestant Prussia as the leading power in Germany. At the same time they expected a disruption of the Triple Alliance, because a German government based on the Center party would lend its support to the establishment of temporal powers of the pope and thus alienate Italy. (The same threat and fear of a Catholic conspiracy at home and abroad that Bismarck himself had so successfully propagated during the *Kulturkampf* was now used by the emperor's supporters against him.) The gains of the Social Democrats, on the other hand, meant to the conservatives that the revolution was just around the corner. In this very confusing situation it was reasonable for Bismarck to assume that his position would be strengthened and that no thought would be given to his dismissal; for who else in Germany would be able to master these chaotic political conditions and still preserve the established order?

But apparently Bismarck's plans went still further. He appears to have considered the possibility of serious and continuing trouble inside Germany and to have prepared for it in two ways: constitutionally and militarily. The chancellor explained at a ministerial council on March 2, 1890, that the federation on which the Reich was based had been formed by an agreement between the federal princes and not by the individual states, and therefore it would be possible for the princes to

BISMARCK'S DISMISSAL

withdraw from this agreement and get rid of the Reichstag if elections continued to turn out badly for the government.[5] The military aspects were dealt with in a directive drafted on March 12, 1890, by General Verdy, the minister of war. It pertained to supervision of the activities of the Social Democratic party and was submitted to Bismarck for his approval. The directive advised the commanders of the major military districts to watch the Social Democratic clubs in their areas and to be ready to proclaim a state of emergency or war as soon as necessary. In such an event, the constitution and civil rights were to be suspended, ringleaders arrested, newspapers suppressed, and war tribunals established. Preparations for such an emergency were to be made covertly, and included gathering sufficient troops to crush a revolt at its very beginning and providing prison facilities to detain suspects.[6] The most efficient use of firearms during such an emergency was also considered. Bismarck approved these measures and it can be inferred that he and the minister of war looked upon these precautions as rational responses to an immediate threat to the safety of the country.

There can be little doubt that Bismarck would have implemented these plans had circumstances warranted. It can also be assumed that he was willing and able to manipulate events to suit his policies. Thus Bismarck's readiness to stage a coup d'état to secure his position and prolong his tenure should be recognized as a major factor in the dismissal crisis.[7]

These maneuvers make it clear that party politics were much more involved in the crisis than has hitherto been assumed. Bismarck's dismissal should not be seen as a popular vote of no confidence, nor as indication of the Reichstag's power, but rather as a matter of power politics. The *Kartell*, an alliance of eastern landowners and western industrialists, felt threatened by what it perceived as erratic domestic and misguided foreign policies; by exerting sufficient pressure and supporting the young emperor, the *Kartell* was able to oust the chancellor.

There was, in addition, the personal conflict between Wilhelm II and Bismarck. Wilhelm wished to be his own master and a popular monarch. He wanted to appear progressive and, having successfully intervened in a miner's strike in 1889, he intended to introduce comprehensive labor legislation to forestall social upheavals. To this Bismarck was strongly opposed. He was still fighting the Social Democrats, and rather than settle the conflict, he intended to intensify it. By March 1890, with the election results indicating a clear victory for the chancellor and an equally clear defeat for the emperor, an open break was only a matter of time. On March 15, Wilhelm had Bismarck dragged out of bed at nine o'clock in the morning, accused him of negotiating behind his back with Windthorst, the Center party's leader, and ordered him to repeal the Prussian Cabinet order of September 8, 1852. This order, which Bismarck had recently called to the attention of his ministerial colleagues because of their intrigues against him, required that the Prussian prime minister be informed before cabinet ministers made important presentations to the king. Bismarck defended himself against these trumped-up charges, as well as against accusations of having withheld reports on changes in Russian policy,[8] but to no avail—Wilhelm wanted his resignation. Bismarck was trapped. His letter of resignation of March 18, 1890, a memorable document which blames the crisis and his retirement squarely on the emperor, was accepted on March 20. Wilhelm suppressed its publication and instead published his own reply, which indicated that the chancellor had insisted on retiring because of ill health, much against the emperor's wishes.[9]

Bismarck's dismissal marked the end of an era. There was, however, no immediate popular reaction, and public opinion seemed indifferent. The bureaucracy was content to be rid of an autocratic chief and the army remained loyal to the emperor. At seventy-five, after twenty-eight years of faithful service, Bismarck was effectively isolated. His dismissal, like his appointment, was brought about by the personal wish of the monarch; perhaps here more than anywhere else, the tragedy and failure of Bismarck's accomplishments can be seen. Despite his considerable political and diplomatic skill, he had no base of support in the country or among the people. At a time when popular support for domestic and foreign policy was becoming increasingly important, as he himself recognized, Bismarck deliberately shunned becoming involved in party politics. He considered himself throughout his term of office a loyal subject of his master and a faithful servant to his king. This feeling is reflected in the epitaph which he chose to have inscribed on his tombstone: "A faithful German servant of Emperor Wilhelm I."

Bismarck took his retirement with bad grace. He considered his health good enough to carry on for some time, and he expected to be recalled at any moment. He began to loathe the emperor and freely predicted disastrous consequences for his policies. In support of his own views, Bismarck wrote and inspired articles in the *Hamburger Nachrichten* and, with the help of Lothar Bucher, prepared his memoirs. Originally planned for six volumes, only two appeared after Bismarck's death. A third, dealing with his dismissal, was released after the fall of the monarchy in 1919.[10]

Soon after Bismarck's dismissal popular opinion rallied around the former chancellor and a constant stream of visitors came to see him at Varzin and Friedrichsruh. Delegations of students, fraternities, and corporations bestowed honorary memberships, politicians sought advice, and journalists and historians asked for interviews. For a while Bismarck tried to exploit these occasions to express his opposition to the emperor, and in one famous speech at Jena he recalled Goethe's *Goetz von Berlichingen.*[11] All of these gestures did not succeed. The emperor was anxious for a reconciliation, and when Bismarck became ill in January 1894, Wilhelm took the occasion to send him a bottle of wine with his adjutant. A return visit by Bismarck to the emperor in Berlin publicly reconciled the two. On November 27, 1894, Bismarck's wife died, and from then on Bismarck's health, none too good for most of his life, declined steadily; on July 30, 1898, he died.

Bismarck
Reassessed

The nineteenth century was for Germany more than for any other country a period of change. At its beginning—at the Congress of Vienna—a German state did not even exist; instead, there was a conglomeration of medium and small states, monarchies, dukedoms, ecclesiastical states, and free cities, most of them impoverished and rural, with few large towns, connected by a few major rivers and some ill-kept roads. By the end of the century, on the eve of the First World War, Germany was the foremost industrial country on the continent, unified, strong, largely urban, bursting at its seams with energy and expanding its trade and commerce to the four corners of the globe.

These social, economic, and political changes, from a rural to an urban society, from an agricultural to an industrial economy, and from particularism to unification in a period of less than fifty years may explain the problems as well as the challenges which Bismarck faced during his term of office. Combining in his ancestry the two dominant strands of German society—the bureaucratic bourgeoisie and the military nobility—Bismarck's fighting nature and strong will led him to the premiership of Prussia in a time of grave constitutional crisis. By sheer force of personality, cold calculation, and favorable circumstances, he was able to unify Germany under Prussian leadership with considerable popular support. Propelled from the provincial German to the cosmopolitan European stage, and performing simultaneously on both, Bismarck managed for two decades to guide his country through increasingly difficult situations.

At home, he maintained the power of the old order—monarchy, aristocracy, army—in the face of major economic and social changes. His two major struggles against the Catholic church and the Social Democratic party ended in failure and left the country deeply divided. In foreign affairs he preserved Germany's preeminent position and the peace of Europe until his dismissal. To do so he created a system so complicated and contradictory that it began to disintegrate even before he left office. His less able successors, unwilling to follow his tortuous path and dealing with vastly different circumstances, were unable to reconcile the opposing factions within Germany or to agree on a sensible policy abroad.

Bismarck, like most men, had some noticeable blind spots. His creative imagination and energy and his rare political insight were marred by an apparent inability to assess correctly such powerful contemporary trends as socialism and industrialization. He believed throughout his career that he could control and direct these forces and maintain the established order with only minor changes. On a more personal level (and affecting domestic policy more than foreign affairs), his willingness to use moral and immoral means, truth or falsehood, and his intense suspicion and lack of respect for people made it difficult for him to attract and work with bright and independent men.

The great hopes of 1870–71, that the Reich would become a stable and integrated modern state, were not fulfilled. Bismarck failed to adjust to the new and changing order and was unwilling (or perhaps unable) to provide even for an orderly and lasting succession.

How different is the picture of Bismark that emerges from the recent reappraisals and reexaminations? His stature, still impressively large, is marred by serious flaws and shortcomings. His work can no longer be looked upon as the perfect creation it once was believed to be. Instead, it should be regarded as one man's attempt to solve the monumental problem of creating a German state in the latter part of the nineteenth century, an attempt which, in the end, was conceived too narrowly and maintained too rigidly for too long. He was also responsible for setting Germany on her future course, though his successors had ample time to change or modify that course and chose not to do so. That the state Bismarck created lasted less than a century is ample testimony to its basic flaws.

Notes

*Bibliographical
Essay*

Index

Notes

PREFACE

1. The best comprehensive survey of historians' views on Bismarck from the 1920s to the 1950s is by Otto Pflanze, *Bismarck and the Development of Germany*, vol. 1, *The Period of Unification, 1815–1871* (Princeton, 1963), pp. 3–8. I have indicated some of the more significant changes of the recent historical literature in notes.
2. To those familiar with American history and the writings of Charles A. Beard, it will seem strange that economic, social, and constitutional aspects in German historical writings were neglected for so long. A survey of the most popular pre-1940 books on Bismarck and the German unification will show, however, that the overwhelming majority dealt with political history to the neglect of all other.
3. M. Stuermer, ed., *Bismarck und die Preussisch-Deutsche Politik, 1871–1890,* (Munich, 1970), p. 25.
4. For a review of new writings on recent German history see Geoffrey Barraclough, "Mandarins and Nazis: Part I," *The New York Review of Books*, Oct. 19, 1972, pp. 37–43; "The Liberals and German History: Part II," ibid., Nov. 2, 1972, pp. 32–38; "A New View of German History: Part III," ibid., Nov. 16, 1972, pp. 25–31.

1. BISMARCK'S YOUTH

1. E. R. Huber, *Deutsche Verfassungsgeschichte seit 1789* (Stuttgart, 1957), 1:583–84.
2. There was, strictly speaking, no "Germany" before 1871, and the correct reference should either be "in the Germanies" or "in central Europe." Both are awkward and I have used "Germany" whenever it seems more convenient.
3. W. L. Langer, *Political and Social Upheaval, 1832–1852* (New York, 1969), pp. 12–14.
4. "In return for abolition of feudal dues the peasants paid with one-third to one-half of their land, while in the enclosure of the common lands they received only 14 percent, mostly wasteland. Large numbers of small holdings were completely liquidated and absorbed in the larger estates." (Langer, *Political and Social Upheaval, 1832–1852*, p. 12.) See also the excellent article by Jerome Blum, "The Conditions of the European Peasantry on the Eve of Emancipation," *Journal of Modern History* 46, no. 3 (Sept. 1974):395–424, especially 418–20.
5. "In the provinces East of the Elbe, agrarian reforms worked almost invariably to the advantage of the large landowners. The peasantry as a whole was weak-

ened." (H. J. Puhle, *Agrarische Interessenpolitik und Preussischer Konservatismus* [Hannover 1966], p. 18.)

6. Erich Marcks, *Bismarcks Jugend, 1815–1848* (Stuttgart, 1915), pp. 12–18.
7. Ibid., pp. 22–23.
8. Some recent Bismarck studies using a psychoanalytic approach have tried to trace the parental influence on Bismarck's later development and to explain his intense drive for power by pointing to his failure to integrate the two different traditions which his parents represented. Otto Pflanze, "Toward a Psychoanalytic Interpretation of Bismarck," *American Historical Review* 77, no. 2 (Apr. 1972):419–44, and Charlotte Sempell, *Otto von Bismarck* (New York, 1972).
9. Marcks, *Bismarcks Jugend*, pp. 54–64.
10. For a fictionalized description of Bismarck's life in Goettingen see Motley's *Morton's Hope* (New York, 1839), where Otto von Rabenmark is unmistakably Bismarck. Marcks, *Bismarcks Jugend*, pp. 94–95.
11. Marcks, *Bismarcks Jugend*, pp. 131–33.
12. Bismarck's parents had left Schoenhausen a year after Otto was born and moved to their recently acquired estate, Kniephof, near Naugard in Pomerania. Marcks, *Bismarcks Jugend*, p. 41.
13. "Ich will aber Musik machen, wie ich sie fuer gut erkenne, oder gar keine." Marcks, *Bismarcks Jugend*, p. 167.
14. C. Sempell, "Unbekannte Briefstellen Bismarcks," *Historische Zeitschrift* 207, no. 3 (Dec. 1968):610–11.
15. At the beginning of 1847, Kniephof was still indebted by 45,000 thaler and Schoenhausen by 60,000. Sempell, "Unbekannte Briefstellen Bismarcks," p. 613.
16. A plot of April 3, 1833, to seize Frankfurt, dissolve the Diet and unify Germany along liberal lines. G. A. Rein, *Die Revolution in der Politik Bismarcks* (Goettingen, 1957), p. 53.
17. Marcks, *Bismarcks Jugend*, p. 198.
18. Ibid., pp. 237–38.
19. Ibid., pp. 293–305.
20. Ibid., pp. 306–94.
21. H. Kober, *Studien zur Rechtsanschauung Bismarcks* (Tuebingen, 1961), pp. 21–32.
22. Pflanze, "Toward a Psychoanalytic Interpretation of Bismarck," p. 424. Older and more traditional studies and biographies, e.g., E. Marcks, *Der Aufstieg des Reiches: Deutsche Geschichte von 1807–1871/78*, 2 vols. (Stuttgart, 1936), E. Brandenburg, *Reichsgruendung*, 2 vols. (Leipzig, 1916), A. O. Meyer, *Bismarck: Der Mensch und der Staatsmann* (Stuttgart, 1949), take the chancellor's religious pronouncements at face value, if they deal with them at all.
23. H. A. Kissinger, "The White Revolutionary: Reflections on Bismarck," *Daedalus* (Summer 1968), p. 897.
24. Ibid., p. 898.
25. Ibid.
26. See F. Stern, *Gold and Iron: Bismarck, Bleichröder, and the Building of the German Empire* (New York, 1977), p. 12.

2. BISMARCK AND THE REVOLUTION OF 1848

1. The equivalent American slogans were "that government is best that governs least," and "the government of business is no business of government." "The coin-

age of the attractive and celebrated phrase laissez-faire is generally attributed to J. C. M. Vincent de Gournay, an eighteenth century French businessman and economic administrator. It was in an impatient outburst against the clutter of regulations and internal barriers to trade that Gournay is said to have said 'Laissez-faire, morbleu, laissez-passer! le monde va de lui-meme! ('Leave things alone, for heaven's sake, let things move! things will take care of themselves!). The heart of laissez-faire as a precept, as the tag for a whole doctrine and as a trend in policy and practice that promised to dominate the western world in the nineteenth century, was the proposition that any interference by the state must inevitably yield less than the optimum allocation of resources, which would result from the decision of competing individuals guided by a rational calculation of their interests. Exceptions had to be made to preserve internal order and national security, but it was hoped that the progressively unimpeded extension of division of labor and the flow of international trade would eventually produce a world at peace." (E. O. Golob in *Handbook of World History*, ed. J. Dunner [New York, 1967], p. 496.)

2. Langer, *Political and Social Upheaval, 1832–52*, pp. 54–56.

3. Jost Hermand, ed., *Das Junge Deutschland: Text und Dokumente* (Stuttgart, 1966), pp. 370 ff.

4. O. J. Hammen, *The Red '48ers: Karl Marx and Friedrich Engels* (New York, 1969), pp. 20 ff. The Cologne disturbances started in November 1837 when Archbishop Clemens August von Droste-Vischering, following papal guidance, declined to carry out the government's policy regarding mixed marriages. When the archbishop also refused to resign, "the Prussian government had him arrested and incarcerated in the fortress of Minden. . . . This arbitrary action, which lacked any legal justification, caused enormous sensation." The Rhinelanders, who already chafed under the government's anti-Catholic attitude, now took to the streets. The conflict was not settled until Friedrich Wilhelm IV ascended the throne in 1840, when most of the anti-Catholic measures were abandoned. (H. Holborn, *A History of Modern Germany, 1684–1840*, [New York 1964], pp. 505, 508.)

5. Hammen, *The Red '48ers*, pp. 68–69.

6. T. S. Hamerow, *Restoration, Revolution, Reaction* (Princeton, N.J., 1958), p. 124. German historians of the interwar period looked upon the delegates to the Frankfurt Parliament either as impractical idealists (E. Marcks, *Bismarck und die deutsche Revolution, 1848–1851*, published posthumously [Stuttgart, 1939]), or humanitarian liberals (V. Valentine, *Geschichte der deutschen Revolution*, 2 vols. [Berlin, 1939]). During the Nazi period the Frankfurt Assembly was scorned and its failure and lack of real power were emphasized (R. Suchenwirth, *Deutsche Geschichte* [Leipzig, 1937]). Historians in the Federal Republic, after the Second World War, held differing views on the Frankfurt Assembly. F. Meinecke believed that the threat of the mob and its communistic slogans played a major role in the deliberations of the representatives in the Paulskirche by frightening them into compromises with the established authorities. ("The Year of 1848 in German History. Reflections on a Centenary," *Review of Politics* 10 [1948], pp. 475–92.) H. Rothfels maintains that the delegates' efforts and devotion to liberal ideals should be commemorated. ("1848—One Hundred Years After," *Journal of Modern History* 2, no. 4, Dec. 1948.) Historians of the German Democratic Republic, on the other hand, point out that the petit bourgeois democrats at Frankfurt were strong on speeches and declarations, but weak in their determination for revolutionary action. They were divided among themselves and incapable of revolutionary leadership. (H. J. Bartmuss et al., *Deutsche Geschichte*, 3 vols. [Berlin, 1967–68].) Of non-German historians, A. J. P. Taylor in his *Course of German History* (New York, 1946),

believes that the Frankfurt Assembly "suffered from too much experience rather than too little: too much calculation, too much foresight, too many elaborate combinations, too much statesmanship" and that "the essence of Frankfurt was the idea of unity by persuasion." To L. B. Namier, "the aim of the Frankfurt Parliament was a real Pan Germany, not a Greater Prussia or Great Austria" (L. B. Namier *Vanished Supremacies* [London, 1958], p. 28; see also L. B. Namier, *1848: The Revolution of the Intellectuals* [London, 1946], an expanded version of his Raleigh Lecture of 1944). The most detailed and balanced account is provided by F. Eyck, *The Frankfurt Parliament, 1848–1849* (New York, 1968). According to him, the moderate liberals and the radicals considered "unification and constitutional progress . . . aspects of the same problem." The Frankfurt Assembly failed to unify Germany because of insufficient public support and lack of interest by either Prussia or Austria. Friedrich Wilhelm IV's rejection of the crown was not so much a failure by the Frankfurt delegates to write a proper constitution, but rather his realization "that his acceptance would involve Germany and possibly Europe in a war."

7. Langer, *Political and Social Upheaval, 1832–1852*, p. 412. The Czechs of Bohemia and Moravia, led by Frantisek Palacky, refused to attend the Assembly. "The rulers of our people," he wrote to the Assembly on April 11, 1848, "have for centuries participated in the Federation of German Princes but the *people* [emphasis added] never looked upon itself as part of the German nation." (Quoted by Namier, *1848: The Revolution of the Intellectuals*, p. 91.)

8. R. Pascal, "The Frankfurt Parliament, 1848, and the Drang nach Osten" *Journal of Modern History* 18 (1946), p. 115; see also Namier, *1848: The Revolution of the Intellectuals*, passim.

9. G. A. Rein, "Bismarcks gegenrevolutionaere Aktion in den Maerztagen 1848," *Die Welt als Geschichte* 18 (1953), pp. 246–62; see also E. Eyck, *Bismarck: Leben und Werk*, 3 vols. (Zuerich, 1941–44), 1: 85–90.

10. Rein, "Bismarcks gegenrevolutionaere Aktion," p. 261.

11. Rein, *Die Revolution in der Politik Bismarcks*, pp. 71–75. As Fritz Stern has pointed out, no one has assessed the impact of the 1848 Revolution on Bismarck. "The Revolution gave Bismarck (like Marx) a new élan and a new direction. The death of a woman he loved brought a new religious commitment to his life: the near death of his monarchy left him with a new political resolve. The first had taught him the powerlessness of all men; the second, the frailty of most men. Both together gave him a stronger sense of his own duty and destiny." (Stern, *Gold and Iron*, p. 13.)

12. O. Becker, *Bismarcks Ringen um Deutschlands Gestaltung* (Heidelberg, 1958), pp. 59–69.

13. For details see Meyer, *Bismarck*, pp. 66 ff.

14. Ibid., p. 67.

15. Bismarck, *Die Gesammelten Werke*, 19 vols. (Friedrichsruh, 1924–32), 10: 101 ff.; henceforth cited *GW*.

16. Quoted by Stern, *Gold and Iron*, p. 14.

17. Quoted by Meyer, *Bismarck*, p. 74.

3. FRANKFURT, ST. PETERSBURG, PARIS, 1851–1862

1. O. Becker, *Bismarcks Ringen um Deutschlands Gestaltung*, pp. 68–69.

2. Quoted by Meyer, *Bismarck*, pp. 76–77.

3. Ibid., p. 89.

4. H. Boehme, *Deutschlands Weg zur Grossmacht* (Cologne, 1966), pp. 23–41.
5. Meyer, *Bismarck*, pp. 98–100.
6. Bismarck's memorandum of April 6, 1853, *GW*, 1:323, n. 1.
7. A. O. Meyer, *Bismarcks Kampf mit Oesterreich am Bundestag zu Frankfurt, 1851 bis 1859* (Berlin, 1927), pp. 189–206.
8. Quoted by Meyer, *Bismarck*, p. 105.
9. In concluding the alliance Austria meant to secure her flank in case of complications with Russia. Prussia, largely pro-Russian in her sympathies, was bent on neutrality and by concluding the alliance hoped to influence Austrian policy toward this goal.
10. Meyer, *Bismarck*, pp. 106–7.
11. Ibid., pp. 108–10.
12. Ibid., pp. 107–11.
13. For details see Meyer, *Bismarcks Kampf*, pp. 324–66.
14. The king's insanity disabled him in October 1857, and Prince Wilhelm had been acting regent since that time.
15. *GW*, 3:302–23.
16. Meyer, *Bismarck*, pp. 119–24.
17. Ibid., p. 126.
18. O. Becker, *Bismarcks Ringen um Deutschlands Gestaltung*, p. 74; *GW*, 14, pt. 1, p. 517; 3:37, 38.
19. Meyer, *Bismarck*, pp. 127–30.
20. Ibid., pp. 145–47.
21. H. Oncken, "Die Baden-Badener Denkschrift Bismarcks," *Historische Zeitschrift* 145 (1932), pp. 124 ff.
22. He criticized the negative and defensive aspects of the conservative program and ridiculed the idea of a solidarity of conservative interest throughout Europe. He characterized the existing constitution of the Confederation as a hothouse for dangerous revolutionary and particularist ideas and expressed surprise that people should be so sensitive to the idea of popular representation in the Confederate Diet or in the Customs Union Parliament. (Bismarck to Alexander Below-Hohendorf, Sept. 18, 1861 [*GW*, 14, pt. 1, p. 578].)
23. Meyer, *Bismarck*, p. 161 and reference.
24. Ibid., pp. 162–68.

4. BISMARCK'S APPOINTMENT AND THE CONSTITUTIONAL CONFLICT IN PRUSSIA

1. Meyer, *Bismarck*, p. 172.
2. Ibid., p. 171.
3. Ibid., p. 172.
4. *GW*, 15:179.
5. Ibid.
6. *Fuerst Bismarcks Briefe an seine Braut und Gattin*, ed. H. Bismarck (Stuttgart, 1900), pp. 513–14.
7. Huber, *Deutsche Verfassungsgeschichte seit 1789*, 3:280.
8. M. Messerschmidt, "Die Armee in Staat und Gesellschaft—Die Bismarckzeit," in M. Stuermer, *Das kaiserliche Deutschland: Politik und Gesellschaft, 1870–1918* (Duesseldorf, 1970), pp. 90–94.
9. O. Becker, *Bismarcks Ringen um Deutschlands Gestaltung*, p. 94.
10. Huber, *Deutsche Verfassungsgeschichte seit 1789*, 3:278. See also W. Sauer, "Das

Problem des deutschen Nationalstaates," in H. U. Wehler, ed., *Moderne deutsche Sozialgeschichte* (Cologne, 1968), p. 427.

11. O. Becker, *Bismarcks Ringen um Deutschlands Gestaltung*, p. 96.

12. Ibid., p. 97. Transcending the military and financial question was a fundamental split between the outlooks of the bourgeoisie and the nobility: "as the political representatives of an economically emancipated middle class, the Prussian liberals had little understanding of the remnants of the old regime, of its political and financial privileges, of the burden of unproductive military expenditures on the economy and of its often patronizing attitude toward the bureaucracy. To get rid of these chains they [the liberals] needed, according to their views, not only economic but political power. These were the issues of the 1860's." (H. A. Winkler, *Preussischer Liberalismus und Deutscher Nationalstaat: Studien zur Geschichte der Deutschen Fortschrittspartei 1861–1866*, [Tuebingen, 1964], p. 20.)

13. Huber, *Deutsche Verfassungsgeschichte seit 1789*, 3:280–87.

14. O. Becker, *Bismarcks Ringen um Deutschlands Gestaltung*, p. 98.

15. Huber, *Deutsche Verfassungsgeschichte seit 1789*, 3:291–93.

16. Winkler, *Preussischer Liberalismus*, pp. 14–15.

17. Wilhelm was crowned king of Prussia at Koenigsberg on January 2, 1861.

18. Huber, *Deutsche Verfassungsgeschichte seit 1789*, 3:294–97.

19. Ibid., pp. 298–99.

20. L. Reiners, *Bismarcks Aufstieg, 1815–1864* (Munich, 1965), pp. 354–56.

21. T. S. Hamerow, *The Social Foundations of German Unification, 1858–1871: Struggles and Accomplishments*, 2 vols. (Princeton, N.J., 1972), 2:158.

22. O. Becker, *Bismarcks Ringen um Deutschlands Gestaltung*, p. 103.

23. Huber, *Deutsche Verfassungsgeschichte seit 1789*, 3:305.

24. Ibid., pp. 306–7; O. Pflanze, "Juridical and Political Responsibility in 19th Century Germany," In L. Krieger and F. Stern, eds., *The Responsibility of Power* (Garden City, N.Y., 1967), p. 179.

25. *GW*, 10:140.

26. Huber, *Deutsche Verfassungsgeschichte seit 1789*, 3:308–9.

27. Ibid., p. 318–19.

28. Quoted by K. S. Pinson, *Modern Germany* (New York, 1954), pp. 130–31.

29. The constitutional conflict in Prussia is probably the best and clearest issue with which to demonstrate the disparate views of historians over the last half century. Erich Marcks, Bismarck's defender and one of the foremost German nationalist historians of the older generation, believed that the chancellor's theory of the constitutional gap could not be considered legally wrong, though the government was in effect exercising dictatorial powers. According to Marcks, the liberals and the moderates, supported by public opinion, were aiming for west European parliamentarism. Bismarck, unable to achieve a compromise, threw himself into the fight with great enthusiasm and carried the king with him. The opposition, in turn, was ready to deny its support even in case of war. The liberals were convinced that without the people's support, Prussia would be defeated in such a war. This stand was necessary to get rid of Bismarck and the hated government. The liberals' fight against their own state was a heavy and tragic responsibility, according to Marcks, but in the end, they vastly overestimated their strength because the Prussian people, basically patriotic, did not follow them. (E. Marcks, *Der Aufstieg des Reiches*.)

Presenting the traditional, liberal point of view, Eugene N. Anderson, an American historian who has written extensively on modern European and Germany history, closely analyzes the parties and issues involved in his *Social and Political Conflict in Prussia, 1858–1864* (Lincoln, Nebr., 1954). He believes "that the Prussian people overwhelmingly opposed the preservation of the vestiges of the Old Regime and desired reform." They understood the issues involved but because of their inexperience in self-government and their fear of using force, they failed in their aims. The liberals did not surrender, however, until the Austro-Prussian War provided the basis for one of their major objectives, German unity. Bismarck, according to Anderson, was not only adept at using power, he was also lucky in benefiting from an upswing of the economy.

Focusing on the Progressive party, Heinrich August Winkler, in his *Preussischer Liberalismus und Deutscher Nationalstaat: Studien zur Geschichte der Deutschen Fortschrittspartei, 1861–1866* (Tuebingen, 1964), believes that the issues involved were more complicated than either Marcks or Anderson will admit. He disputes the latter's judgment on the election of July 1866 (Winkler, *Preussischer Liberalismus*, p. 92, n. 4) and asserts that the Liberal's views on foreign policy in the 1860s were "considerably more aggressive and militant than those of Bismarck" (p. 112, fn. 59). Winkler also maintains that the so-called capitulation of German liberals in 1866 has been misinterpreted by the older historians, E. Marcks (*Der Aufstieg des Reiches*) and E. Brandenburg (*Die Reichsgruendung*), and by the more recent ones, F. C. Sell (*Die Tragoedie des deutschen Liberalismus* [Stuttgart, 1953]) and H. Kohn (*The Mind of Germany* [New York, 1960]). According to Winkler, the resistance to the rise of liberalism was much stronger in Germany than in western Europe because of the greater power and firmer foundation of the various local dynasties; the Reformation and the strong particularistic feeling throughout Germany had also established close ties between the people and their princes, closer ties than those between other people in western Europe and their local nobility. For these reasons, the Prussian liberals were justified, according to Winkler, in trusting the nobility which, under Stein and Hardenberg, had effected a revolution from above (pp. 115–16).

Breaking new ground by getting away from the usual preoccupation with diplomatic and political affairs, Theodore S. Hamerow focuses on the social and economic aspects of nineteenth-century history in his two-volume study *The Social Foundations of German Unification, 1858–1871*. From a vast array of hitherto neglected sources and statistical data, he concludes that the majority of people were indifferent to the constitutional conflict. "The struggle between Crown and Parliament did not arise out of a deliberate confrontation. It was rather the inadvertent result of political strategems whose effect had not been foreseen." Bismarck, according to Hamerow, "rejected the possibility of an overt coup d'état. He felt that under the political conditions of modern society, parliamentary institutions were essential for monarchical rule. Prussia's experience with constitutionalism convinced him of the compatibility of a representative assembly with royal authority." For the latest study see M. Gugel, *Industrieller Aufstieg und buergerliche Herrschaft: Soziooekonomische Interessen und politische Ziele des liberalen Buergertums in Preussen zur Zeit des Verfassungskonflikts, 1857–1867* (Cologne, 1975).

30. Winkler, *Preussischer Liberalismus*, pp. 24–27.
31. Shlomo Na'aman, *Lassalle* (Hannover, 1970), p. 431.

5. BISMARCK'S THREE WARS

1. Quoted by R. H. Lord, "Bismarck and Russia in 1863," *American Historical Review* 29 (October 1923), p. 26.
2. Gorchakov mentioned the Convention to the French ambassador, while Bismarck

bragged to Behrend, vice-president of the Prussian Diet, about Prussian incursions into Poland as far as Warsaw; in addition, German newspapers had printed several stories about Russia's inability to cope with the revolt. (E. Eyck, *Bismarck*, 1:469.)

3. Ibid., p. 472. On the attitude of the liberals to the Polish question, see Winkler, *Preussischer Liberalismus*, pp. 34–41.

4. Lord, "Bismarck and Russia in 1863," p. 32.

5. W. E. Mosse, *The European Powers and the German Question, 1848–1871* (Cambridge, 1958), pp. 115–16.

6. Lord, "Bismarck and Russia in 1863," p. 24; see also A. Hillgruber, *Bismarcks Aussenpolitik* (Freiburg, 1972), pp. 49 ff., and W. Bussmann, *Das Zeitalter Bismarcks* (Frankfurt, 1968), pp. 71 ff.

7. It has been suggested that Bismarck might have wanted to use the crisis and an ensuing war to alleviate and perhaps solve the constitutional crisis at home. (Lord, "Bismarck and Russia in 1863," pp. 47–48.)

8. See chap. 2.

9. Boehme, *Deutschlands Weg zur Grossmacht*, pp. 100–117.

10. The standard work is still L. D. Steefel, *The Schleswig-Holstein Question* (Cambridge, Mass., 1932).

11. See chap. 2.

12. K. A. P. Sandiford, *Great Britain and the Schleswig-Holstein Question, 1848–1864* (Toronto, 1975), pp. 67 ff.

13. For a detailed account of the Prussian liberals' concern regarding the Schleswig-Holstein question, see Winkler, *Preussischer Liberalismus*, pp. 41 ff.

14. F. Thimme, editor of Bismarck's political writings (*GW*, vols. 4–6b), believed that Bismarck's foreign policy toward Austria was strongly influenced by domestic conservative considerations (the desire to repress liberal opposition and reestablish and increase royal power) and that his cooperation with Austria in the Schleswig-Holstein question was not designed to achieve greater power for Prussia. Bismarck's real aim, according to Thimme, was an alliance with Austria to gain Austria's trust and favor, and in this way achieve Prussian predominance in North Germany. With Prussia's vital interests secured, and a trusting and long-lasting cooperation between the two German powers established, they could both fight against the common enemy: constitutionalism and revolution. It was only after the Gastein Convention that Bismarck considered all possibilities for cooperation with Austria lost. Austria's secret agreement with France was a much stronger indication of her pro-war policy than Bismarck's earlier agreement with Italy was in the case of Prussia. (Introduction to *GW*, 5:x–xii).

15. Boehme, *Deutschlands Weg zur Grossmacht*, p. 165.

16. *GW*, 5:96–103.

17. In an interesting and penetrating study on the possibility of war in the summer of 1865 ("Kriegsgefahr und Gasteiner Konvention: Bismarck, Eulenburg und die Vertagung des preussisch-oesterreichischen Krieges im Sommer 1865," in I. Geiss and B. J. Wendt, eds., *Deutschland in der Weltpolitik des 19. und 20. Jahrhunderts* [Duesseldorf, 1973], pp. 89–103), J. C. G. Roehl agrees with R. Stadelmann, who believes that the European political situation in the summer of 1865 was an ideal moment for Bismarck to declare war on Austria. Britain was preoccupied with the American Civil War, France with her Mexican adventure, and Russia with internal affairs in the aftermath of the Crimean War. None of these powers could have come to Austria's assistance and, in addition, Austria had constitutional and financial troubles of her own. Since this situation could not be expected to last, time was against Bismarck; why he failed to take advantage of this favorable moment is an

intriguing question. Either he genuinely wanted to avoid war and come to terms with Austria, or he had already decided on war but had not completed all his preparations. Stadelmann tends toward the latter explanation, though he also considers the influence of public opinion and the possibility that Bismarck may have pursued both courses simultaneously. (Stadelmann shows that Wilhelm I and his advisors favored a much stronger anti-Austrian policy than German historians of the older school have heretofore assumed. R. Stadelmann, *Das Jahr 1865 und das Problem von Bismarcks deutscher Politik, Historische Zeitschrift* supplement no. 29 [Munich, 1933], quoted by Roehl, "Kriegsgefahr," pp. 90–91.)

Roehl concludes, on the basis of newly discovered letters from Bismarck to the Prussian minister of the interior, Eulenburg, that Bismarck's reasons for postponing war in July 1865 were predominantly financial. The failure of some important financial transactions, for which he blamed the Prussian finance minister Bodelschwingh and the Prussian minister for trade Itzenpiltz, left the government short of funds for the war effort. "During the year 1865, Bismarck did not honestly work for an understanding with Austria. The Convention of Gastein cannot be judged as proof of a desire to achieve a peaceful dualism; it was nothing but an attempt to gain time." (Roehl, "Kriegsgefahr," p. 103.)

18. E. Eyck, *Bismarck*, 2:68–69.
19. Ibid., p. 86.
20. *GW*, 5:307–11.
21. Quoted by E. Eyck, *Bismarck*, 2:101.
22. *GW*, 5:365–68.
23. E. Eyck, *Bismarck*, 2:112.
24. Ibid., p. 124.
25. Stern, *Gold and Iron*, p. 69. The property involved was the Cologne-Minden Railroad.
26. Although Bleichroeder's relationship to Bismarck had been known for a long time, the details of their relationship and the importance of Bleichroeder's role has only been dealt with recently by Fritz Stern in his penetrating and well-written study, *Gold and Iron*.
27. Ibid., chaps. 3 and 4.
28. A. J. P. Taylor, *The Struggle for Mastery in Europe, 1848–1918* (Oxford, 1954), pp. 163–65.
29. *GW*, 5:416–19.
30. Ibid., pp. 432–34, 447–49.
31. See chap. 3.
32. E. Eyck, *Bismarck*, 2:162.
33. Ibid., p. 169.
34. On July 20, 1858, Napoleon III and Cavour met at Plombières and agreed to join forces in a war against Austria. For details see Taylor, *The Struggle for Mastery in Europe*, pp. 103–4.
35. E. Eyck, *Bismarck*, 2:170–72.
36. The motives which caused Bismarck to consider the plan at all are not entirely clear. They were probably part of his two-track effort to gain Prussian supremacy in Germany. One track followed a warlike policy, the other a peaceful one. The Gablenz plan was part of the second track and also served to strengthen the king's resolve, should the peaceful policy fail. (E. Eyck, *Bismarck*, 2:174–81.) For a presentation of various views by historians on the Gablenz mission and Bismarck's attitude toward it, see O. Becker, *Bismarcks Ringen um Deutschlands Gestaltung*, chap. 4, n. 4, pp. 843–44.

37. Reorganization of the Prussian army in connection with the constitutional conflict played no part in the army's effectiveness, for victory could also have been achieved by employment of the militia and other Boyen reforms. O. Becker, *Bismarcks Ringen um Deutschlands Gestaltung*, p. 98.

38. Pflanze, *Bismarck and the Development of Germany*, vol. 1, pp. 301–3. "Bleichroeder . . . transmitted 400,000 thaler to the Hungarian revolutionaries" (F. Stern, *The Failure of Illiberalism* [New York, 1972], p. 62). See also Stern, *Gold and Iron*, pp. 89–90.

39. On Bismarck's treatment of Frankfurt, see Stern, *Gold and Iron*, pp. 90–91.

40. *GW*, 6:120. Pflanze, *Bismarck and the Development of Germany*, vol. 1, pp. 306–10.

41. Winkler, *Preussischer Liberalismus*, pp. 91–92.

42. Huber, *Deutsche Verfassungsgeschichte seit 1789*, 3:353, 358.

43. On the split of the liberals, see Winkler, *Preussischer Liberalismus*, pp. 93 ff.

44. G. A. Kertesz, "Reflections on a Centenary," *Historical Studies of Australia and New Zealand* 12 (Oct. 1966), pp. 333–42.

45. K. G. Faber, "Realpolitik als Ideologie," *Historische Zeitschrift* 203 (Aug. 1966), pp. 1–45. Winkler believes it would be wrong to accuse the liberals of having opted for power and against freedom in 1866. From their point of view it was quite reasonable to hope that Prussia's strongly authoritarian position would be diluted by the unification of Germany. (Winkler, *Preussischer Liberalismus*, p. 122). See also G. R. Mork, "Bismarck and the 'Capitulation' of German Liberalism," *Journal of Modern History* 43, no. 1 (March 1971): 59–75.

46. Bismarck spent the latter part of October and early November at Putbus on the Baltic Sea, recuperating from an illness. Bussman, *Das Zeitalter Bismarcks*, p. 96.

47. Pflanze, *Bismarck and the Development of Germany*, vol. 1, p. 338.

48. H. Hefter, *Die deutsche Selbstverwaltung im 19. Jahrhundert*, 2d ed. (Stuttgart, 1969), believes that Prussian hegemony in the North German Confederation and later in the Reich preserved Prussian particularism. By the same token, the particularism of the lesser German states was preserved, and the door was left open for the South German states to enter the Confederation later on (p. 468).

49. The text of this clause provided that "the regulations and decrees of the Federal President are issued in the name of the Confederation and require for their validity the counter signature of the Federal Chancellor who accepts with it the responsibility." Article 172/2 as quoted by R. Morsey, *Die oberste Reichsverwaltung unter Bismarck, 1867–1890* (Muenster, 1957), p. 19. See also E. Hahn, "Ministerial Responsibility and Impeachment in Prussia 1848–63," *Central European History* 10, no. 1 (Mar. 1977): 3–27.

50. Morsey, *Die oberste Reichsverwaltung*, pp. 20–21.

51. During Bismarck's term of office he was responsible neither to the Reichstag nor to the Federal Council, only to the king. His dismissal in 1890 was not for any loss of confidence by any legislative bodies, but only because the king had lost confidence in his minister. Morsey, *Die oberste Reichsverwaltung*, pp. 21–23; Pflanze, "Juridical and Political Responsibility," p. 173, n. 17. For Bismarck's views on ministerial responsibility, see Hahn, "Ministerial Responsibility," pp. 24–25.

52. Quoted by G. P. Gooch, *Studies in Modern History* (New York, 1968), p. 227.

53. Pflanze, *Bismarck and the Development of Germany*, vol. 1, p. 361.

54. Morsey, *Die oberste Reichsverwaltung*, pp. 24, 25.

55. J. Becker, "Zum Problem der Bismarckschen Politik in der Spanischen Thronfrage 1870," *Historische Zeitschrift* 212, no. 3 (June 1971): 529–607.

56. E. Eyck, *Bismarck*, 2:424.

57. Taylor, *The Struggle for Mastery in Europe*, p. 185.

58. Alexander had come to Paris in June 1867 to visit the exhibition and to meet his mistress, Princess Catherine Dolgoruky. W. E. Mosse, *The European Powers and the German Question, 1848–1871*, p. 270, n. 3.

59. There were firm indications of a French-Austrian understanding at the time (November 1867–January 1869) and rumors of an Austro-Prussian rapprochement. The latter was strongly denied by Bismarck. W. E. Mosse, *The European Powers*, pp. 279–83.

60. Ibid., pp. 284–90.

61. Following the defeat of the republican forces under Garibaldi, French forces occupied Rome in 1849 to ensure the future safety of the pope and of the Church. By 1864 Napoleon III changed his policy, to the dismay of many Catholics in France and, in an attempt to curry favor with the Italians, he signed the September Convention with the Italian government. By its terms, the Italians promised not to attack papal territory and, in return, the French government agreed to withdraw its troops within two years, which it did in December 1866. By October of the following year, French troops returned after an insurrection in Rome had failed and volunteers under Garibaldi had defeated the papal forces. The combined French and papal forces defeated the volunteers in the battle of Mentana, November 3, 1867, and Garibaldi was captured. The Italians were deeply resentful and though Napoleon tried to come to terms with them, French public opinion, spurred by the Church, precluded any concessions. Thus, the Roman question remained a major point of dispute and crippled Franco-Italian relations until the fall of the Second Empire.

62. E. Eyck, *Bismarck*, 2: 342–46, 348–51, 355–58.

63. The Spanish throne had become vacant after Queen Isabella fled to France, September 29, 1868, following the defeat of the royal forces. In May 1869, the Spanish Parliament voted for a constitutional monarchy and looked for a suitable candidate for the Spanish throne among the royal houses of Europe.

    The material on the Hohenzollern candidature is voluminous; the original German documents, with minor exceptions, were kept secret until the Second World War when Allied troops captured them as part of the German Foreign Ministry archives. The documents on the Hohenzollern candidature plus some documents from the Hohenzollern-Sigmaringen archives were compiled and edited by Georges Bonnin in *Bismarck and the Hohenzollern Candidature for the Spanish Throne: The Documents in the German Diplomatic Archives* (London, 1957). Bonnin's introduction is a fascinating account of how German Foreign Office officials suppressed the key documents. The publication of Bonnin's volume was welcomed by most historians as an important contribution and clarification of a major problem in modern European history. Only Gerhard Ritter, the doyen of German national historians, was unimpressed. In his introduction to J. Dittrich's book (see below) he asserted that most of the material that Bonnin had discovered had been known to German historians since 1913. (One can only wonder why German historians did nothing with the material in that interval.) He deplored the fact that the documents had been translated into English and regretted that they were published by a foreigner.

    Historical opinion on Bismarck's role in this crisis can be roughly divided into three views: historians who believed that Bismarck used the Hohenzollern candidature from the very beginning to go to war with France, those who considered Bismarck completely blameless in the affair, and those who believed that while he did not cause or even want the war, he took advantage of the situation and confronted France with a choice of war or diplomatic defeat.

    To the first group belong the French historians who published prior to World War

I. E. Ollivier, *L'Empire Liberal*, 16 vols. (Paris 1895–1912); H. Welschinger, *La Guerre de 1870: Causes et Responsibilités*, 2 vols., (Paris, 1875); A. Sorel, *Histoire Diplomatique de la Guerre Franco-Allemande* (Paris, 1875); P. de la Gorce, *Histoire du Second Empire*, 7 vols. (Paris, 1896–1903). German historians whose studies came out after World War II also shared this view. E. Eyck, *Bismarck*, believed Bismarck set a trap for Napoleon III from which there was no escape but war (2:487). H. U. Wehler, *Bismarck und der Imperialismus* (Cologne, 1969), sees in Bismarck's policy a "revolution from above" with aspects of Bonapartism designed to preserve the existing order through foreign diversions and limited concessions at home (p. 456). J. Becker, "Zum Problem der Bismarckschen Politik in der Spanischen Thronfrage 1870," in *Historische Zeitschrift* 212, no. 3 (June 1971): 529–607, the most recent and most comprehensive account, concludes that Bismarck was determined that his policy should lead to war with France from the very beginning (pp. 604–5).

The second group, which considers Bismarck blameless, is composed of historians, mostly Germans, who wrote before or after World War I, but there are some who, even after 1945 and the considerable amount of new evidence, still consider Bismarck innocent of an aggressive policy toward France. H. v. Sybel, the official historian of German unification, asserted in his *Die Begruendung des deutschen Reiches durch Wilhelm I*, 7 vols. (Munich, 1913), that Bismarck had nothing to do with the Hohenzollern candidature. Hans Delbrueck, in "Das Geheimnis der Napoleonischen Politik im Jahre 1870," in his *Erinnerungen, Aufsaetze und Reden* (Berlin, 1902) and H. Oncken, in *Das deutsche Reich und die Vorgeschichte des Weltkrieges* (Leipzig, 1933), believed that Bismarck's policy was primarily defensive and a reaction to Napoleon's attempt to encircle Prussia by his alliances with Austria and Italy. This is also E. Brandenburg's opinion in *Die Reichsgruendung*. L. Reiners, *Bismarck gruendet das Reich, 1864–1871* (Munich, 1957), asserts that although Bismarck favored Leopold's candidacy, he had no intention of letting it lead to war, nor did he want to set a trap for Napoleon III (p. 381). A. J. P. Taylor, *Bismarck: The Man and the Statesman* (London, 1955), considers the question of Bismarck's involvement "the most difficult to answer" and concludes that "there is not a scrap of evidence that he worked deliberately for a war with France, still less that he timed it precisely for the summer of 1870 . . . the Hohenzollern Candidature, far from being designed to provoke a war with France which would complete the unification with Germany, was intended rather to make German unification possible without war. . . . He [Bismarck] had neither planned the war nor foreseen it. But he claimed it as his own once it became inevitable. He wished to present himself as the creator of Germany, not as a man who had been mastered by events" (pp. 115, 116, 118, 121).

The third and largest group consists of those historians who occupy a position between the two extremes; they are Germans, Americans, and Englishmen, most of whom have reevaluated old evidence or have used new documents appearing since the end of World War II.

H. Geuss, in *Bismarck und Napoleon III* (Cologne, 1959), believes that Bismarck estimated that a Hohenzollern in Spain would tie up 40,000–80,000 French soldiers; that is, one-eighth to one-quarter of the French wartime army. The diversion of such a large part of his army would persuade Napoleon to abandon the French war faction in the government and turn toward a liberal course in domestic policies. This, in turn, would have allowed Bismarck to pursue a peaceful policy of German unification. "The Hohenzollern Candidature was thus primarily a lever for Bismarck to move the uncertain French domestic situation . . . toward German unification and peace as he had intended all along" (p. 266). The plan misfired because one of its key factors—total secrecy—was not maintained. B. Schot, "Die Entstehung des deutsch-franzoesischen Krieges und die Gruendung des deutschen Reiches," in H. Boehme, ed., *Probleme der Reichsgruendungszeit, 1848–1879* (Cologne, 1968), pp. 269–95, maintains that Bismarck did not plan a war from the beginning, but at the same time, he did nothing to calm the excitement aroused by the premature news of the candidature; on the contrary, he cleverly utilized the situation created by the exaggerated French demands. And he confronted the French government with the alternatives of war to save French national prestige or diplomatic defeat. It was imperative for German and European public opinion that France take the initiative and appear as the disturber of the peace. Bismarck had achieved his aim, but in a different way than he had originally imagined (p. 291). J. Dittrich, *Bismarck, Frankreich und die spanische Thronkandidature der Hohenzollern: Die "Kriegschuldfrage" von 1870* (Munich, 1962), concludes that Bismarck engineered (*gemacht*) the candidature and that he used it to bring about a decision (p. 2), but does not believe that Bismarck wanted war (p. 289). L. D. Steefel, *Bismarck, the Hohenzollern Candidacy and the Origins of the Franco-German War of 1870* (Cambridge, Mass., 1962), states that "the Franco-German War of 1870 was not the product of reasoned long-term policy" (p. 221). He stresses repeatedly that France declared war and that war was not inevitable until then. "Bismarck did not create the Hohenzollern Candidacy as a countermine to explode the projected triple alliance, but the fear of such an alliance was a major factor, perhaps the major factor, in his decision to urge the Spanish offer" (p. 239). "[The candidacy] provided Bismarck with the means to create a European crisis. What form it would take could not be predicted with certainty" (p. 244). Pflanze, *Bismarck and the Development of Germany*, vol. 1, considers that "the Hohenzollern candidature was an offensive, not a defensive act. . . . Bismarck's goal was . . . a crisis with France. He deliberately set sail on a collision course with the intent of provoking either war or a French internal collapse" (pp. 448, 449). W. N. Medlicott, *Bismarck and Modern Germany* (London, 1965), believes that "Bismarck undoubtedly instigated the candidature, and he undoubtedly welcomed the outbreak of war which resulted from it" (p. 81). The Franco-Prussian War was certainly not an unprovoked attack on Prussia's part: "but who can deny that Bismarck's conduct since 1866 had provoked the provocation?" (p. 84). A. Mitchell, *Bismarck and the French Nation, 1848–1890*, (New York, 1971), calls attention to Bismarck's concern with French domestic policies, especially the outcome of the national election for the legislature in May 1869, which returned a liberal majority. Contrary to some opinion which feared that the election results heralded a return to domestic unrest and foreign adventures, Bismarck believed it "strengthened Napoleon's throne." Mitchell believes that this was unsettling to Bismarck, because he "would no longer be able to count on a maladroit French initiative to provide a convenient diplomatic complication to be exploited" (p. 51). In his forword to G. Bonnin, ed., *Bismarck and the Hohenzollern Candidature for the Spanish Throne. The Documents in the German Diplomatic Archives* (London, 1957), G. P. Gooch writes that "Bismarck welcomed the prospect of a conflict with France in which military victory seemed reasonably certain and which he believed would remove the last obstacle to the voluntary incorporation of the south German states in a federal empire with the King of Prussia at its head. Of his desire for war there is of course not a trace in his letters and dispatches" (pp. 10–11).

64. J. Becker, "Zum Problem der Bismarckschen Politik in der Spanischen Thronfrage 1870," pp. 569–70.

65. D. W. Houston, "Emile Ollivier and the Hohenzollern Candidature," *French Historical Studies* 4 (Fall 1965), pp. 125–49.
66. W. L. Langer, "Bismarck as a Dramatist," in A. O. Sarkissian, ed., *Studies in Diplomatic History and Historiography in Honor of G. P. Gooch* (New York, 1962), pp. 199–216. The original of this famous dispatch, with Bismarck's corrections, is missing, if it ever existed. J. Becker, "Zum Problem der Bismarckschen Politik in der Spanischen Thronfrage 1870," p. 531.
67. A correct appraisal would shed important light on Bismarck's personality and methods, and would also clarify his policy toward German unification and explain subsequent German-French relations prior to World War I. For the following, I have relied heavily on J. Becker, "Zum Problem der Bismarckschen Politik in der Spanischen Thronfrage 1870."
68. Quoted by J. Becker, "Zum Problem der Bismarckschen Politik in der Spanischen Thronfrage 1870," p. 597.
69. The "iron budget" of 1867, "provided for an army equivalent to 1 per cent. of the population, supported by an automatic annual grant of the 225 thaler per man. Originally scheduled to expire in December 1871, this law was extended for an additional three years." G. Craig, *The Politics of the Prussian Army, 1640–1945* (Oxford, 1955), p. 220.
70. Pflanze, *Bismarck and the Development of Germany*, vol. 1, p. 449.
71. J. Becker, "Zum Problem der Bismarckschen Politik in der Spanischen Thronfrage 1870," p. 605. Mitchell, *Bismarck and the French Nation*, pp. 51–52.
72. The best account of the war is M. Howard, *The Franco-Prussian War* (New York, 1961).
73. E. Kolb, "Kriegsfuehrung und Politik 1870/71," in T. Schieder and E. Deuerlein, eds., *Reichsgruendung 1870/71* (Stuttgart, 1970), pp. 95–118.
74. Quoted by Taylor, *The Struggle for Mastery in Europe*, p. 212.
75. Ibid., pp. 212–14.
76. R. I. Giesberg, *The Treaty of Frankfort* (Philadelphia, 1966), pp. 87–98.
77. Ibid., pp. 107–26.
78. The unified German state, Bismarck's greatest achievement, did not survive the Second World War. The methods Bismarck used to unify Germany were admired and praised during his lifetime, but were increasingly questioned as the Reich failed to meet a series of external and domestic crises and was finally crushed.

   Before and during the First World War, historians stressed the patriotic and national aspects of the unification movement and praised Bismarck and Wilhelm I, thus indirectly criticizing Wilhelm II. Some writers during the Weimar Republic, which followed World War I, attempted to discover whether faults in the founding of the Reich could explain its recent defeat, while others extolled Bismarck's glorious achievements, which they compared favorably to the petty and harmful policies of the politicians of the Republic.

   In the Third Reich Nazi historians compared Bismarck's establishment of a lesser German Reich unfavorably to Hitler's Greater Germany; some saw in Bismarck's creation the forerunner to Hitler's Reich. After the collapse in 1945, German historians have tried to reassess the unification of 1871.

   The following is but a sample of some historians' views. H. v. Treitschke in his *Historische und Politische Aufsaetze*, 3 vols. (Leipzig, 1911–15), written in 1886, credited the Prussian monarchy with the creation of the Reich; accomplished by military might, it had the power of a *fait accompli* and the irresistible force of awakened national feeling behind it (2:551). But the masses played no part in the unification movement, "it was not even desirable that they should do so," according to Treitschke, "because such a movement on German soil usually produced a lot of noise and anarchy" (3:544). Nor did the Customs Union parliament play a constructive role in the larger movement. Particularism and the hatred of Prussia among the South German states made German unity appear unattainable for a long time. At this point, "a kind providence sent us the war with France. And indeed, only such a tremendous event, only such an act of violence, so brutal and impudent that it would arouse even the most indolent conscience, was able to lead the South back into the greater fatherland" (3:548).

E. Brandenburg, in *Die Reichsgruendung*, believed that while leading statesmen and generals played an important role in the unification and military and diplomatic events may have been decisive, the national feeling and the cooperation of the German people should not be underestimated; the existence of a strong national movement was the indispensable basis for the achievements of the statesmen. Everyone who had carried a gun during the struggles from 1813 to 1870, or had fought for national ideals by making speeches and writing pamphlets, had participated in the founding of the new Germany. The decisive deeds, however, came from the men around King Wilhelm, and the biggest among them was Bismarck (2:413, 417–18).

J. Ziekursch, in the *Politische Geschichte des neuen deutschen Kaiserreiches*, 3 vols. (Frankfurt, 1925–30), asserted that Bismarck's work was accomplished against the wishes of a majority of the German people. It was done in the interests and with the help of the Hohenzollern dynasty, the Prussian nobility, the officer corps, and high civil servants. This created tensions at home and pressures from abroad. In spite of these difficulties Bismarck led Germany to glory and power, but when he was forced to resign, nobody was able to continue his work or take his place (1:328–29).

Writing only a few years later, E. Marcks, a nationalist and an ardent admirer of Bismarck, completed the first part of his Bismarck biography and his life's work with *Der Aufstieg des Reiches: Deutsche Geschichte von 1807–1871/78*, 2 vols. (Stuttgart, 1936). He believed that Germany's unification was Bismarck's own work; and while others, such as the king, Moltke, Roon, the army, public opinion, and the German people were involved, it was Bismarck who unified the country (1:xii–xiii; 2:514–15).

H. v. Srbik, the Austrian historian and foremost proponent of the all-German historical view (*gesamtdeutsche Geschichtsauffassung*), asserted in his *Deutsche Einheit: Idee und Wirklichkeit von Villafranca bis Koeniggraetz*, 4 vols. (Munich, 1940–42), that it was on the battlefield of Sadowa/Koeniggraetz in 1866 rather than in the palace of Versailles in 1871 that the German empire was founded (4:464). And Srbik regretted Bismarck's failure to establish a Greater German Reich.

Writing during World War II, W. Mommsen, in "Bismarcks kleindeutscher Staat und das grossdeutsche Reich" originally printed in the *Historische Zeitschrift* (vol. 167, pp. 66–82), now reprinted in H. Boehme, ed., *Probleme der Reichsgruendungszeit, 1848–1879* (Cologne, 1968), pp. 355–68, saw Bismarck's Germany as a direct antecedent to Hitler's Greater Germany, not a detour. And he believed that the particular form which German unification took was the only possible solution at the time (p. 356).

L. v. Muralt, in *Bismarcks Verantwortlichkeit* (Goettingen, 1955), sees the problem in a similar light. "Bismarck created the German Reich in the only way possible at that time, i.e., under the leadership of Prussia's power" (p. 33).

Golo Mann, on the other hand, in his *Deutsche Geschichte des 19. und 20. Jahrhunderts* (Frankfurt, 1958), believes that German unification was accomplished by the states, that is by Prussia, the big state, forcing the lesser states to follow its lead. Prussia's coercion was hidden by the fact that large segments of the population wanted and worked for unity though the people themselves did not achieve it. Once unity was accomplished, only a minority was satisfied with the results (p. 378). In the end it was not even a real national state, inasmuch as large parts of the nation remained outside forever (p. 386).

H. Bartel, an east German historian, in "Zur Stellung der Reichsgruendung von 1871 und zum Charakter des preussisch-deutschen Reiches," in H. Bartel and E. Engelberg, eds., *Die grosspreussische militaeristische Reichsgruendung 1871*, 2 vols. (Berlin, 1971), pp. 1–20, sees the founding of the Reich primarily as the result of successful capitalism. Quoting Engels, he asserts that trade and industry had developed in Germany to such a high level and German trade relations were so extensive that particularism at home and lack of protection abroad could no longer be tolerated. The path toward unification proceeded along bourgeois, counter-revolutionary lines and ended without a complete victory for the people. The old monarchy was transformed into a bourgeois-imperialist monarchy with the privileges of the nobility intact, to the great disadvantage of the workers. Thus, class differences were reinforced and the divergence between the character of the state and the developing needs of the nation was further accentuated which led, among other things, to an aggressive foreign policy (2:4–6).

Among non-German historians, G. Barraclough in his *Origins of Modern Germany* (New York, 1946), states "that the new Reich of 1871—whatever the theory—was in practice a Prussian Reich, shaped to accord with Prussian interests, constructed in conformity with Prussian tradition, ruled by the dynasty of the Hohenzollern, and dominated by the Prussian Junker class" (pp. 442–23).

A. J. P. Taylor, in *The Course of German History* (New York, 1946), asserts that "the Bismarck Reich was a dictatorship imposed on the conflicting forces, not an agreement between them. The parties did not compromise; they were manipulated by Bismarck—pushed down when they threatened to become strong, helped up when they appeared weak. Bismarck stood at the center of a multiple seesaw tilting it now this way, now that in order to keep his artificial creation in some sort of equilibrium; but the inevitable result was to give Germany ever more violent and uncontrollable oscillations" (pp. 115–16).

In *The Catholics and German Unity, 1866–1871* (Minneapolis, 1954), G. G. Windell writes that "the particularists had lost, but only by the slimmest of margins. The nationalists had won but only with the aid of some who were in their hearts chagrined at what they had done . . . throughout the country many individuals of both faiths had come to regard the war, and the future of Germany, as another stage in the centuries-old struggle between Wittenberg and Rome" (pp. 273–74).

T. S. Hamerow in *The Social Foundations of German Unification, 1858–1871* believes that, "even in the hour of its greatest triumph the policy of centralization was received by most Germans with indifference and suspicion. National unification was the achievement of a determined, influential, prosperous, intelligent, and indefatigable minority. . . . Bismarck had succeeded in adapting the structure of the state to the needs of an economy which was increasingly industrialized. He had negotiated an unwritten compromise between aristocracy and bourgeoisie through which the interests of the old order would be safe within the framework of the new. Authoritarian rule was disguised by a facade of parliamentary control, while material progress was assured by the achievement of economic integration. Military and political success enabled Germany to satisfy the demands of industrial capitalism without altering her traditional class system" (pp. 425–26).

79. Pflanze, *Bismarck and the Development of Germany*, vol. 1, p. 491. On attempts by

some representatives of the lesser states to weaken the predominance of Prussia in the new Reich and strengthen the federal aspects of the new constitution, see R. Dietrich, "Das Reich, Preussen und die Einzelstaaten bis zur Entlassung Bismarcks," in D. Kurze, ed., *Aus Theorie und Praxis der Geschichtswissenschaft: Festschrift fuer Hans Herzfeld*, (Berlin, 1972), pp. 236–56. For details on the negotiations with Bavaria and especially Bleichroeder's role, see Stern, *Gold and Iron*, pp. 133–34.

80. Pflanze, *Bismarck and the Development of Germany*, vol. 1, pp. 480–90.
81. K. Bosl, "Die Verhandlungen ueber den Eintritt der Sueddeutschen Staaten in den Norddeutschen Bund und die Entstehung der Reichsverfassung," in Schieder and Deuerlein, eds., *Reichsgruendung 1870/71*, pp. 148–63.

6. THE NEW REICH

1. W. Heyderhoff and P. Wentzke, eds., *Deutscher Liberalismus im Zeitalter Bismarcks* (Bonn, 1925), 1:494.
2. G. O. Kent, *Arnim and Bismarck* (Oxford, 1968); F. B. M. Hollyday, *Bismarck's Rival: A Political Biography of General and Admiral Albrecht von Stosch* (Durham, N.C., 1960).
3. Stern, *The Failure of Illiberalism*, pp. 50–51.
4. L. Gall, ed., *Das Bismarck-Problem in der Geschichtsschreibung nach 1945* (Cologne, 1971), p. 106.
5. Ibid., p. 134.
6. Ibid., p. 338.
7. Stern, *The Failure of Illiberalism*, pp. 47–48.
8. For text see J. Lepsius, A. Mendelssohn Bartholdy, F. Thimme, eds., *Die Grosse Politik der Europaeischen Kabinette, 1871–1914*, 40 vols., (Berlin, 1922–27), vol. 1, no. 17, pp. 38–43, henceforth cited *GP*.
9. The annexation of Alsace-Lorraine after the war of 1870–71 became one of the major problems in German-French relations, and contributed to the outbreak of the First World War. The question of responsibility for the annexation has long interested historians and has understandably focused on Bismarck. Lately the controversy over Bismarck's role has been revived and a series of articles in the *Historische Zeitschrift* and elsewhere has produced some interesting opinions.

The latest account, by H. U. Wehler, "Das 'Reichsland' Elsass-Lothringen von 1870 bis 1918," in H. U. Wehler, ed., *Krisenherde des Kaiserreichs, 1871–1918* (Goettingen, 1970), with an exhaustive bibliography tucked away in footnotes, shows that far from resisting the annexation of Alsace (which no serious historian ever proposed), Bismarck favored it. The question of how much and how openly he favored it has aroused a certain amount of controversy. W. Lipgens, in two articles in the *Historische Zeitschrift* ("Bismarck, die oeffentliche Meinung und die Annexion von 1870," *HZ* 199 (1964): 31–112, and "Bismarck und die Frage der Annexion von 1870," *HZ* 206 (1968): 486–617, believes that Bismarck stimulated popular demand for annexation through a well-coordinated press campaign in July–August 1870. Arguing against this are L. Gall, "Zur Frage der Annexion von Elsass-Lothringen 1870," *HZ* 206 (1968): 265–326, and E. Kolb, "Bismarck und das Aufkommen der Annexionsforderungen 1870," *HZ* 209 (1969): 318–56. The latter, also supported by J. Becker, "Baden, Bismarck und die Annexion von Elsass und Lothringen," in *Zeitschrift fuer die Geschichte des Oberrheins* 115 (1967): 167–204, shows convincingly that rather than encouraging annexation demands, Bismarck had no influence on public opinion, at least until the middle of August 1870. On the contrary, the recovery of Alsace was demanded unanimously by all sections of German public opinion from the end of July, and with increasing frequency as German military successes mounted (E. Kolb, *Bismarck und das Aufkommen*, p. 353).

While Wehler does not touch upon these finer points, he mentions that German public opinion was strongly reinforced by the views of prominent professors and publicists such as Sybel, Treitschke, Mommsen, Maurenbrecher, and Lenz, who warned the people not to repeat the mistakes of 1815. Wehler also believes that Bismarck kept these annexation demands alive and manipulated them for political purposes. The army demanded annexation for military and strategic reasons, though the extensive economic and industrial benefits of the Longwy-Brie iron ore deposits were not known at the time. (See, however, G. W. F. Hallgarten, *Imperialismus vor 1914*, 2d ed., 2 vols. [Munich, 1963], 1:157–58; H. Boehme, *Deutschlands Weg zur Grossmacht* [Cologne, 1966], pp. 301–2; and R. Hartshorne, "The Franco-German Boundary of 1871," *World Politics* 2 [1949–50], pp. 209–50.) From the military point of view Alsace-Lorraine and the fortresses of Belfort, Metz, and Strasbourg were the keys to the defense of northeastern France, which the German high command wanted to use as a jumping off point in the next war. The two provinces and the fortresses also provided a much needed defense for southwestern Germany, especially Baden and the Palatinate.

That Bismarck always believed in strong safeguards against French revenge is also stated by. G. Ritter, *The Sword and the Scepter*, 4 vols. (Coral Gables, Fla., 1969–73). "Bismarck himself . . . helped fan the flames of nationalist passions," though he himself was never swayed by it, "and proclaimed from the outset as one of the war aims . . . the slogan that Alsace-Lorraine must become German." According to Ritter, Bismarck's primary aim was a durable peace, and the annexation of the provinces was "not to vindicate old property rights . . . but to protect [Germany] . . . against the next attack" (1:226, 254, 258).

R. I. Giesberg in *The Treaty of Frankfort* (Philadelphia, 1966) also believes that military strategic considerations were uppermost in Bismarck's mind, that he was not swayed by national sentiments and had no intention of resisting popular demands (pp. 24–25).

The only Germans who were not persuaded by military arguments were Marx and Engels. The latter wrote that only "the asses of the official Prussian press" would believe that France could be held back by Germany's annexation of Alsace-Lorraine (quoted by Wehler, "Das 'Reichsland' Elsass-Lothringen," p. 22); while Marx believed that rather than guarantee the peace, as some German generals and publicists maintained, the annexation of Alsace-Lorraine would lead either to total German dependency on Russia or to a "racial war against the allied Roman and Slav races." (Karl Marx, *Der Buergerkrieg in Frankreich* [Berlin, 1949], p. 36.)

Seventeen years later, in 1887, Bismarck himself admitted that there was a possibility that Germany might have to fight both France and Russia in the not too distant future (*GW*, 7:378).

Wehler believes that annexations were inevitable, considering the overwhelming military victory and the nationalistic sentiments of German public opinion. This thought was also expressed by Wilhelm I. "I did not ask for Alsace-Lorraine at the beginning of the last war," he said to his reading companion, "but, at the same time, I would not have dared to let it go if I wanted to keep my army and my people." (Quoted by Wehler, "Das 'Reichsland' Elsass-Lothringen," p. 330, n. 16.)

See also D. P. Silverman, *Reluctant Union: Alsace-Lorraine and Imperial Germany, 1871–1918* (University Park, Pa., 1972), pp. 29–30 and n. 37.

10. L. Gall, "Das Problem Elsass-Lothringen," in Schieder and Deuerlein, eds., *Reichsgruendung 1870/71*, pp. 366–85; the quotation is on p. 375, n. 26.
11. On Bismarck's realpolitik, see the essays under this title by O. Pflanze, in *The Review of Politics* 20 (Oct. 1958), pp. 492–514; and H. Holborn, in *The Journal of the History of Ideas* 21 (Jan., Mar. 1960), pp. 84–98.
12. On the rapid development of industrialization, see K. E. Born, "Structural Changes in German Social and Economic Development at the End of the 19th Century," in J. J. Sheehan, ed., *Imperial Germany* (New York, 1976), pp. 17–18.
13. For a very detailed account, see Wehler, *Bismarck und der Imperialismus*, pp. 53–84; also Stern, *Gold and Iron*, pp. 182–83.
14. See chap. 7.
15. Boehme, *Deutschlands Weg zur Grossmacht*, pp. 354–59.
16. H. Rosenberg, "The Political and Social Consequences of the Great Depression of 1873–96 in Central Europe," *The Economic History Review* 13 (1943), pp. 58–73. Rosenberg expanded this topic in his *Grosse Depression und Bismarckzeit: Wirtschaftsablauf, Gesellschaft und Politik in Mitteleuropa* (Berlin, 1967). In this study Rosenberg links Bismarck's cautious foreign policy and his aggressive domestic policy to the consequences of the depression of 1873–79, which coincided with Kondratiev's "long wave" of 1873–96. For a different view, see A. Gerschenkron, "The Great Depression in Germany," in his *Continuity in History and Other Essays* (Cambridge, Mass., 1968), pp. 405–8.
17. Up to that time, 1874, the army budget was governed by the so-called iron budget of 1867. Craig, *The Politics of the Prussian Army*, pp. 219 ff.
18. D. S. White, *The Splintered Party: National Liberalism in Hessen and the Reich, 1867–1918* (Cambridge, Mass., 1976), pp. 55 ff.
19. A good example is the attempt to reform the Prussian district administration (*Kreisordnung*). After 1866 there was general agreement that reform and a certain measure of decentralization were necessary, and Bismarck supported this trend. The measure failed in 1869 because of conservative opposition in the upper house; in 1872, when it came up again, Bismarck had lost his interest and insisted that reforms of the upper house—where there was considerable opposition to his policies—take precedent. In this instance he was outmaneuvered by Count Eulenburg, the Prussian minister of the interior, and the new *Kreisordnung* became law on December 13, 1872. Contrary to general expectations, it did not liberalize or decentralize the established power structure in the country districts as the municipal order (*Staedteordnung*) had done in the cities. (Hefter, *Die Deutsche Selbstverwaltung in 19. Jahrhundert*, pp. 489–555.)
20. See chap. 7.
21. Boehme, *Deutschlands Weg zur Grossmacht*, pp. 380–86.
22. The development from free trade to protectionism was, of course, much more complicated than described in this short survey. For details see, *inter alia*, H. Boehme, "Big-Business Pressure Groups and Bismarck's Turn to Protectionism 1873–79," *Historical Journal* 2 (1967); I. Lambi, *Free Trade and Protection in Germany, 1868–1879*, (Wiesbaden, 1963), and Born, "Structural Changes in German Social and Economic Development at the End of the 19th Century."
23. Knut Borchardt, "The Industrial Revolution in Germany, 1700–1914," in C. M. Cipolla, ed., *The Fontana Economic History of Europe*, (London, 1971–), 4, pt. 1, p. 155.
24. Aside from economic interests, Center party officials believed that by favoring protectionism they might force Bismarck to terminate the *Kulturkampf*.
25. Boehme, *Deutschlands Weg zur Grossmacht*, pp. 419, 566–67. The single most deci-

sive shift in recent German historiography is the change of emphasis from 1871, the founding of the empire, to 1879, the turn toward protectionism. This new attitude de-emphasizes the political and organizational aspects connected with 1870–71 and stresses the economic, social, and domestic changes that took place after 1875 as a result of the depression of 1873. The foremost proponent of this new view is H. Boehme, who sees Bismarck's shift in the years 1875–81 from laissez-faire to protectionism and from cooperation with the liberals to alliance with the conservatives as more significant in the development of Prussia-Germany than the unification and founding of the Reich at Versailles in 1871. "The reconciliation with the Center and, most of all, the change-over by the large landowners to protectionism constituted [important] points on the road to the reorganization of the Prussian-German state by Bismarck; a reorganization which was equivalent to a new founding of the Reich." (Boehme, *Deutschlands Weg zur Grossmacht*, p. 419.)

26. Promulgated at the Vatican Council on July 18, 1870, it asserted that the pope, when speaking *ex cathedra*, was infallible in matters of faith and morals.

27. Quoted by Stern, *The Failure of Illiberalism*, p. 53.

28. On Augusta's pro-Catholic sympathies, see, *GW*, 15:336 and M. Busch, *Bismarck, Some Secret Pages of His History*, 3 vols. (London, 1893), 2:416. Interpretations of the *Kulturkampf* and Bismarck's motives for embarking on this fateful struggle have been influenced by religious and ideological considerations, and no balanced, definitive study has appeared so far.

One of the earliest works by a Catholic historian, J. B. Kissling, *Geschichte des Kulturkampfes im Deutschen Reiche*, 3 vols. (Freiburg, 1911–16), is sharply antiliberal. In Kissling's opinion, Bismarck's alliance with the liberals after 1871 led to concessions in religious and educational matters and sacrificed conservative Christian principles in the process. The chancellor's support of the liberal government in Bavaria was another reason for the struggle (1:365, 390). But there was no overall definite plan; it started very gradually. Neither the Polish question nor the Center party had any real influence on Bismarck's policies, contrary to what he may have said later on (3:357, 360). Originally, Bismarck had no intentions of fighting the Center; instead, he wanted to reconcile the Center and the National Liberals, and maintain friendly relations with the pope. But when the National Liberals introduced the question of German intervention in behalf of the pope's temporal powers, Bismarck had to take sides. He still hoped, however, to get the Center's support, and asked Antonelli, the papal secretary of state, to direct the Center along those lines. When Antonelli refused, Bismarck labeled the pope a *Reichsfeind* (enemy of the state) and applied this by extension to the Center party (3:361–63).

Following World War I and the publication of 40 volumes of pre-1914 German Foreign Office documents, German historical writing concentrated on foreign policy. In this vein, A. Wahl, *Vom Bismarck der siebzieger Jahre* (Tuebingen, 1920) and *Deutsche Geschichte, 1871–1914*, 4 vols. (Stuttgart, 1926–36), believed that Bismarck started the *Kulturkampf* primarily to isolate France and to tie Russia and Italy (which had their own troubles with the Church) closer to Germany. No domestic political considerations played a role in this decision.

Paul Sattler, "Bismarcks Entschluss zum Kulturkampf," in F. Hartung and W. Hoppe, eds., *Forschungen zur Brandenburgischen und Preussischen Geschichte*, vol. 52 (Berlin, 1940), writing during the Nazi period, saw the *Kulturkampf* as a struggle against the forces of internationalism (represented by the Center and the Social Democratic parties) in which Bismarck was unsuccessful; only Hitler had been able to overcome these enemies of the state. The immediate causes of the

Kulturkampf were the first Vatican Council and its consequences, the Roman question and the loss of the pope's temporal power, and the appearance of a political party organized along confessional lines (pp. 66–67).

Writing during the same period but taking a less extreme position, E. Schmidt, *Bismarcks Kampf mit dem politischen Katholizismus* (Hamburg, 1942), believed that political Catholicism tried to put its own imprint on the newly established Reich and, when this failed, joined the opposition against Bismarck. Thus, Bismarck was forced into the *Kulturkampf* to defend his life's work (p. 6).

A more balanced view is presented by H. Bornkamm, *Die Staatsidee im Kulturkampf* (Munich, 1950), who maintains that domestic as well as foreign considerations influenced Bismarck. Domestically, Bismarck was threatened by the Center's use of parliamentary tactics to further its program. For the safety of the new Reich, this party had to be destroyed, and this was Bismarck's only aim in the struggle. His motives were not based on any theory of state, nor on ideological grounds, but rested entirely on political considerations. "He fought for no ideas, nor in the name of a Protestant, Hegelian, National Liberal, or critical philosophy in which modern science was pitted against medieval dogma. His only principle was to achieve a clear-cut division between the religious and political sphere, which he saw dangerously mixed-up by the very existence and policy of the Center Party . . . [to him], the *Kulturkampf* was a preventive war on the domestic scene" (pp. 65–66).

F. Nova, "The Motivation in Bismarck's Kulturkampf," *Dusquesne Review* 10 (Spring 1965), sees the essence of the *Kulturkampf* in the collision between the pope's desire to reaffirm his preeminent position after his loss of temporal power in 1870, and "the similar dynamic demands and aspirations of modern civilization, nationalism, statism, liberalism, materialism and secularism, manifested most clearly in the newly established German Empire" (p. 43).

J. Becker, on the other hand, sees Bismarck's *Kulturkampf* primarily as a political device. The chancellor used it to unite the diverse liberal parties for his own purpose, while at the same time corrupting their ideals and diverting them from their constitutional goals. (J. Becker, *Liberaler Staat und Kirche in der Aera der Reichsgruendung und Kulturkampf* [Mainz 1973], pp. 375–76.)

29. Bornkamm, *Die Staatsidee im Kulturkampf*, p. 9.
30. Bussmann, *Das Zeitalter Bismarcks*, p. 158.
31. Ibid., pp. 166–67.
32. A. Constable, *Vorgeschichte des Kulturkampfes* (Berlin, 1956), passim.
33. Kent, *Arnim and Bismarck*, pp. 124, 127.
34. Bussmann, *Das Zeitalter Bismarcks*, p. 216.
35. Ibid., p. 215. Talks between the Prussian government and the papal nuncio started in July 1878.
36. Bornkamm, *Die Staatsidee im Kulturkampf*, pp. 65–71.
37. Ibid.
38. Bismarck had accused leaders of the SDP of high treason for opposing the annexation of Alsace-Lorraine and expressing sympathy with the Paris Commune.
39. V. Lidtke, *The Outlawed Party: Social Democracy in Germany, 1878–90* (Princeton, 1966), pp. 70 ff.
40. "Fear of the revolution, fear of losing economic status, fear of the future—these were the basic underlying presumptions of the election in the summer of 1878." (M. Stuermer, *Regierung und Reichstag im Bismarckstaat, 1871–1880* [Duesseldorf, 1974], p. 231.)
41. Lidtke, *The Outlawed Party*, p. 74.

42. Ibid., p. 78.
43. The following is based on M. Stuermer, "Staatsstreichgedanken im Bismarckreich," *Historische Zeitschrift* 209 (Dec. 1969), pp. 566–615, esp. 582 ff.
44. Ibid., p. 593, n. 66.
45. Ibid., p. 599, n. 77.
46. Ibid., p. 601.
47. This was primarily in the colonial sphere; see H. P. v. Strandmann, "Domestic Origins of Germany's Colonial Expansion under Bismarck," *Past and Present* 42 (Feb. 1969); and H. U. Wehler, "Bismarck's Imperialism, 1862–90," *Past and Present* 48 (Aug. 1970).
48. According to Steuermer, *Regierung und Reichstag im Bismarckstaat*, p. 291, the essence of the German constitutional problem during the empire revolved around the unresolved conflict between parliamentarianism and Caesarism. Bismarck used some aspects of the latter to undermine parliamentary representation, while at the same time appealing for popular plebiscites and threatening a coup d'état.
49. O. Vossler, "Bismarcks Ethos," *Historische Zeitschrift* 171 (Mar. 1951), p. 290.
50. H. J. Steinberg, "Socialismus,. Internationalismus und Reichsgruendung," in Schieder and Deuerlein, eds., *Reichsgruendung 1870/71*, pp. 319–44.
51. Quoted by H. U. Wehler, *Das Deutsche Kaiserreich, 1871–1918* (Goettingen, 1973), p. 136.
52. E. Eyck, *Bismarck*, 3: 368–75.
53. Lidtke, *The Outlawed Party*, p. 159.
54. Ibid., p. 160.
55. Ibid., pp. 74, 185.
56. Ibid., pp. 241–44.
57. Ibid., pp. 256–301.
58. Quoted by Stern, *The Failure of Illiberalism*, p. 13.
59. Ibid., p. 15.
60. F. K. Ringer, *The Decline of the German Mandarins: The German Academic Community, 1890–1933* (Cambridge, Mass., 1969), p. 121.
61. Ibid., p. 128.
62. Quoted by Stern, *Gold and Iron*, pp. 205–6.
63. Stuermer, *Regierung und Reichstag im Bismarckstaat*, pp. 296–308. For an interesting and stimulating article on the idea that Napoleon III and Guizot were models for Bismarck, see A. Mitchell, "Bonapartism as a Model for Bismarckian Politics" and subsequent comments by O. Pflanze, C. Fohlen, and M. Stuermer, in *Journal of Modern History* 49, no. 2 (June 1977): 181–209.
64. J. J. Sheehan, "Conflict and Cohesion among German Elites in the 19th Century," in Sheehan, ed., *Imperial Germany*, pp. 62–92; the quotation is on pp. 82–83.
65. Bussman, "Europa und das Bismarckreich," in Gall, ed., *Das Bismarck-Problem*, pp. 325–27.
66. F. Fischer, *Der Krieg der Illusionen* (Duesseldorf, 1969), p. 64.
67. E. Deuerlein, "Die Konfrontation von Nationalstaat und national bestimmter Kultur," in Schieder and Deuerlein, eds., *Reichsgruendung 1870/71*, pp. 226–58.
68. G. L. Mosse, *The Crisis of German Ideology* (New York, 1964); F. Stern, *The Politics of Cultural Despair* (Berkeley, Calif., 1961), passim.
69. D. Gasman, *The Scientific Origins of National Socialism* (New York, 1971), p. xxiii. See also H. G. Zmarzlik, "Social Darwinism in Germany, Seen as an Historical Problem" in H. Holborn, ed., *Republic to Reich* (New York, 1973), pp. 435.
70. Gasman, *The Scientific Origins of National Socialism*, passim.

71. P. Pulzer, *The Rise of Political Anti-Semitism in Germany and Austria* (New York, 1964), pp. 76–96.
72. See chap. 1.
73. M. Busch, *Tagebuchblaetter*, 3 vols. (Leipzig, 1902), 2:33.
74. Stern, *Gold and Iron*, p. 528. See also W. T. Angress, "Prussia's Army and the Jewish Reserve Officer Controversy before World War I," in Sheehan, ed., *Imperial Germany*, pp. 97–100.
75. Messerschmidt, "Die Armee in Staat und Gesellschaft—Die Bismarckzeit," pp. 102–7.
76. K. H. Hoefele, *Geist und Gesellschaft der Bismarckzeit, 1870–1890* (Goettingen, 1967), pp. 22 ff.

7. BISMARCK'S FOREIGN POLICY

1. F. Fischer, *Der Krieg der Illusionen*, chaps. 4–6 passim.
2. *GP* vol. 2, no. 294. This is known as the Kissingen Memorandum.
3. Mitchell, *Bismarck and the French Nation*, p. 74.
4. The appraisal of Bismarck's foreign policy, similar to that of his policy at home, has undergone considerable change since the publication of the *Grosse Politik* in the 1920s. W. L. Langer, in his *European Alliances and Alignments* (New York, 1931) believed that "no other statesman of his standing had ever before shown the same great moderation and sound political sense of the possible and the desirable" (pp. 503–4). Twenty-five years later, and after another world war, opinions were not quite as favorable. A. J. P. Taylor considers the chancellor's "'system' . . . something of a conjuring trick, a piece of conscious virtuosity. Once started on the path of alliances, Bismarck treated them as the solution for every problem." (*The Struggle for Mastery in Europe*, p. 278.) And W. N. Medlicott in *Bismarck, Gladstone and the Concert of Europe* (London, 1956), writes that "if Bismarck wanted peace, it was on his own terms; his philosophy of international life remained fundamentally combative and pessimistic, and he could discover no reliable basis for national survival other than the accumulation and manoeuvering of superior force. . . . Bismarck was singularly unconvincing as the great architect of peace: foreign states were mainly conscious of the aggressive potentialities of his diplomacy. . . . A considerable problem that faces the student of his later diplomacy is, indeed, to decide how far he was alarmed by nightmares of his own creation" (pp. 11, 12).

Beyond political and diplomatic considerations, there were attempts, especially after 1945, to look at Bismarck's foreign policy from wider perspectives. The dogma of the primacy of foreign policy expressed by Ranke in the first half of the nineteenth century and upheld by German historians well into the second half of the twentieth century, was challenged for the first time by E. Kehr in his *Schlachtflottenbau und Parteipolitik, 1894–1901* (Berlin, 1930). His innovative method of examining domestic problems and policies and their influence on foreign policy was not well received at the time, and his lead was not followed until after World War II. Since then such West German historians as Rosenberg, Boehme, and Wehler have linked economic and social conditions with foreign policy, while in East Germany, Jerusalimski, Wolters, Kumpf-Korfes, and Engelberg followed the tradition of Marxist historiography which has traditionally considered economic and social conditions as the basis of foreign policy. (H. Wolters, "Neue Aspekte in der Buergerlichen Historiographie der BRD zur Bismarckschen Aussenpolitik 1871 bis

1890," *Jahrbuch fuer Geschichte* 10 [1974], pp. 507–39, and G. G. Iggers, *New Directions in European Historiography* [Middletown, Conn., 1975], pp. 96–98.)

5. After Austria's defeat at Koeniggraetz in 1866, a new constitutional system was established and under the terms of the Compromise of 1867 Hungary was given a large measure of autonomy within the empire. Its official title from then until 1918 was the Austro-Hungarian Monarchy. Throughout this study the more convenient term, "Austria," will be used to describe the empire and its government.

6. A. J. P. Taylor, *Bismarck*, p. 143.

7. Kent, *Arnim and Bismarck*, pp. 117 ff.

8. Craig, *The Politics of the Prussian Army*, p. 275, n. 2.

9. E. Eyck, *Bismarck*, 3:160–61: For a recent treatment of the crisis, see Hillgruber, *Deutsche Grossmacht-und Weltpolitik* (Duesseldorf, 1977), pp. 35–52.

10. For Henri de Blowitz's role in this affair, see H. S. de Blowitz, *My Memoirs* (London, 1903), pp. 106 ff., and F. Giles, *A Prince of Journalists: The Life and Times of Henri Stefan Opper de Blowitz* (London, 1962), pp. 80 ff.

11. *GW*, 11:476.

12. N. Rich and M. H. Fisher, eds., *The Holstein Papers*, 4 vols. (London, 1955–63), 1:124.

13. "Pan Slavism was a poorly coordinated movement among the Slavic-speaking peoples of Europe (Great Russians, Byelorussians, Ukrainians, Lusatians, Poles, Czechs, Slovaks, Serbs, Croats, Slovenes, Macedonians, and Bulgarians), chiefly during the 19th century, in which they affirmed their cultural unity and sometimes expressed the desire for political union. Pan-Slavism was not Russian in origin. Nevertheless, it was widely regarded and feared in western Europe, usually without justification, as Russian instigated and directed, as a device to strengthen Russia's hand in international affairs and facilitate its expansion on the Continent." (J. Dunner, ed., *Handbook of World History* (New York, 1967), pp. 680–81.)

14. R. Wittram, "Bismarcks Russlandpolitik nach der Reichsgruendung," *Historische Zeitschrift* 186 (Dec. 1958), pp. 261–84.

15. Taylor, *The Struggle for Mastery in Europe*, p. 229.

16. The Russian inquiry of October 1, 1876, was a result of Wilhelm's letter to the czar, in which the German emperor expressed his appreciation for Russia's policy toward Prussia from 1864 to 1870–71. This attitude, Wilhelm wrote, "will determine my policy toward Russia whatever may come." (Quoted by Bussman, *Das Zeitalter Bismarcks*, p. 133; see also Wittram, "Bismarcks Russlandpolitik," pp. 269–70.)

17. M. S. Anderson, *The Eastern Question, 1774–1923* (New York, 1966), p. 193.

18. See W. N. Medlicott, *The Congress of Berlin and After* (London, 1938), pp. 10–13.

19. Ibid., chaps. 2 and 3. Why Berlin was chosen and who suggested this site are not quite clear. It seems that Andrassy proposed Vienna at the end of January 1878 and, when Russia objected, suggested Brussels or Baden-Baden. According to another version it was Bismarck who suggested Vienna, and Andrassy, Berlin; Gorchakov, too, apparently suggested Berlin. The choice of Berlin was, without a doubt, a concession to Russia to induce her to participate in the Congress, and Gorchakov appreciated this gesture. (A. Novotny, *Quellen und Studien zur Geschichte des Berliner Kongresses 1878* [Graz, 1957], 1:51–52.)

20. E. Eyck, *Bismarck*, 3:253; see, however, Medlicott, *The Congress of Berlin and After*, p. 22, "Bismarck played an essentially negative part during this crisis in Russia's fortunes, and if Russia had no right to claim his support, she also had no reason to be grateful for his friendship."

21. E. Eyck, *Bismarck*, 3:267. Bismarck's support for Britain was in recognition of the close cooperation between Andrassy and Disraeli and the existing agreements be-

tween Russia and Austria. His aim was to avoid a general war but to keep the Balkan question open so that Germany, by holding back, would profit from it. (Hillgruber, *Bismarcks Aussenpolitik*, p. 152.)

22. Various explanations for the Dual Alliance with Austria have been offered by historians. The old school, as represented by Erich Brandenburg, saw it as a simple and straightforward foreign policy matter: Bismarck concluded the alliance as a defensive measure against a threatening Russian attack, though he did not intend to make Russia a permanent enemy. (*Von Bismarck zum Weltkrieg*, 2d ed. [Berlin, 1924], p. 11.) A similar point is made by W. Windelband, *Bismarck und die europaeischen Grossmaechte, 1879–1885* (Essen, 1942) who, on the basis of much new and hitherto unpublished material, concluded that Bismarck was forced to look to Austria because of the greatly increased size of the Russian army and the possibility that Russia might join an anti-German coalition (p. 54).

A. J. P. Taylor cites more complicated causes in his masterful and provocative study on nineteenth-century European diplomacy. Bismarck, according to Taylor, would have preferred to recreate the Holy Alliance, but Austrian suspicion of Russia prevented it; he was more afraid of Austria's restlessness than Russia's aggression and one way to control Austria was to conclude an alliance with her. It "was a sop to the liberals whom he was deserting in home affairs. Though he did not give them 'greater Germany,' he gave them a union of the two German powers, based on national sentiment." (*The Struggle for Mastery in Europe*, p. 259.) Walter Bussman, in *Das Zeitalter Bismarcks*, believes the alliance embodies the concept of *Mitteleuropa*. The possible threat of an Austro-French-Russian alliance, the old Kaunitz coalition of the Seven Years' War, compelled Bismarck to form the Dual Alliance (pp. 140–41). In A. Hillgruber's opinion, Bismarck concluded the alliance at the very moment when Russia was approaching Germany to reestablish friendly relations, and the purpose of the alliance with Austria was to hasten the formalization of the good relationship with Russia (*Bismarcks Aussenpolitik*, p. 156). The most recent and detailed treatment of the Dual Alliance is presented by B. Waller, *Bismarck at the Crossroads* (London, 1974). Waller believes that a personal feud between Bismarck and Gorchakov, combined with the Rumanian question, made a German alliance with Austria desirable (chaps. 4, 7–9).

23. Waller, *Bismarck at the Crossroads*, pp. 102–5.

24. Ibid., pp. 135–44.

25. Stern, *Gold and Iron*, pp. 351 ff.

26. For example, at the Congress of Berlin, Bismarck encouraged French ambitions in Tunisia, which would simultaneously embroil her with Italy, distract her from Alsace-Lorraine, and preoccupy her in case of Russo-German difficulties in Europe. Another example was Bismarck's backing of Britain in Egypt, designed to involve Britain with France and, at the same time, make Britain dependent on Bismarck's good will and assistance. Both cases illustrate Bismarck's thinking as outlined in the Kissingen Memorandum.

27. An ill-tempered letter by Alexander to Wilhelm of August 15, 1879, complaining about the deterioration of Russo-German relations and foreseeing disastrous consequences, did not change Bismarck's decision, but was used by him to persuade the emperor that an alliance with Austria was necessary. Bismarck also used the announcement of Andrassy's pending resignation to convince Wilhelm that under Andrassy's successor Austria might change her policy and turn toward Russia. (Waller, *Bismarck at the Crossroads*, pp. 183 ff.; Hillgruber, *Bismarcks Aussenpolitik*, pp. 155 ff.; Bussmann, *Das Zeitalter Bismarcks*, pp. 139 ff.)

28. It was a defensive treaty directed against Russia, providing for the partners to

come to each other's aid if one or the other were attacked by Russia. It contained no similar provision for an attack by France. In that or any other instance, the party not directly involved would remain neutral.

29. Taylor, *The Struggle for Mastery in Europe*, p. 261. For Bismarck's struggle with the emperor, see Waller, *Bismarck at the Crossroads*, p. 192 and n. 40.

30. *GP*, vol. 4, pp. 7 ff.

31. Taylor, *The Struggle for Mastery in Europe*, pp. 267–69.

32. Ibid., pp. 270–71.

33. General Skobelev, a hero of the Russo-Turkish war and a Pan-Slavist, went on a mission to Paris in January 1882 and made several belligerent speeches which were well received by French nationalists but had no visible effects on either French or Russian policies. (Taylor, *The Struggle for Mastery in Europe*, pp. 272–76.)

34. Hillgruber, *Bismarcks Aussenpolitik*, p. 161.

35. See, in this connection, Hallgarten, *Imperialismus vor 1914*, 1:227 ff.

36. Medlicott, *Bismarck, Gladstone and the Concert of Europe*, pp. 335–36.

37. There was an Anglo-Russian crisis over Afghanistan from March 1885 to June 1886.

38. For the views of the pro-German and pro-French factions within the Russian government and at the Russian court, see S. Kumpf-Korfes, *Bismarcks "Draht nach Russland"* (Berlin, 1968), pp. 77 ff.

39. Gall, ed., *Das Bismarck-Problem*, p. 40; the first two quotations are in Wittram, "Bismarcks Russlandpolitik," pp. 261–84. For a defense of the Reinsurance Treaty, see H. Krausnick, "Rueckversicherungsvertrag und Optionsproblem 1887–90," in M. Goehring and A. Scharff, eds., *Geschichtliche Kraefte und Entscheidungen: Festschrift fuer Otto Becker* (Wiesbaden, 1954), pp. 210–32.

40. It has been suggested that Bismarck, not Giers, inserted the Straits clause, and there are some indications that Bismarck favored Russian aspirations toward the Straits. The possibility that Bismarck wanted Russia to embroil herself in a drive toward Constantinople is expressed in a letter of May 3, 1888, to Prince Reuss, German ambassador in Vienna, and in another one of May 9, 1888, to the crown prince. In the former, Bismarck expressed the belief that Germany could hasten Russia's disintegration by encouraging her to get involved in the "oriental [that is, Balkan] dead end street." To the latter he wrote that the secret treaty (the Reinsurance Treaty) guaranteed that Russia would in the future be trapped in the cul-de-sac of Constantinople, as she would already have been but for German restraint of Austria. (Wittram, "Bismarcks Russlandpolitik," p. 278, n. 1.)

41. For the following, I rely on H. U. Wehler, "Bismarcks spaete Russlandpolitik 1879–90," in Wehler, ed., *Krisenherde des Kaiserreichs, 1871–1918*, pp. 163–80, based on an exhaustive and exhausting source collection, and on Kumpf-Korfes, *Bismarcks "Draht nach Russland."*

42. Kumpf-Korfes, *Bismarcks "Draht nach Russland,"* p. 162.

43. W. L. Langer, *The Diplomacy of Imperialism*, 2d ed. (New York, 1951), chap. 1 passim.

44. Craig, *The Politics of the Prussian Army*, p. 268.

45. Kumpf-Korfes, *Bismarcks "Draht nach Russland,"* pp. 115 ff.

46. Wehler, *Krisenherde des Kaiserreichs, 1871–1918*, p. 176.

47. Ibid., p. 178. See also Stern, *Gold and Iron*, pp. 440–50.

48. Wehler, *Krisenherde des Kaiserreichs, 1871–1918*, pp. 179–80, esp. n. 44. I do not believe, as Wehler does, that Bismarck's action set Germany on her fatal course. Bismarck may indeed have pointed German policy in this direction, but his successors chose to reinforce, rather than reverse, this trend.

49. Quoted by G. W. F. Hallgarten, "War Bismarck ein Imperialist?" *Geschichte in Wissenschaft und Unterricht* (May 1971), p. 262.
50. Rich and Fisher, eds., *The Holstein Papers*, 2:138.
51. Strandmann, "Domestic Origins of Germany's Colonial Expansion under Bismarck," p. 149, n. 36; *GW*, 13:383.
52. Wehler, "Bismarck's Imperialism, 1862–90," p. 129, n. 17.
53. Ibid., p. 129, n. 18. The argument whether Bismarck was or was not an imperialist has aroused much interest among historians. (For one of the more recent exchanges, see the Hallgarten-Wehler articles listed in the Bibliographical Essay.) In A. J. P. Taylor's view, Bismarck used the colonial issue in 1884 for his own ends. "If it is absurd to suppose that Bismarck allowed a few colonial enthusiasts to divert and injure his foreign policy, it is even more absurd to believe that Bismarck, who refused to condone German ambitions in Europe, himself succumbed to ambitions overseas." (*The Struggle for Mastery in Europe*, pp. 293–94.) According to K. Buettner, *Die Anfaenge der deutschen Kolonialpolitik in Ostafrika* (Berlin, 1959), however, Bismarck's initial opposition to and later enthusiasm for colonies was entirely in the spirit of the period. His opposition in 1868 was in line with the prevailing mood of laissez faire and his later conversion to colonies followed the changing trends of business and commercial interests. Bismarck had no blueprint for acquiring colonies, and until the 1880s the German flag followed German trade. The attitude toward colonies was but an expression of domestic political struggles and, as a practical politician, Bismarck changed his views around 1885 (pp. 23–25).

   G. W. F. Hallgarten in *Imperialismus vor 1914* believes that it was von Kusserow, an official in the German Foreign Office, who established the major lines of German colonial policy and persuaded a reluctant Bismarck to follow them (1:206–22). H. U. Wehler, in "Bismarck's Imperialism 1862–90," in Wehler, ed., *Krisenherde des Kaiserreichs, 1871–1918*, pp. 113–34, considers Bismarck's imperialism the result of an insolvable tension at home. According to Wehler, there was no break in Bismarck's views in 1884–86; he still believed that an informal empire was preferable to state-directed colonial administration. Bismarck was a pragmatic imperialist, not motivated by prestige, a German mission, or world power. He believed that colonies would assure safe and secure economic growth and preserve the existing social hierarchy and political structure. To alleviate the effects of the economic crisis in the fall of 1882, the government had little choice but to accelerate overseas expansion, which it did by providing subsidies for exports and steamship lines, and by promoting new trade agreements. The end of free trade policies by other nations and increased commercial competition made direct state intervention inevitable. There was also a feeling in German government circles and among the business community that the international race for colonies was just about over, and if Germany did not act quickly, she would be too late. To Bismarck, colonies were a means to assist German export trade and thus the German economy. He also used colonial policies for election purposes, to cover up serious social and political tensions, to strengthen his Bonapartist-dictatorial power position, and to enhance the dwindling popularity and prestige of the government. See also P. M. Kennedy, "German Colonal Expansion," *Past and Present* 54 (Feb. 1972), pp. 134–41, and K. J. Bade, *Friedrich Fabri und der Imperialismus in der Bismarckzeit: Revolution-Depression-Expansion* (Zuerich, 1975), passim.
54. P. M. Kennedy, *The Samoan Tangle: A Study in Anglo-German-American Relations, 1878–1900* (New York, 1973), passim.
55. For an interesting study of the development of business and industrial organizations

in Germany, and their relationship to the government and their attitude toward colonies, see W. Fischer, *Wirtschaft und Gesellschaft im Zeitalter der Industrialisierung* (Goettingen, 1972), especially p. 211.
56. Wehler, "Bismarck's Imperialism, 1862–90," p. 129, n. 18.
57. Hallgarten, "War Bismarck ein Imperialist?" p. 261.
58. Strandmann, "Domestic Origins of Germany's Colonial Expansion under Bismarck," p. 158, n. 74.
59. Bussmann, *Das Zeitalter Bismarcks*, pp. 148–51.

8. BISMARCK'S DISMISSAL

1. M. Balfour, *The Kaiser and His Times* (New York, 1972), pp. 139–40; Craig, *The Politics of the Prussian Army*, p. 239.
2. Quoted by Bussman, *Das Zeitalter Bismarcks*, p. 236.
3. The following is based on J. C. G. Roehl, "The Disintegration of the Kartell and the Politics of Bismarck's Fall from Power 1887–89," *Historical Journal* 9 (1966), pp. 60–89; and by the same author, "Staatsstreichplan oder Staatsstreichbereitschaft? Bismarcks Politik in der Entlassungskrise," *Historische Zeitschrift* 203 (Dec. 1966), pp. 610–24.
4. One of the earliest books on the dismissal crisis, P. Liman, *Fuerst Bismarck und seine Entlassung* (Berlin, 1904), gives a most adulatory account of the chancellor and his policies and blames Bismarck's dismissal on the difference in age and temperament between the emperor and the chancellor. The book is based primarily on Bismarck's memoirs and is only mildly critical of Wilhelm II. Liman blames the crisis on bureaucratic and court intrigues.

G. Freiherr von Eppstein, *Fuerst Bismarcks Entlassung* (Berlin, 1920), using the private posthumous papers of the former minister of state and state secretary of the interior, Boetticher, and the former chief of the Reich Chancellery, Rottenburg, believes that the clash between youth impatiently forging ahead and cautious old age accounts for Bismarck's removal, but he discounts intrigue as a factor. Boetticher, one of Bismarck's closest collaborators during the chancellor's last ten years in office, was suspected and accused by Bismarck of having intrigued against him. Boetticher denied these accusations in his papers and, in turn, accused Herbert Bismarck, the chancellor's oldest son, of having created bad blood between the emperor, the chancellor, and himself.

The first comprehensive account of the dismissal crisis is by W. Schuessler, *Bismarcks Sturz* (Berlin, 1922). It presents the chancellor's fall partly in terms of a morality play: "Who can doubt that our calamities started at that time? . . . [It was] a tragedy because the hero—guilty or innocent—was the victim of his fate which was partly created by himself, partly by the Gods . . . but all this, the many misunderstandings, the loneliness of the genius, the passing of an age, and the struggle for power, cannot absolve Wilhelm II who was found guilty before history: the day of judgment was November 9, 1918" (pp. vii–viii).

Schuessler's account, written in a time of humiliation and distress, was also meant to remind his countrymen of their great past. In this context he saw the conflict between the emperor and the chancellor essentially as a struggle for power (p. 185).

Wilhelm Mommsen, *Bismarcks Sturz und die Parteien* (Berlin, 1924), looks at the problem from the point of view of the political parties. Had the parties supported Bismarck, Wilhelm II would not have dared to let him go. None of the chancellor's opponents, according to Mommsen, would have been able to justify his dismissal and in the end his fall was due to the combined pressure of various personal interests and demands (pp. 7–9). The petty and self-serving policies of party hacks and politicians, some of whom (like Miquel) saw the dangers ahead but were afraid to mention them and followed the rest, reassured the emperor of his rightness in this matter and thus made future criticism of his policies extremely difficult. The politicians' lack of responsibility and courage made them at least partially responsible for Germany's future fate (pp. 155–59).

Egmont Zechlin, *Staatsstreichplaene Bismarcks und Wilhelm II, 1890–1894* (Stuttgart, 1929) concentrates on Bismarck's plan for a coup d'etat as outlined in the state council's meeting of March 2, 1890. According to the protocol of this meeting, Bismarck intended to have the German princes and representatives of the Free Cities who had signed the federal treaty establishing the Reich revoke the treaty and establish a new constitution for the Reich if the parliamentary elections continued to turn out badly for the government. The chancellor also intended to neutralize the Reichstag by refusing to nominate federal members (*Bundesratsmitglieder*) to attend its sessions (p. 47). Zechlin considers Bismarck's fall the result of the conflict between chancellor and Reichstag, a conflict which Bismarck saw as inevitable. Bismarck hoped to eliminate the Reichstag, or at least the Social Democrats, in this conflict. The emperor, however, decided finally to postpone or avoid such a conflict with the Reichstag.

5. Roehl, "Staatsstreichplaene," p. 610, n. 1.
6. For the text of this directive, see Roehl, "Staasstreichplaene," pp. 623–24.
7. Bismarck's willingness to use the threat of coup d'état throughout his term of office is persuasively presented by Stuermer, "Staatsstreichgedanken im Bismarckreich," pp. 566–615.
8. Bussmann, *Das Zeitalter Bismarcks*, p. 244.
9. Balfour, *The Kaiser and His Times*, p. 132.
10. A critical, up-to-date edition of the *Reflections and Reminiscences* can be found in the *Gesammelten Werke*, vol. 15.
11. *Goetz von Berlichingen*, one of Goethe's earliest and best known dramas, deals with Goetz, the freedom-loving, independent knight during the Peasant Wars who, though disrespectful of laws and lesser men, remained loyal to the emperor.

Bibliographical Essay

This essay deals primarily with books and articles published after 1945; those in English appear first, followed by those in German.

The literature on Bismarck and the unification of Germany is continuously expanding and there seems to be no end in sight. On Bismarck alone, a listing published several years ago mentioned over six thousand items (Karl E. Born, *Bismarck Bibliographie* [Cologne, 1966]).

In English the foremost biography is O. Pflanze, *Bismarck and the Development of Germany* (Princeton, 1963–), but only the first volume covering the period 1815–71 has been published to date. Shorter biographies include: A. J. P. Taylor, *Bismarck: The Man and the Statesman* (New York, 1955), a provocative and stimulating study; W. N. Medlicott, *Bismarck and Modern Germany* (Mystic, Conn., 1965), a concise, well-informed account; E. Eyck, *Bismarck and the German Empire* (London, 1950), a condensed translation of his three-volume work (see below); W. M. Simon, *Germany in the Age of Bismarck* (New York, 1968), an introductory essay with a documentary section; and C. Sempell, *Otto von Bismarck* (New York, 1972), which concentrates on the chancellor's personality.

The economic, intellectual, and social aspects of the period prior to unification are covered by the excellent volumes of T. S. Hamerow: *Restoration, Revolution, Reaction: Economics and Politics in Germany, 1815–1871* (Princeton, 1958); *The Social Foundations of German Unification, 1858–1871*, vol. 1, *Ideas and Institutions* (Princeton, 1969), vol. 2, *Struggles and Accomplishments* (Princeton, 1972).

On the Customs Union, A. Price, *The Evolution of the Zollverein* (Ann Arbor, 1949) deals with ideas and institutions between 1815 and 1833 and supplements W. O. Henderson, *The Zollverein* (Chicago, 1939). I. N. Lambi, *Free Trade and Protection in Germany, 1868–1879* (Wiesbaden, 1963), is a reexamination of Bismarck's tariff policy and its consequences, and H. Rosenberg, "Political and Social Consequences of the Great Depression of 1873–96 in Central Europe," *Economic History Review* 12 (1943), is an excellent survey of a hitherto much neglected subject. Frank B. Tipton, "The National Consensus in German Economic History," *Central European History* 7 (Sept. 1974), pp. 195–224, points out the lack of agreement on industrial and economic development in nineteenth-century Germany. This is further developed in his study *Regional Variations in the Economic Development of Germany During the Nineteenth Century* (Middletown, Conn., 1976). Three review articles are of more than passing interest: Klaus Epstein, "The Socio-Economic History of the Second German Empire," *Review of Politics* 29 (1967), deals with E. Kehr's *Der Primat der Innenpolitik* (Berlin, 1965) and H. Boehme's *Deutschlands Weg zur Grossmacht* (Cologne, 1966); O. Pflanze, "Another Crisis among German Historians? Helmut Boehme's *Deutschlands Weg zur Grossmacht*: A Review Article," *Journal of Modern History* 40 (1968); and J. F. Harris, "Social-Economic Analysis and the Bismarckzeit," *Maryland Historian* 2 (Fall 1971), which reviews Boehme, H. Rosenberg's *Grosse Depression und Bismarckzeit* (Berlin, 1967), and T. S. Hamerow's *The Social Foundations of German Unification*, vol. 1.

There is no recent, comprehensive study of Bismarck's foreign policy in English. Special studies are: W. E. Mosse, *The European Powers and the German Question, 1848–1871* (Cambridge, 1958); Richard Millman, *British Foreign Policy and the Coming of the Franco-Prussian War* (Oxford, 1965); R. I. Giesberg, *The Treaty of Frankfort: A Study in Diplomatic History, September 1870–September 1873* (Philadelphia, 1966); G. O. Kent, *Arnim and Bismarck* (Oxford, 1968); A. Mitchell, *Bismarck and the French Nation, 1848–1890* (New York, 1971); W. N. Medlicott, *The Congress of Berlin and After* (London, 1938), and *Bismarck, Gladstone, and the Concert of Europe* (London, 1956); B. Waller, *Bismarck at the Crossroads: The Reorientation of German Foreign Policy after the Congress of Berlin, 1878–1880* (London, 1974); E. A. Pottinger, *Napoleon III and the German Crisis, 1865–1866* (Cambridge, Mass., 1966); G. Bonnin, ed., *Bismarck and the Hohenzollern Candidature for the Spanish Throne: The Documents in the German Diplomatic Archives* (London, 1957); L. D. Steefel, *Bismarck, the Hohenzollern Candidacy and the Origins of the Franco-German War of 1870* (Cambridge, Mass., 1962); and his *The Schleswig-Holstein Question* (Cambridge, Mass., 1932), and K. A. P. Sandiford, *Great Britain and the Schleswig-Holstein Question, 1848–1864* (Toronto, 1975); L. Cecil, *The German Diplomatic Service, 1871–1914* (Princeton, 1976).

There are some articles on Bismarck's foreign policy that should be mentioned. W. L. Langer, "Bismarck as a Dramatist," in A. O. Sarkissian, ed., *Studies in Diplomatic History and Historiography in Honour of G. P. Gooch* (New York, 1962), is a gem on Bismarck and the Ems dispatch. O. Pflanze, "Bismarck's Realpolitik," *The Review of Politics* 20 (1958), and H. Holborn, "Bismarck's Realpolitik," *Journal of the History of Ideas* 21 (1960), are the best treatments of a difficult subject. R. H. Lord, "Bismarck and Russia in 1863," *American Historical Review* 29 (Oct. 1923), evaluates the Alvensleben

BIBLIOGRAPHICAL ESSAY

Convention on the basis of Russian documents. G. A. Kertesz, "Reflections on a Centenary: The Austro-Prussian War of 1866," *Historical Studies of Australia and New Zealand* (1966), is well written and includes some interesting material. S. W. Halperin, "The Origins of the Franco-Prussian War Revisited: Bismarck and the Hohenzollern Candidature for the Spanish Throne," *Journal of Modern History* 45 (1973), is a critical review of E. Kolb, *Der Kriegsausbruch 1870* (see below). On Bismarck's colonial policies, H. P. v. Strandmann, "Domestic Origins of Germany's Colonial Expansion under Bismarck," *Past and Present* 42 (1969), and H. U. Wehler, "Bismarck's Imperialism 1862–90," *Past and Present* 48 (1970), are the most recent contributions. A good collection of essays appears in P. Gifford and W. R. Louis, eds., *Britain and Germany in Africa* (New Haven, 1967). Also of considerable interest are P. M. Kennedy, "German Colonial Expansion," *Past and Present* 54 (1972), and by the same author, *The Samoan Tangle: A Study in Anglo-German-American Relations, 1878–1900* (New York, 1973). H. D. Andrews, "Bismarck's Foreign Policy and German Historiography 1919–1945," *Journal of Modern History* 37 (1965), is a useful survey. G. Ritter, *The Sword and the Scepter: The Problem of Militarism in Germany*, 4 vols. (Coral Gables, Fla., 1969–73) covers the Bismarckian period in the first volume in a traditional and conservative nationalistic manner.

There are a great number of studies on Bismarck's domestic policies; some of the more noteworthy are the following: F. Stern, *Gold and Iron: Bismarck, Bleichröder, and the Building of the German Empire* (New York, 1977); F. Stern, "Money, Morals, and the Pillars of Bismarck's Society," *Central European History* 3 (1970); H. Boehme, "Big-Business Pressure Groups and Bismarck's Turn to Protectionism 1873–79," *Historical Journal* 2 (1967); A. Dorpalen, "The German Historians and Bismarck," *Review of Politics* 11 (1953); H. A. Kissinger, "The White Revolutionary: Reflections on Bismarck," *Daedalus* (Summer 1968); V. L. Lidtke, "German Social Democracy and German State Socialism 1876–84," *International Review of Social History* 9 (1964). On anti-Semitism, P. Pulzer, *The Rise of Political Anti-Semitism in Germany and Austria* (New York, 1964), is the best study. There are a number of interesting essays on Jewish life in Germany during the nineteenth century in the recent volumes of the Leo Baeck Institute; one of the more noteworthy is M. A. Mayer, "The Great Debate on Anti-Semitism: Jewish Reaction to New Hostility in Germany, 1879–81," *Leo Baeck Institute Yearbook* 9 (1966). G. R. Mork, "Bismarck and the 'Capitulation' of German Liberalism," *Journal of Modern History* 43 (1971); J. L. Snell and H. A. Schmitt, *The Democratic Movement in Germany, 1789–1914* (Chapel Hill, N.C., 1976); O. Pflanze, "Juridical and Political Responsibility in 19th Century Germany," in L. Krieger and F. Stern, eds., *The Responsibility of Power* (Garden City, N.Y., 1967); O. Pflanze, "Bismarck and German Nationalism," *American Historical Review* 60 (1955); H. Pross, "Reflections on German

BIBLIOGRAPHICAL ESSAY

Nationalism, 1866–1966," *Orbis* (Winter 1967); S. A. Stehlin, "Bismarck and the New Province of Hanover," *Canadian Journal of History* 4 (1969); A. Vagts, "Bismarck's Fortune," *Central European History* 1 (1968); F. Nova, "The Motivations in Bismarck's *Kulturkampf*," *Dusquesne Review* 1 (1965); F. B. M. Hollyday, *Bismarck's Rival: A Political Biography of General and Admiral Albrecht von Stosch* (Durham, N.C., 1960); V. Lidtke, *The Outlawed Party: Social Democracy in Germany, 1878–1890* (Princeton, 1966); and J. C. G. Roehl, "The Disintegration of the Kartell and the Politics of Bismarck's Fall from Power, 1887–90," *Historical Journal* 9 (1966). For an excellent essay on the effects of the Bismarck legend, see M. Stuermer, "Bismarck in Perspective," *Central European History* 4 (Dec. 1971), pp. 291–331, and the follow-up comments by Hans A. Schmitt and M. Stuermer, ibid. 6 (Dec. 1973), pp. 363–72. A good and readable account of Wilhelm II is M. Balfour, *The Kaiser and His Times* (Boston, 1964).

J. J. Sheehan, ed., *Imperial Germany* (New York, 1976), is a useful and interesting collection of essays on German domestic and foreign policy. D. S. White, *The Splintered Party: National Liberalism in Hessen and the Reich, 1867–1918* (Cambridge, Mass., 1976), and D. P. Silverman, *Reluctant Union: Alsace-Lorraine and Imperial Germany, 1871–1918* (University Park, Pa., 1972), are notable studies on much-neglected topics. G. Craig, *The Politics of the Prussian Army, 1640–1945* (Oxford, 1955), is still the standard work on the subject.

Of biographies and collections of personal papers of major figures of the Bismarck era, only the one on Holstein has been published in English. N. Rich and M. H. Fisher, eds., *The Holstein Papers*, 4 vols. (Cambridge, 1955–63), and N. Rich, *Friedrich von Holstein*, 2 vols. (Cambridge, 1965).

In German a study of Bismarck should start with his writings, *Bismarck: Die Gesammelten Werke*, 15 vols. (Berlin, 1924–35). Edited by the foremost scholars of the period (Gerhard Ritter, H. v. Petersdorff, F. Thimme, W. Andreas, W. Schuessler, and others), the work is not complete. Many of the chancellor's letters and directives on foreign policy before 1871 are in *Die auswaertige Politik Preussens, 1858–1871*, 10 vols. (Munich, 1932–45); after 1871, they are to be found in the first six volumes of *Die Grosse Politik der Europaeischen Kabinette*, 40 vols. (Berlin, 1922–27). This collection, too, is incomplete. His speeches are in H. Kohl, ed., *Bismarcks Reden*, 14 vols. (Berlin, 1892–95), and there are many published collections of his letters. A small part of the unpublished material has been microfilmed. (For a listing of these films and their locations, see *A Catalogue of Files and Microfilms of the German Foreign Ministry Archives, 1867–1920* [Oxford, 1959].) A good factual account of Bismarck's chancellorship is W. Bussman, *Das Zeitalter Bismarcks* (Frankfurt, 1968); this should be supplemented with H. U. Wehler, *Das deutsche Kaiserreich, 1871–1918* (Goettingen, 1973).

There is an extensive memoir literature by Bismarck's contemporaries (for a

BIBLIOGRAPHICAL ESSAY

listing, see Born's bibliography); one of the more interesting memoirs is *Das Tagebuch der Baronin Spitzemberg*, edited by R. Vierhaus (Goettingen, 1960). Of private paper collections (*Nachlaesse*), the ones of E. L. von Gerlach, Grand Duke Frederick I of Baden, and P. Eulenburg, are the most important: H. Diwald, ed., *Von der Revolution zum Norddeutschen Bund. Aus dem Nachlass von Ernst Ludwig von Gerlach*, 2 vols. (Goettingen, 1970); W. P. Fuchs, ed., *Grossherzog Friedrich I von Baden und die Reichspolitik, 1871–1907*, 3 vols. (Stuttgart, 1968–); and J. C. G. Roehl, ed., *Philipp von Eulenburgs Politische Korrespondenz* (Boppard, 1976), the first of a three-volume work.

Of the many major biographies those of E. Eyck, *Bismarck: Leben und Werk*, 3 vols. (Zuerich, 1941–44), and A. O. Meyer, *Bismarck: Der Mensch and der Staatsmann* (Stuttgart, 1949), present two opposing views. The former presents a liberal interpretation, while the latter reflects the traditional, conservative-national approach. The two works appeared almost simultaneously in the early post–World War II period and triggered a spirited debate among German historians. Some of the more important contributions to this debate are: F. Schnabel, "Das Problem Bismarck," *Hochland* 42 (1949); H. Rothfels, "Probleme einer Bismarck Biographie," *Deutsche Beitraege* 2 (1948); G. Ritter, "Das Bismarckproblem," *Merkur* 4 (1950); H. v. Srbik, "Die Bismarck-Kontroverse: Zur Revision des deutschen Geschichtsbildes," *Wort und Wahrheit* 5 (1950); W. Bussman, "Wandel und Kontinuitaet der Bismarck Wertung," *Welt als Geschichte* 15 (1955); and M. v. Hagen, "Das Bismarckbild der Gegenwart," *Zeitschrift fuer Politik*, n.s. 6 (1959). Some of these essays are printed in L. Gall, ed., *Das Bismarck-Problem in der Geschichtsschreibung nach 1945* (Cologne, 1971).

On Bismarck's early period, E. Marcks, *Bismarcks Jugend, 1815–1848* (Stuttgart, 1915), is still the best, and K. Groos, *Bismarck im eigenen Urtel: Psychologische Studien* (Stuttgart, 1920), is a valuable contribution. Bismarck's views and activities during the 1848 Revolution are well described by G. A. Rein, "Bismarcks gegenrevolutionaere Aktion in den Maerztagen 1848," *Welt als Geschichte* 13 (1953). An indispensable source for contemporary literature on the unification is K. G. Faber, *Die nationalpolitische Publizistik Deutschlands von 1866 bis 1871: Eine kritische Bibliographie*, 2 vols. (Duesseldorf, 1963), which is a continuation of Hans Rosenberg, *Die nationalpolitische Publizistik Deutschlands vom Eintritt der Neuen Aera in Preussen bis zum Ausbruch des Deutschen Krieges* (Munich, 1935).

The centenary of the founding of the German Reich has produced a large number of articles and essays; some of these are printed in: T. Schieder and E. Deuerlein, eds., *Reichsgruendung, 1870/71: Tatsachen, Kontroversen, Interpretationen* (Stuttgart, 1970); W. Hofer, ed., *Europa und die Einheit Deutschlands: Eine Bilanz nach 100 Jahren* (Cologne, 1970); H. Boehme, ed., *Probleme der Reichsgruendungszeit, 1848–1879* (Koeln, 1968); M. Stuermer,

BIBLIOGRAPHICAL ESSAY

ed., *Das kaiserliche Deutschland: Politik und Gesellschaft, 1870–1918* (Duesseldorf, 1970); H. Bartel and E. Engelberg, eds., *Die grosspreussisch-militaerische Reichsgruendung 1871*, 2 vols. (Berlin [East], 1971).

O. Becker, *Bismarcks Ringen um Deutschlands Gestaltung* (Heidelberg, 1958), is a detailed and thorough study of political and constitutional developments from the Revolution of 1848 to the unification. H. Boehme, *Deutschlands Weg zur Grossmacht: Studien zum Verhaeltnis von Wirtschaft und Staat waehrend der Reichsgruendungszeit* (Cologne, 1966), is a similar treatment of economic policies and their impact on the unification from 1848 to 1878. The most comprehensive work on German constitutional history is E. R. Huber, *Deutsche Verfassungsgeschichte seit 1789*, 4 vols. (Stuttgart, 1957–69). (See, however, R. Dietrich's criticism of Huber's work in his "Das Reich, Preussen und die Einzelstaaten bis zur Entlassung Bismarcks," in D. Kurze, ed., *Aus Theorie und Praxis der Geschichtswissenschaft: Festschrift fuer Hans Herzfeld* [Berlin, 1972], pp. 236–56, especially p. 242, fn. 6, and pp. 246–47.) E. W. Boeckenfoerde, ed., *Moderne Deutsche Verfassungsgeschichte, 1815–1918*, (Cologne, 1972) is a collection of essays; of particular interest for the Bismarck period is T. S. Hamerow, "Die Wahlen zum Frankfurter Parlament," pp. 215–36; K. Griewank, "Ursachen und Folgen des Scheiterns der deutschen Revolution von 1848," pp. 40–62; and H. O. Meisner, "Bundesrat, Bundeskanzler, und Bundeskanzleramt (1867–71)," pp. 76–94. K. H. Hoefele, *Geist und Gesellschaft der Bismarckzeit, 1870–1890* (Goettingen, 1967), presents a good selection of interesting readings of the period.

One of the best historiographical essays on the German unification is E. Fehrenbach, "Die Reichsgruendung in der deutschen Geschichtsschreibung," in the Schieder and Deuerlein collection. Other noteworthy articles on the unification are L. Gall, "Staat und Wirtschaft in der Reichsgruendungszeit," *Historische Zeitschrift* 209 (1969), and W. Zorn, "Wirtschafts- und Sozialgeschichtliche Zusammenhaenge der deutschen Reichsgruendungszeit 1850–70," *Historische Zeitschrift* 197 (1963), which deal with the social and economic aspects. H. Bartel, "Die Reichseinigung in 1871 in Deutschland—ihre Geschichte und Folgen," *Zeitschrift fuer Geschichtswissenschaft* 16 (1968), is an East German appraisal, as is E. Engelberg, ed., *Im Widerstreit um die Reichsgruendung: Eine Quellensammlung zur Klassenauseinandersetzung in der deutschen Geschichte von 1849 bis 1871* (Berlin [East], 1970). G. Ritter, "Grossdeutsch und Kleindeutsch im 19. Jahrhundert," in W. Hubatsch, ed., *Schicksalswege deutscher Vergangenheit* (Duesseldorf, 1950), is a review of the greater and lesser German solutions leading toward unification.

The centenary of the Austro-Prussian War of 1866 also produced a number of interesting articles. H. J. Schoeps, "Der Frankfurter Fuerstentag und die oeffentliche Meinung in Preussen," *Geschichte in Wissenschaft und Unterricht* 19 (1968), and W. Real, "Oesterreich und Preussen im Vorfeld des Frankfurter Fuerstentages," *Historisches Jahrbuch* 2 (1966), deal with the meeting of the German princes at Frankfurt in August 1863. T. Schieder, W. Bussmann, H. Hantsch, "Entscheidungsjahr 1866," *Das Parlament* 24 (1966), and E. Deuerlein, W. Poels, "Entscheidungsjahr 1866," *Das Parlament* 25 (1966), discuss the significance of 1866 for German history. Also on this subject are: K. G. Faber, "Realpolitik als Ideologie: Die Bedeutung des Jahres 1866 fuer das politische Denken in Deutschland," *Historische Zeitschrift* 203 (1966); K. Bosl, "Die deutschen Mittelstaaten in der Entscheidung von 1866," *Zeitschrift fuer Bayerische Landesgeschichte* 3 (1966): and K. H. Hoefele, "Koeniggraetz und die Deutschen von 1866," *Geschichte in Wissenschaft und Unterricht* 17 (1966). H. A. Winkler, *Preussischer Liberalismus und deutscher Nationalstaat, 1861–1866* (Tuebingen, 1964), deals with the split among German liberals in the wake of the constitutional conflict and Prussia's victory over Austria, while M. Gugel, *Industrieller Aufstieg und buergerliche Herrschaft: Soziooekonomische Interessen und politische Ziele des liberalen Buergertums in Preussen zur Zeit des Verfassungskonflikts, 1857–1867*, (Cologne, 1975), examines the political aims and the social and economic interests of the liberal bourgeoisie in connection with the constitutional conflict.

On the Prussian-Italian alliance of 1866, its origins and subsequent relations, R. Lill has written three interesting pieces. "Die Vorgeschichte der preussisch-italienischen Allianz (1866)," *Quellen und Forschungen aus italienischen Archiven und Bibliotheken* 42–43 (1963); "Beobachtungen zur preussischitalienischen Allianz (1866)," ibid. 44 (1964); and "Die italienisch-deutschen Beziehungen 1869–76," ibid. 46 (1966).

The Hohenzollern candidature for the Spanish throne and the origins of the Franco-Prussian War of 1870 have attracted the interest of German historians, especially in view of newly discovered documents. J. Dittrich, "Ursachen und Ausbruch des deutsch-franzoesischen Krieges 1870/71," in Schieder and Deuerlein, eds., *Reichgruendung 1870/71* (Stuttgart, 1970), contains a good historiography of the origins of the war, while his larger, earlier study, *Bismarck, Frankreich und die spanische Thronkandidature der Hohenzollern: die "Kriegsschuldfrage" von 1870* (Munich, 1962), presents new documents from the Sigmaringen archives. J. Becker, "Zum Problem der Bismarckschen Politik in der Spanischen Thronfrage 1870," *Historische Zeitschrift* 212 (1971), is based on newly discovered material. E. Kolb, *Der Kriegsausbruch 1870: Politische Entscheidungsprozesse und Verantwortlichkeiten in der Julikrise 1870* (Goettingen, 1970), a defense of Bismarck, is critically reviewed by S. W. Halperin (*Journal of Modern History* 45 [1973]).

New interpretations and a lively exchange of opinions have arisen on the topic of the annexation of Alsace-Lorraine following the Franco-Prussian War: W. Lipgens, "Bismarck, die oeffentliche Meinung und die Annexion von Elsass und Lothringen 1870," *Historische Zeitschrift* 199 (1964); L. Gall, "Zur Frage der Annexion von Elsass und Lothringen 1870," *Historische Zeitschrift* 206 (1968); W. Lipgens, "Bismarck und die Frage der Annexion 1870: Eine Erwiderung," *Historische Zeitschrift* 206 (1968); and E. Kolb, "Bismarck und das Aufkommen der Annexionsforderung 1870," *Historische Zeitschrift* 209 (1969).

The most recent study of Bismarck's foreign policy is by A. Hillgruber, *Bismarcks Aussenpolitik* (Freiburg, 1972). A. S. Jerussalimski, *Bismarck: Diplomatie und Militaerismus* (Berlin [East], 1970) looks at the chancellor and his foreign policy from a Marxist point of view. A detailed criticism of the West German, bourgeois historiography of Bismarck's foreign policy is H. Wolter, "Neue Aspekte in der buergerlichen Historiographie der BDR zur Bismarckischen Aussenpolitik 1871 bis 1890," in *Jahrbuch fuer Geschichte* 10 (1974), pp. 507–39. A. Novotny, *Quellen und Studien zur Geschichte des Berliner Kongresses 1878*, vol. 1, *Oesterreich, die Tuerkei und das Balkanproblem im Jahre des Berliner Kongresses* (Graz and Cologne, 1957), presents a summary of documents and a useful historiographical account of the literature up to 1957. H. U. Wehler's interpretation of the chancellor's colonial policy, in *Bismarck und der Imperialismus* (Cologne, 1969), gave rise to a keen controversy. (See, in this connection, G. W. F. Hallgarten, "War Bismarck ein Imperialist? Die Aussenpolitik des Reichsgruenders im Licht der Gegenwart," *Geschichte in Wissenschaft und Unterricht* 22 [1971]; H. U. Wehler, "Noch einmal: Bismarcks Imperialismus. Eine Entgegnung auf G. W. F. Hallgarten," ibid. 23 [1972]; and G. W. F. Hallgarten, "Wehler, der Imperialismus und ich: Eine geharnischte Antwort," ibid. 23 [1972].) From the German Democratic Republic, K. Guettner, *Die Anfaenge der deutschen Kolonialpolitik in Ostafrika* (Berlin [East], 1959) presents new material from the Potsdam archives on the beginnings of German colonial policy in East Africa, and M. Nussbaum, *Vom "Kolonialenthusiasmus" zur Kolonialpolitik der Monopole* (Berlin [East], 1962), deals with colonial policies from Bismarck to Hohenlohe. K. J. Bade, *Friedrich Fabri und der Imperialismus in der Bismarckzeit: Revolution-Depression-Expansion* (Zuerich, 1975), focuses on the father of the German colonial movement who, for a time, became Bismarck's informal advisor.

More specialized studies of Bismarck's foreign policy are: F. Schnabel, "Bismarck und die klassische Diplomatie," *Aussenpolitik* 3 (1952); R. Wittram, "Bismarcks Russlandpolitik nach der Reichgruendung," *Historische Zeitschrift* 186 (1958); S. Kumpf-Korfes, *Bismarcks "Draht nach Russland": Zum Problem der sozial-oekonomischen Hintergruende der russischdeutschen Entfremdung im Zeitraum von 1878 bis 1891* (Berlin [East], 1968); H. Philippi, "Beitraege zur Geschichte der diplomatischen Beziehungen zwischen dem Deutschen Reich und dem Heiligen Stuhl 1872–1909," *Historisches Jahrbuch* 82 (1963); M. Winckler, "Der Ausbruch der 'Krieg-in-Sicht' Krise vom Fruehjahr 1875," *Zeitschrift fuer Ostforschung* 14 (1965); and M. Winckler, "Zur Entstehung und vom Sinn des Bismarckschen Buendnissystems," *Die Welt als Geschichte* 2 (1963).

BIBLIOGRAPHICAL ESSAY

On domestic policy, H. Rosenberg, *Grosse Depression und Bismarckzeit: Wirtschaftsablauf, Gesellschaft und Politik in Mitteleuropa* (Berlin, 1967), is a significant extension of the author's article mentioned earlier. R. Morsey, *Die oberste Reichsverwaltung unter Bismarck, 1867–1890* (Muenster, 1957), is a thorough study of the higher levels of administration of the Bismarck period. M. Stuermer, *Regierung und Reichstag im Bismarckstaat, 1871–1880. Caesarismus oder Parlamentarismus* (Duesseldorf, 1974), deals with the constitutional dilemma and the role of the Reichstag and is a major contribution toward a better understanding of Bismarck's domestic policies. The question of Bonapartism in Bismarck's policies is discussed by A. Mitchell, "Bonapartism as a Model for Bismarckian Politics," with comments by O. Pflanze, C. Fohlen, and M. Stuermer, in the *Journal of Modern History* 49, no. 2 (June 1977): 181–209.

A significant study on German local government and administration is H. Heffter, *Die Deutsche Selbstverwaltung im 19. Jahrhundert* (Stuttgart, 1969). W. Fischer, *Wirtschaft und Gesellschaft im Zeitalter der Industrialisierung* (Goettingen, 1972), deals with the development of business and industrial organizations and their relationship to the government.

On the *Kulturkampf*, A. Constabel, *Die Vorgeschichte des Kulturkampfes: Quellenveroeffentlichung aus dem Deutschen Zentralarchiv* (Berlin [East], 1956), presents a collection of documents from the East German state archives. H. Bornkamm, *Die Staatsidee im Kulturkampf* (Muenchen, 1950), is a short account of Bismarck's motives and the political ideas surrounding this struggle. G. Franz, *Kulturkampf: Staat und Katholische Kirche in Mitteleuropa von der Saekularisation bis zum Abschluss des Preussischen Kulturkampfes* (Muenchen, 1954), puts the struggle into its European context and stresses the domestic as well as the international aspects. R. Ruhenstroth-Bauer, *Bismarck und Falk im Kulturkampf* (Heidelberg, 1944), uses the Falk *Nachlass*, the reports of the Wuerttemberg and Baden representatives, and material from the files of the former Prussian Secret State Archives.

On Bismarck's anti-Socialist crusade and on Germany's Social Democratic party in general, most of the more recent studies have been published in the German Democratic Republic. E. Kundel, *Marx und Engels im Kampf um die revolutionaere Arbeitereinheit: Zur Geschichte des Gothaer Vereinigungskongresses von 1875* (Berlin [East], 1962), deals with the Gotha Congress. K. A. Hellfaier, *Die deutsche Sozialdemokratie waehrend des Sozilistengesetzes, 1878–1890* (Berlin [East], 1959), describes the activities of the party during its illegal period. Outside the DDR, W. Pack, *Das parlamentarische Ringen um das Sozialistengesetz Bismarcks, 1878–1890* (Duesseldorf, 1961), presents a balanced account of the parliamentary struggle over the anti-Socialist laws, and W. Poels, "Staat und Sozialdemokratie im Bismarckreich," *Jahrbuch fuer die Geschichte Mittel- und Ostdeutschlands* 13–14 (1965), is a useful survey.

Bismarck's relationship with the German press is dealt with by E. Naujoks,

BIBLIOGRAPHICAL ESSAY

"Bismarck und die Organisation der Regierungspresse," *Historische Zeitschrift* 206 (1967), and by D. Brosius, "Welfenfonds und Presse im Dienste der preussischen Politik in Hannover nach 1866," *Niedersaechsisches Jahrbuch fuer Landesgeschichte* 36 (1964). N. v. d. Nahmer, *Bismarcks Reptilienfonds* (Mainz, 1968), discusses the chancellor's secret press fund.

There is a considerable amount of literature on Bismarck's personality, his political and social views, his religion, and anything else that might explain his actions and thoughts. L. v. Muralt, *Bismarcks Verantwortlichkeit* (Goettingen, 1955), describes him as a responsible, Christian statesman. G. A. Rein, *Die Revolution in der Politik Bismarcks* (Goettingen, 1957), deals with the "revolutionary" aspects of the chancellor's policies, such as his introduction of universal manhood suffrage, a possible alliance with Lassalle's workers' movement, and the workmen's insurance and compensation legislation of the 1880s. H. Kober, *Studien zur Rechtsanschauung Bismarcks* (Tuebingen, 1961), discusses Bismarck's attitude toward law, while H. Loesener, *Grundzuege von Bismarcks Staatsauffassung* (Bonn, 1962), deals with his political and constitutional views. G. A. Rein, "Bismarcks Royalismus," *Geschichte in Wissenschaft und Unterricht* 5 (1954), examines his attitude toward the monarchy.

Some attention has been paid in recent years to Bismarck's alleged plans for a coup d'état. W. Poels, *Sozialistenfrage und Revolutionsfurcht in ihrem Zusammenhang mit den angeblichen Staatsstreichplaenen Bismarcks* (Luebeck, 1960), treats this subject in connection with the Socialist question in the late 1880s and early 1890s. J. C. G. Roehl, "Staatsstreichplaene oder Staatsstreichbereitschaft? Bismarcks Politik in der Entlassungskrise," *Historische Zeitschrift* 203 (1966), looks at it at the time of Bismarck's dismissal, while M. Stuermer, "Staatsstreichgedanken im Bismarckreich," *Historische Zeitschrift* 209 (1969), examines the implications of the idea of a coup d'état throughout Bismarck's tenure of office.

Index

INDEX

INDEX